REGREENING THE NATIONAL PARKS

Michael Frome

Regreening

the National Parks

THE UNIVERSITY

OF ARIZONA PRESS

TUCSON & LONDON

The University of Arizona Press
Copyright © 1992
Michael Frome
All Rights Reserved
♾ This book is printed on acid-free, archival-quality paper.
Manufactured in the United States of America

97 96 95 94 93   6 5 4 3 2

LIBRARY OF CONGRESS CATALOGING-IN-PUBLICATION DATA
Frome, Michael.
  Regreening the national parks / Michael Frome.
    p. cm.
  Includes bibliographical references and index.
  ISBN 0-8165-0956-5 (cloth)   ISBN 0-8165-1288-4 (paper)
    1. National parks and reserves—United States.   2. National parks and reserves—
Government policy—United States.   3. United States. National Park Service.   4.
National parks and reserves—United States—Management.   5. Nature conserva-
tion—Government policy—United States.   6. Concessions (Amusements, etc.)—
United States. I. Title.
SB482.A4F76 1991   91-17477
333.78'0973—dc20   CIP
British Library Cataloging in Publication data are available.

To the memory of my parents

Contents

Acknowledgments

I am reminded by Gregory McNamee, my editor at the University of Arizona Press, that six-plus years elapsed from conception to completion of this book. But I can look back a lot further to say that it began when I first became seriously involved in national parks. I still feel singularly blessed by the kindness of the people who got me started, particularly S. Herbert Evison, Ronald F. Lee, Conrad L. Wirth, all in the Washington headquarters of the National Park Service, and Sam P. Weems, superintendent of the Blue Ridge Parkway. In those same early days I met Horace M. Albright, who was forever generous with encouragement and inspiration.

Through the years I have benefited from contact with an abundance of individuals associated in various ways with national parks, many of them quoted or otherwise cited in the pages of this book. I feel particularly indebted for counsel in preparation or review of the manuscript to Devereux Butcher, Russell E. Dickenson, Boyd Evison, Paul Fritz, John Miles, Clay Peters, Mark Peterson, Alfred S. Runte, Mack Prichard, Paul C. Pritchard, and Gilbert F. Stucker. I also appreciate support provided by the institutions where I have worked while writing the book: the College of Forestry at the University of Idaho, the Sigurd Olson Environmental Institute at Northland College in Wisconsin, and Huxley College of Environmental Studies, Western Washington University, with a special word of gratitude to

Karen Foisy, Nancy Johnson, and the Bureau of Faculty Research at the last named. Two talented graduate students in environmental writing at Western Washington University have worked with me: Sara Olason, indefatigable, meticulous researcher and reviewer, and Lisa Friend, the creative indexer. May they both write books of their own before long.

I am grateful also to Lynn Seligman, formerly with the Julian S. Bach Literary Agency, who helped to get the book off the ground, and to the incomparable Julian Bach, and to Ann Rittenberg and Emma Sweeney. My work has been aided by grants from the Fund for Investigative Journalism; the National Park Literary Fund, a group of national park personnel coordinated by Raymond Nelson and Douglas Bruce McHenry; and from the late S. Herbert Evison.

Gregory McNamee has been a positive and patient editor who steered me back on track from detours of my own making. Mindy Conner meticulously copyedited redundancies and queried me on picky but important points. I appreciate the warm good spirit extended by Greg, Mindy, Stephen Cox, Marie Webner, and their colleagues at the University of Arizona Press. I share credit for all that is right in this work with those mentioned above, reserving to myself responsibility for the rest.

REGREENING THE NATIONAL PARKS

Introduction

I began my close connection with national parks in the late 1940s and early 1950s. It was simple and straightforward at first, but in time I became something of a double agent—that is, a parks promoter, on the one hand, and a preservationist on the other.

In his book *The National Park Service*, William C. Everhart referred to me as follows:

> One of the shrewdest and most combative of the conservation writers, Mike Frome, has been scolding the Park Service over a good many years for failing to live up to his stern standards. Frome contributed a commentary to the *Washington Post* in April 1981, "Parks in Peril," which describes conditions in Yellowstone: "Congestion, noise, intrusions of man-made structures, pollution from too many automobiles and vandalism all interfere with enjoyment of the natural scene." Frome also authors the Rand McNally *National Park Guide*, but in this travel-encouraging publication the parks seem much more attractive, American treasures "that inspire, instruct and stimulate spiritual well-being."[1]

I can't accept the notion of contradiction that appears so clear to Everhart. Even after more than forty years, I still feel that national parks inspire and instruct; they certainly do that for me. I encourage others to share the same kind of illuminating experience. But for the sake of us all I want the parks to be free of congestion, noise, intrusions, pollution, and vandalism.

Believe me, when I began, I hardly thought of myself as a preservationist. I didn't know what the word meant. In those days I worked for the American Automobile Association at its headquarters in Washington, D.C., as a writer and publicist. The AAA and its affiliated clubs had a considerable background of interest in the parks and of collaboration with the National Park Service. As a case in point, the Automobile Club of Tennessee was instrumental in establishing Great Smoky Mountains National Park. The manager of the Automobile Club of Kentucky, Eugene Stuart, was a prime champion of Mammoth Cave National Park. The auto clubbers' role may have been pure boosterism, but Stuart introduced me to one of his strong allies, Tom Wallace, editor of the *Louisville Times*, who *was* a preservationist. One day at his home in Louisville, Stuart showed me and commended a book, *A Thousand Mile Walk to the Gulf*, by an author, John Muir, whom I had barely known but whose works subsequently became a beacon in my life.

The late 1940s and 1950s were marked by a surge of tourism. The parks were principal targets, but they were wholly unprepared, having spent the World War II years virtually in cold storage. When the postwar push began, park buildings were run-down and staffs were inadequate. Auto club members returned from their trips with a variety of complaints, and they were not alone. Bernard DeVoto, for one, wrote a classic piece, "Let's Close the National Parks," in *Harper's* of October 1953. My work through most of the 1950s enabled me to visit the parks to observe and write about conditions there, and I met many individuals in and out of government (including DeVoto) with particular roles in park policy. Park people impressed me as protectors of the public heritage, guardians of sacred trust. Most conservationists impressed me, too, though they were beyond my depth.

But everybody begins somewhere, and that was where I came in. I believed in the leaders of the National Park Service—the parks as I saw them were evidence of their commitment to good deeds. I believed it was right to encourage tourism in the parks, the finest recreational resource America offers its people, and therefore right to support the development of facilities to properly accommodate the rising tide of tourists.

Something happened along the way to change my perspective. In the mid-1960s I went south to write a book about the Great Smokies. My idea was to make it a combined history and travel guide. Just then, however, the National Park Service was proposing to construct a major highway across the Smokies and a network of massive campgrounds in the park. That struck me as a nightmarish scheme to destroy the values that people came there to enjoy. I joined the opponents of the road, whose reasoning made much more sense, and I wanted my book to help, to show why the Smokies should not be disfigured merely to rush people through from one tourist town to another. Happily, we succeeded in saving the wilderness.

In the same period I was engaged by Kodak to write a guide to photography in the national parks. Midway through, I received a phone call from the project supervisor complaining that I was making it too difficult in my script for people to take pictures. I didn't see it that way. I insisted that national parks must be treated not as tourist attractions in the ordinary sense, but as exalted places deserving time and patience. I wrote a photography guide with an ecological approach, encouraging perception of native life communities—trees, birds, animals, fish, shrubs, flowers, soil, water, and air, all interdependent, dynamic, and changing. I counseled patience in photographing wildlife, considering that national parks are meant for animals on their own terms; unlike zoo animals, those in the wild move about with season, time of day, weather, availability of food, and other reasons they have chosen not to disclose.

Whether or not I convinced any readers, I succeeded in convincing myself. National parks *are* exalted places. On entering a national park I feel uplifted and renewed. "Man has lost the capacity to foresee and forestall," wrote Albert Schweitzer. "He will end by destroying the earth." Yes, there is much cause for gloom in our age, almost as though humankind as a species has lost its home and direction. But national parks I see in ideal form as the antidote to pessimism, the affirmation of hope.

Forty-plus years after I came in, I recognize that I've changed. So have the parks and the people who administer them, and so too the country and the world, and essentially not for the better. Civilization in our time is driven by materialism and troubled by pollution, overpopulation, corruption, and violence. National parks can hardly be uncoupled from the society around them, but that only makes it more important to protect them and keep them whole and pure. As long as a park is sustained with self-respect, then there is hope for the surrounding environment. Or, as Theodore Roosevelt, after camping in 1903 with John Muir among the giant sequoias in Yosemite, told an assemblage at Stanford University, "There is nothing more practical than the preservation of beauty, than the preservation of anything that appeals to the higher emotions of mankind."[2]

Many, many words have been written and spoken about problems in the national parks. They're overcrowded, underfunded, and politicized. Americans are loving the parks to death. Too many automobiles cause congestion and pollution. Low-flying airplanes and helicopters pollute the wilderness with noise. It isn't safe to go to the parks. Toxic chemicals ruin the air and water. Park personnel are demoralized. All these and more—all true, and no secret.

I've examined the issues in interviews with public officials, conservation leaders, park rangers, scientists, concessionaires, and park visitors. I've been to the parks again and again and again, reviewing the scenes, facilities, and activities. Certain improvements have been made, largely to the credit of people who work in the parks. On the whole, however, it's been downhill, with new illusions substituted for the old reality. For example, when Virgin Islands National Park was established in 1956, coral reefs were its particular pride. The reefs were equated with Yellowstone's geysers and Yosemite's waterfalls. Now they are mostly shadows of themselves, deteriorated and dying as a consequence of diverse human disturbances and abuses. There isn't much coral along the Trunk Bay underwater nature trail, which once was a showplace. But snorkelers can still read the labels etched on submerged glass plates describing reef life and imagine they are seeing it.

This isn't right. It leads me to ask whether each generation must know less of the real thing and accept less, settling for an increasingly degraded and crowded world, and whether it will all be taken for granted, as though nothing serious has been lost, without realizing that as the environment is altered, so too are we.

I don't mean to be combative or a scold, but I envision national parks as cathedrals of spirituality and emotion; as models of respect for all land and water and all of life; as a powerfully creative social ideal. I want those responsible for the parks—Congress, the executive branch, the National Park Service, the concessionaires who do business for profit in the parks, and the people who "love the parks to death"—to raise their sights and standards. This is the right thing to do, for the common good and the good of the parks. In the pages that follow I trace park history from the original greening, through growth, to the ungreening in our time. I discuss the roles of principal institutions and individual players, including the executive branch of government and Congress; the leadership, or directorate, of the National Park Service in Washington; the field force of park superintendents and rangers; plus park concessionaires and conservationists. My account gives credit for the great deal of good in our parks, but criticism, too, where it belongs. Finally, I offer a course of action, a set of specific proposals for regreening the national parks.

Women Should Not Go Hiking Alone

Raising the sights and standards of society, by appealing to and serving the higher emotions of humankind, is the singular mission of the national parks. This can hardly be an easy mission, however, when standards of society everywhere are declining; when materialism, violence, and corruption prevail; and when the earth has been reduced from mother of life to a commodity to be bought and sold and exploited. I think of what Thomas Merton called "The Time of the End," which he described as "the time when everyone is obsessed with lack of time, lack of space, with saving time, conquering space, projecting into time and space the anguish produced within them by the technological furies of size, volume, quantity, speed, number, price, power and acceleration."[1]

That is an apt profile of our age. Nevertheless, Oscar Wilde had a great line: "We are all in the gutter, but some of us are looking at the stars." National parks are special places for looking at stars—for touching stars and being touched and empowered by them. National parks are sources of caring based on inner feeling, on emotional concern for wolf, bear, insect, tree, and plant, and hopes for the survival of these and all species. National parks are schools of awareness, personal growth, and maturity, where the individual learns to appreciate the sanctity of life and to manifest distress and love for the natural world, including the human portion of it.

This particular concept may be questioned as a subjective value judgment, but history shows that from the very beginning national parks have been established to appeal to and serve the higher human emotions. Consider the legislation President Lincoln signed in July 1864 granting the prized natural wonders of Yosemite Valley and the Mariposa grove of giant sequoias to California for safekeeping from exploitation and destruction (until, in due course, they were returned to the federal government as portions of Yosemite National Park). Consider further the establishment of Yellowstone National Park in 1872, a monumental act of idealism that sparked a new kind of land ethic and a preservation movement around the world. And when President William Howard Taft in 1912 urged Congress to place a new bureau in charge of the parks, he said it was "essential to the proper management of those wonderful manifestations of nature, so startling and so beautiful that everyone recognizes the obligations of the government to preserve them for the edification and recreation of the people."[2]

Thus in 1916 the National Park Service was established, headed by Stephen T. Mather, who defined national parks as "America's most inspiring playgrounds and best equipped nature schools."[3] Mather had been a journalist and supersalesman who made a fortune in the borax business. When he took over, the entire Washington staff consisted of himself, his young assistant and fellow Californian Horace M. Albright, and a stenographer. Mather proceeded to promote the parks like a product, encouraging Americans to visit and explore the far-flung natural wonders. He saw promotion as the expeditious way to build a public constituency to influence Congress to support the bureau, enhance its prestige, and add new areas to its jurisdiction. He collaborated with the railroads, encouraging them to advertise their routes to the parks, and he personally escorted editors and publishers on field trips. There was plenty of room for everybody, and the bigger the crowd the better.

Mather meant well and repeatedly showed that he cared about the out-of-doors. He faced the reality that his successors would be obliged to face, that bears and trees don't vote and wilderness preserved doesn't bring revenue to the federal treasury.

The early leaders of the Park Service established parks and saved wilderness; at the same time, however, they altered important parcels of the land and the way we look at and use them. In 1934 Robert

Marshall, the pioneer in wilderness protection, was sent by Secretary of the Interior Harold L. Ickes to scout the Great Smoky Mountains of North Carolina and Tennessee. In a memo dated August 18 of that year, Marshall reported to Ickes:

> I hiked to Clingman's Dome last Sunday, looking forward to the great joy of undisturbed nature for which this mountain has been famous. Walking along the skyline trail, I heard instead the roar of machines on the newly constructed road just below me and saw the huge scars which this new highway is making on the mountain. Clingman's Dome and the primitive were simply ruined for me.
>
> Returning to where a gigantic, artificial parking place had exterminated the wild mountain meadows in Newfound Gap, I saw papers and the remains of lunches littered all over. There were about twenty automobiles parked there, from at least a quarter of which radios were blaring forth the latest jazz as a substitute for the symphony of the primitive.[4]

A few months later, on March 9, 1935, Marshall wrote his friend Irving Clark of Seattle: "I need only point out the inexcusable fake Hopi watchtower at the brink of the Grand Canyon, the luxurious developments on the floor of Yosemite Valley which have ruined all primitive effect, the skyline drive in the Great Smokies and the elaborate tunnel system in the park through Newfound Gap, the tunnel system which is so boasted about in Zion National Park . . . and the general artificiality everywhere."[5]

Artificiality has been widely implanted throughout the national parks. It dilutes the appeal to higher emotions. It is common fare, despite the best intentions of well-intentioned people. One director of the National Park Service after another has given a little here, or a little there. But history demonstrates that the first step is the worst step, and from then on it's usually downhill.

In May 1980 the National Park Service issued a report titled "State of the Parks." It was long overdue, but at last a systematic attempt had been made to identify critical issues affecting the parks both inside and outside their boundaries. "Threats will continue to degrade and destroy irreplaceable park resources," the report warned.[6] But most officials don't go around looking for threats. In 1988 Director William Penn Mott made speeches assuring the country that the parks were in better shape than ever.[7] This led subordinates to echo their boss. "I get tired of all this 'Chicken Little' stuff," Bob Barbee, superintendent of Yellowstone, told reporters in June 1988. "I would contend that in Yellowstone we are in better shape, biologically, than we were seventy-five years ago. We are more sensitive to the integrity of the resources than we have ever been."[8]

Maybe so, but that depends on how one looks at things, and on who is doing the looking. The National Park Service, as a case in point, has changed, and so have the people in it. The typical ranger conveys an image of tradition and trust, but he, or she, and his or her peers live in a different world from that of the old rangers. Rangers in Yellowstone a generation ago conducted winter patrols on skis. It took a lot of time and energy. Now they scoot around on snowmobiles, covering more ground, saving time, relating increasingly to the machine and less to the natural environs. One winter in the 1980s I snowmobiled around Yellowstone with the chief ranger (see chapter 11). It was a comfortable experience—the handlebars on the machine were even heated to warm the driver's hands and fingers—and a convenient way to see Yellowstone, but hardly to feel it.

The National Park Service as a whole has changed. Mather's brand of promotion is no longer necessary, but the emphasis is still on numbers of visitors and entertaining them, with unhappy consequences. "Women should not go hiking alone," warned a park ranger in an article headlined "Slaying Casts Shadow over Park's Beauty" (*Fresno Bee*, March 24, 1985), reporting the death of a young woman who was visiting Yosemite National Park. Hiking alone at three in the afternoon on a popular trail, within sight of Glacier Point and Half Dome, two principal tourist magnets, she was fatally stabbed by an assailant unknown. This was no isolated incident: during a single year of the 1980s, Yosemite rangers made more than seven hundred arrests for offenses ranging from traffic violations to drug use, assault, rape, and murder.[9]

Law enforcement is now a major activity throughout the parks. The "new breed of ranger" is equipped with handgun, mace, nightstick, radio, and handcuffs; rangers patrol with siren, emergency lights, high-performance engine, and shotgun or rifle, and are competent in hand-to-hand combat, karate, and search procedures.[10]

If it takes armed guards to save us in "our most inspiring playgrounds," then America is sicker than anyone imagines. Something is wrong when a woman cannot hike alone when being alone in nature is the way to experience it best. The rangers advise walking in pairs and groups, which makes me wonder if we are nearing the day when hiking parties will have to be accompanied by an armed ranger. "Aggressive professional law enforcement" doesn't work in cities, or in relations among nations, any more than it can work in national parks.

While a park in principle is a different kind of place, it's difficult for it to survive in a healthy condition within an unhealthy environment. As long as the park is sustained with self-respect, there should be hope for the environment around it. But the spark of that self-respect must come from the people in charge. Over the course of years, however, a professional agency has been transformed into a political agency, leading to an emphasis on recreation, complete with urban malls, supermarkets, superhighways, airplanes and helicopters sightseeing overhead, snowmobiling, rangers who know they can get ahead by being policemen, and nature carefully kept in its place. Park visitors expect comfort, convenience, and short-order wilderness served like fast food.

Horace Albright, the pioneer who began with Mather and then succeeded him, the patriarch of the parks until his death in 1987 (at the age of ninety-seven), observed the hardening of institutional arteries. In 1989 his daughter, Marian Albright Schenck, shared with me a letter he had written years before, in which he warned: "As bureaus grow older and men, too, advance in age and as the bureau inevitably takes on new activities and new responsibilities, it tends to become more 'bureaucratic,' has more red tape and more rules and regulations, and, in time, gets farther away from the people and ultimately will become 'just another bureau.'"[11]

This is apt to happen to any organization or institution, of course. It starts with vigor and youth, sparked by risk takers driven by dreams and goals. In time, manuals and tables of organization are written. Mission-oriented amateurs are replaced by rule-book writers and managers—trained career professionals with college degrees qualifying them as specialists. The institution acquires an organizational culture marked by lack of initiative, lack of leadership with commitment, and lack of an effective process of internal communication and organizational development. Scientific data and valid research are altered or suppressed. There are meetings, memos, task forces, and business trips—everything but creativity, courage, and bold decision making. The system relieves rather than mandates responsibility. Incentive rewards go to the team players, and risk takers are sidelined. Good people are frightened and frustrated.

A review of history shows that the presidential administration of Ronald Reagan, with James G. Watt (followed by Donald Hodel) as secretary of the interior, did more to inhibit individuality and initiative on behalf of national parks preservation than any earlier administration. But I have watched a long-term shift away from bold, active commitment; it has spread, pervasively, through liberal Democratic as well as conservative Republican administrations. Stewart L. Udall, secretary of the interior under John F. Kennedy and Lyndon B. Johnson, received credit for the considerable good he did for national parks, but he did a lot of damage, too. Udall for a long time supported the proposed construction of dams in the Grand Canyon, and personnel at Grand Canyon National Park were unable to speak in defense of the resource in their trust. Udall sanctioned and personally promoted the worst kind of power projects, devastating to Navajo and Hopi Indian cultures and degrading to the national parks of the Southwest.[12] Park Service officials learned to go along or perish. The Black Mesa Project in northeastern Arizona, designed to pump two thousand gallons of water a minute from an already low water table and to construct six power plants and the largest strip mine in the world, presents a clear example. Interpreters at Mesa Verde National Park wanted to tell visitors about Black Mesa while it was still in the proposal stage, so they would know about the potentially severe impact on Navajo and Hopi peoples, the country's last remaining stronghold of traditional Indian life.

On August 16, 1970, a memorandum that read like a military order was distributed to the interpreters by Chief Park Archaeologist Gilbert R. Wenger on behalf of Superintendent Meredith Guillet: "The Superintendent wants the distribution of any literature specifically calling attention to the Black Mesa coal project to be stopped immediately. If interpretive personnel are telling visitors on tours to stop by the museum and pick up such literature these individuals are doing so against direct orders. These orders must be obeyed. I do not want to hear of any more incidents on tours or at campfire programs where the uniformed person removes his badge or covers it and says he is speaking as a private individual on these issues. That individual is still on duty and will be guilty of insubordination."

Whatever the penalty for insubordination in a civilian agency might be, on the following day four rangers turned in their badges and quit. They went out with a public blast: "Morally we felt we could no longer work for an agency whose purpose is to protect our cultural heritage, but whose practice is censorship of major environmental problems which will ultimately affect the very park in which we were working."[13]

That statement tells the story of internal difficulty. Resource professionals are trained at colleges and universities to specialize in principles of "management" rather than in the history, philosophy, and principles of preservation. They are programmed in school and on the job to repress emotions, so they perform as technicians—professionalized, internalized, competent in jargon but not in ability to heed, hear, and respond to voices outside their own ranks. Like the professions of medicine and education, any positive training is weakened by inbreeding. The words about protecting "unspoiled wonders" are much the same as in the past, but visions and courage have dimmed with time; except for some notable exceptions, particularly in the lower ranks, most personnel function with narrow vision and an emphasis on structure rather than on broad helpfulness and a sense of humanity.

It might be surprising if this were otherwise. National parks reflect society. They tend to become what the public wants them to be, through usage as well as law. They are creatures of the American political system, responsive to Congress and the party in power. Now is the time to make the whole system accountable.

2

In the beginning, the very beginning, the whole earth was one big national park, but there was no need to call it Earth National Park. Then humankind came along to conquer and divide the planet. It took a long, long time, but ultimately civilization advanced to recognize the wisdom of setting aside small fragments of the wild original earth. Americans are proud that the national park idea is an American creation, that Yellowstone in 1872 became the first national park anywhere. But Yellowstone and all other parks are creations of the political system, as reflected in Congress and the party in power. Thus the critical weaknesses in the administration of national parks are systemic, derived from the history of the Department of the Interior, which controls the affairs of the national parks and National Park Service as a political instrument of Congress and the party in power.

The department was established to give land away, not to protect it. Scandals and scams have been recurrent, the most infamous being the Teapot Dome oil giveaway of the early 1920s. It was neither the first nor the last, though, and the worst scams may not even be known; they have become almost commonplace. On March 3, 1975, for example, it was revealed that forty-nine officials of the U.S. Geological Survey owned stock in companies holding mineral leases on federal lands supervised by the USGS, and that the Geological Survey itself, a major bureau of the Interior Department, had taken no action to force divestiture.[1] National parks, with their lofty idealistic purpose, are misplaced in this environment. They lend credibility to the entire department, yet the pervasive political sleaze influences all the park personnel; it clouds their perceptions of right and wrong and what it takes to get ahead. Congress, for its part, feeds on the sleaze. Westerners claim a larger share than Easterners, but Republicans and Democrats, conservatives and liberals alike, regard the Department of the Interior as a garden meant for plucking plums.

In September 1985 I sat in the office of the secretary of the interior in Washington, D.C., trying to set aside such irreverent notions. I had been there numerous times before, and always felt this huge and sumptuous room, large enough to accommodate seventy-five or a hundred persons at a stand-up reception, would do any corporate nabob proud. It was designed as a showplace by its first occupant, Harold L. Ickes, the self-styled "curmudgeon" who was secretary during the Franklin D. Roosevelt administration, when the building was erected. The motif was all Western, reflected in the paintings on paneled walls, carvings, sculpture, and carpets. Donald Hodel, the successor to James G. Watt as secretary in the Reagan administration, had a wood fire in the fireplace, although it was a very warm day, and he wore Western boots, as though to create an appropriate outdoorsy mood. Hodel called my attention to a photo on the mantle showing him climbing a rock wall in Yosemite, where he recently had visited. He expressed his fondness for the parks, as all secretaries do, although national parks are pretty small potatoes in the scheme of things. Of much greater significance are the public domain lands with their hard-rock minerals, petroleum, timber, and forage for cows and sheep; the water that flows out of the public lands (including the parks), which is transformed into energy and irrigation; and the outer continental shelf, the OCS, with its submerged petroleum. Those resources are the large potatoes at Interior.

Hodel told me that being the forty-fifth secretary of the interior had piqued his curiosity about his predecessors, and he'd learned that the job had never been a steppingstone to anything of consequence—not even the vice presidency. He was right. The second secretary, who resigned after eleven days, wrote President Millard Fillmore that his particular nervous temperament couldn't stand the stress. Gerald Ford's first secretary of the interior, Stan Hathaway, didn't last much longer. He was so poorly received in Washington that after a month he withdrew to Bethesda Naval Hospital to repair his nerves, then headed back to Wyoming.[2]

When the United States was new, the entire federal government consisted of three departments—State, Treasury, and War—each with clearly defined and necessary functions. By 1849 the country's population had reached twenty-three million. Following expansion of the national borders by the Mexican War, many of the adventurous were ready to press westward across the plains. Thus Congress established the Department of the Interior to help them on their way. One of its major bureaus, the General Land Office, was designed to give land away. Another, the Office of Indian Affairs, was assigned not to protect the interests of Indians but to keep them quiet, and out of the way, while whites proceeded to settle the West.

Following the Civil War the federal government disposed of millions of acres of the public domain—the lands of the Louisiana Purchase, Red River Basin, cessions from Spain and Mexico, the Oregon Compromise, and the Texas, Gadsden, and Alaska purchases. The Homestead Act of January 1, 1863, was intended to be the greatest instrument in history for distributing land to people; it was followed by other land laws ostensibly passed to encourage, assist, and reward average Americans who would open frontier lands and settle the West. Presently, however, land laws were subverted, leading to fraud, land thievery, and land speculation through which something like one-half of the nation's forests passed into private ownership. Complicity of land officials was common.[3]

Carl Schurz, who served as secretary of the interior under Rutherford B. Hayes from 1877 to 1881, was one of the few to protest land theft and resource exploitation. Schurz had come to the United States from Germany in 1852. He settled first in Wisconsin as a twenty-three-year-old, then became a Civil War general, a journalist, an editor, and senator from Missouri. He was a muckraker and reformer who fought patronage and corruption. In his 1879 report Schurz wrote: "The waste and destruction of the redwood (*Sequoia sempervirens*) and 'big trees' (*Sequoia gigantea*) of California have been and continue to be so great as to cause apprehension that these species of trees, the noblest and oldest in the world, will entirely disappear unless some measures be taken soon to preserve at least a portion of them."[4] His plea went unheeded. Timber companies acquired the great stands by fair means and foul. Many years later they would sell bits of them back to the federal government at huge profits for Redwood National Park.[5]

When he became president, Theodore Roosevelt faced much the same scene as had Schurz. Binger Hermann, commissioner of the General Land Office, had already been twice indicted; at best he typified the old philosophy that the choice way to manage land was to give it away. Roosevelt dismissed Hermann and began to surround himself with allies determined to set a new course. One was James Garfield, son of the twentieth president, who was appointed secretary of the interior. Another was Gifford Pinchot, then a young pioneer in forestry headquartered in the Department of Agriculture. Their objectives were to clean up the government and to quit giving away the public domain. Pinchot influenced Roosevelt to support the transfer of many millions of acres of public domain from Interior to Agriculture. As they reasoned, Interior had the land but no foresters. The department was tainted with patronage and scandal. Placing all forest work under Pinchot's wing in Agriculture marked the beginning of the national forest system. Unfortunately, Pinchot's emphasis always was on "preservation through use" rather than on use through preservation, and in due course significant portions of the forest lands would have to be redesignated national parks in order to save them.

William Howard Taft had been handpicked by TR to succeed him in hopes of continuing his policies, but Taft reversed course, dismissing Garfield as secretary of the interior and replacing him with Richard A. Ballinger, a Seattle lawyer and former commissioner of the General Land Office. Pinchot and Ballinger became embroiled in a celebrated controversy over coal leases on public lands in Alaska. Ballinger, first as commissioner of the Land Office, and later as secretary, favored the claimants, despite the protest of his own department's land agents, who had reported unfavorably, even asserting the claims were fraudulent. Pinchot demanded the claims be nullified, insisting the issue was a showdown over Roosevelt's conservation policies. Taft supported Ballinger and fired Pinchot, but not without considerable attendant publicity and congressional inquiry.[6]

The controversy over whether government land should be sold outright in response to valid claims or leased and maintained in government ownership contributed to passage of the Mineral Leasing Act of 1920, which provided access to oil, gas, and coal on public lands on payment of a royalty fee. That much was considered progress, though it scarcely eliminated the temptation, weakness, and corruption that crystallized in Teapot Dome.[7] That connivance began with the election of Warren G. Harding as president and his appointment of Albert B. Fall, a former senator from New Mexico and poker crony from Harding's days in the Senate, as secretary of the interior. In those years there were four naval oil reserves, including Teapot Dome in Wyoming and Elk Hill in California. Fall talked his cabinet colleague, the secretary of the navy, into giving administrative control of the navy's reserves to Interior, a move that Harding approved with a secret executive order on May 31, 1921. Fall then leased Teapot Dome in its entirety to Harry F. Sinclair, a petroleum kingpin, secretly and without bids. Soon after, he leased a large part of the Elk Hill reserve to Edward L. Doheny, again without bids. The leases came to light, the Senate investigated, and Fall's public career was finished. Doheny later told of lending Fall $100,000 on an unsecured note while seeking the Elk Hill leases; the money had been delivered to Fall's office at Interior by Doheny's son in what became known as "the little black bag." Fall left the government and went to work for Sinclair. But that was not the end. Indictments were issued against Fall, Sinclair, and the Dohenys. The courts found the Teapot Dome lease had been obtained through collusion and conspiracy between Fall and Sinclair, and that fraud and corruption were involved in the California case. Doheny was acquitted of charges of bribing Fall; Sinclair was sentenced to six months for contempt of court; while the hapless Fall was sentenced to a year in prison and a $100,000 fine.

Every secretary of the interior has carried the Teapot Dome burden with him, but none tried harder than Harold L. Ickes to overcome history and build an image of integrity for his department.[8] He was a Chicagoan, not a Westerner, a Bull Moose supporter of Theodore Roosevelt in 1912 who had been a journalist and then a lawyer. Ickes served as secretary from 1933 to 1945, longer than any other man before or since. Critics said he didn't know one end of a cow from another, but he worked hard at conservation, championed progressive New Deal causes, and left noteworthy accomplishments. He appointed John Collier as head of the Bureau of Indian Affairs, and Collier endeavored a heroic and historic change in direction (which included hiring Robert Marshall, the champion of wilderness preservation). Ickes abolished racial segregation in the department's restrooms and cafeterias. He provided for Marian Anderson to use the Lincoln Memorial for a concert in 1939 after the Daughters of the American Revolution had refused her the use of Constitution Hall, and he personally introduced her.

Ickes thrived on debate and controversy. He felt he had the president's backing, and he used a variety of construction and conservation projects to build a base of support for the administration and himself. Thus he was emboldened to resist, or even insult, members of the Senate like Kenneth McKellar of Tennessee, a kingpin of Southern patronage politics. Ickes was temperamental, unpredictable, stubborn, given to tantrums, and difficult to understand—the self-styled "America's No. 1 Curmudgeon, or Sour Puss." He could look out his office window and shudder with sentiment at the sight of a tree being removed from Rawlins Park, then turn around and blaspheme a well-intentioned and perfectly competent career professional. Walter Lippman wrote in the *New York Herald Tribune* (February 7, 1952) after Ickes's death: "He was a kind and generous and warmhearted man. The Old Curmudgeon business was a false front to protect him against its being generally realized how violently virtuous, how furiously righteous, how angrily unbigoted he was almost all the time." Maybe so, but it was well known (and he himself later confessed) that he sanctioned spying and eavesdropping in the department. He was especially rough on national parks people, whom he considered ingrained bureaucrats in need of a spanking.

Ickes devoted considerable energy to the National Park Service, including several vacations at Acadia National Park in Maine. In 1938 he married Jane Dahlman, who worked in the historical division of the Park Service. (He was sixty-four, she was twenty-five.) He was suspicious of the Park Service, almost in the same manner as James G. Watt would be a half century later. He inherited the agency as it had been trained by its founders, Stephen T. Mather and Horace M. Albright, and considered it too independent, in need of a lesson in obedience. He complained that the Park Service was stereotyped, with too many incompetent people and in need of new blood. When he received a report about a questionable method of land appraising, he quickly concluded that Park Service personnel were in a conspiracy to defraud the government, not for personal profit, but to build up the park system. He was convinced it was a criminal conspiracy traceable to the Hoover administration, but later it turned out to be a mistake of the Government Accounting Office and no conspiracy at all. He was toughest on Arno B. Cammerer, the director of the Park Service, a thoroughly decent individual whom he belittled unmercifully and ultimately forced out.

Such behavior reflected Ickes's scrappy nature and his relish for tough battles. Although he considered himself a Pinchot apostle in the early years, he became a bitter foe of the Forest Service, insisting that it wasn't fit to administer wilderness and that the only way to protect wilderness was to transfer it to national parks and national monuments. He involved himself in historic campaigns on behalf of Grand Teton, Olympic, and Kings Canyon national parks. He fought the concessionaires and wanted the government itself to operate facilities in the parks.

More than any other secretary of the interior before or after his time, he enunciated a clear policy of preservation and committed himself to make it work. At the Superintendents' Conference in February 1936 he expressed this philosophy on the administration of national parks:

> I do not want any Coney Island. I want as much wilderness, as much nature preserved and maintained as possible. If I could have my way I would have much fewer roads in most of the parks.
>
> I recognize that a great many people, an increasing number every year, take their nature from the automobile. I am more or less in that class on account of age and obesity. But I think the parks ought to be for people who love to camp and love to hike and who like to ride horseback and wander about and have a community of interest, a renewed communion with nature. . . .
>
> Our national parks are intended to be breaks on this route of insane life we have led. But we find ourselves speeding up to keep pace with a life that is lived at too high a rate instead of performing the function that I think we were intended to perform—of slowing down and making it possible for the people to relax.
>
> If people are genuinely interested, we ought to satisfy that interest. But let's don't drum up trade. Let's let people go into the park and be natural. Let them go back to nature. And don't let's try to force the issue as to people being educated. I don't think the parks were intended to be classrooms.
>
> Colonel Thomson [Charles Goff Thomson, park superintendent]

told me when I was out there [Yosemite] that they were beginning to demand shower baths, and running hot and cold water, and all the rest of it. That is perfectly natural. And that is what I am trying to emphasize. There is no limit to it. If you give them hot and cold running water for shower baths, the next thing they will want will be their breakfasts in bed.[9]

No secretary has come close to saying anything like it before or since Ickes's time. He was secure throughout FDR's administration, but he became unhappy with President Harry S Truman, particularly with Truman's nomination of Edwin W. Pauley as under secretary of the navy. Pauley was a California oil man who, as treasurer of the Democratic National Committee, had gathered oil money for the party. Ickes feared a rerun of Teapot Dome and elected to quit. He suggested that he leave on March 31, 1946, but Truman was stubborn, too, and advanced the date to February 15. Thus ended Ickes's twelve years as secretary of the interior. The nomination of Pauley was withdrawn, and the old curmudgeon had done his share to part the heavy clouds of sleaze.

3

During the years I lived and worked in Washington, I spent considerable time at the Interior Department and have many, many telling
recollections. In 1967, for instance, I interviewed Secretary Stewart
L. Udall in his office for a magazine article. "All of us overcompro-
mise," he said during the course of our dialogue, "and therefore fall
short of our ideals." He was frank and open, for which I respected
him. During his eight years in the job Udall showed himself sensitive
to high ethical qualities of national life and earnest in his desire to
contribute positively to them. But when things got tough, politics
transcended principle, as he himself conceded. A stream of slick publications and glowing news releases flowed from Interior during his
tenure. They assured America that all was well in the great new
Kennedy-Johnson conservation wave, even while Udall was supporting extensive leasing of federal and Indian coal lands and environmentally destructive water projects, including the Hooker Dam in
New Mexico, which would have flooded the Gila Wilderness, established by Aldo Leopold in 1924 as the first designated wilderness in
the country.[1] Lofty, high-sounding pledges, in short, were common,
but rhetoric and public relations outran performance.

That, I suppose, is characteristic of government, all government.
Udall's successor, Walter J. Hickel, lasted less than two years, but he
developed a strong perception of leadership derived from the Ickes

model. In his book *Who Owns America* Hickel wrote: "Politics is the art of compromise. If those words were carved out of solid granite in ten-foot letters up each side of the Washington Monument, they would be no more revered than they are already in the American capital. The expression has been used for generations as an excuse for selling out one's belief and 'making a deal.' The man who listens, who finds out the naked truth and goes forward without compromise, is truly a great leader. The real challenge for a leader is to sell those ideas he absolutely believes in from the heart. His greatest achievement is to gain support for those ideas that do not compromise his principles."[2]

Secretaries of the interior are not appointed to be two-fisted leaders, and they are certainly not supposed to be champions of conservation. They're chosen because they are good politicians, party regulars worthy of reward who come from the right part of the country and have an ability to make deals and accept deals. Presidents scarcely, if ever, ask, Who really is best qualified to define and face the tough, inescapable resource challenges?

Udall wanted to confront and deal with challenges, and he arrived on the scene at an opportune moment. National concern for the environment was on the upswing, and conservation groups were gaining significant numerical strength for the first time. The Sierra Club, hitherto headquartered wholly in California, had opened a legislative office in Washington. Congressmen who formerly considered national parks a luxury commodity and derided the National Park Service for "grabbing land," now found that new parks were good politics. During Udall's time in office, from the beginning of the Kennedy administration to the end of the Johnson administration, the park system underwent unparalleled expansion. Important new units were established (Biscayne, Canyonlands, North Cascades, and Voyageurs national parks, to cite a few), with Udall leading the charge. The expansion was heady stuff for parks people. It meant promotions, jobs, bigger budgets, and more political clout. But the parks suffered, too, and so did principles of preservation.

In his book *Rape of the American Virgins* (1972) Edward A. O'Neill called Udall one of the "parfait knights" at Kennedy's Round Table.[3] That seems apt: Udall was a third-term congressman who had worked hard to secure the presidential nomination for Kennedy, and he was a Westerner, which qualified him for the one slot in the cabinet traditionally reserved for the West. I first turned to O'Neill's book for its reference to Virgin Islands National Park, which had been established in 1956 on the island of St. John with land acquired and presented to the government by Laurance Rockefeller. Over the years I've observed continual erosion in the natural qualities the park was established to preserve. O'Neill showed this to be part of the general environmental degradation in the Virgin Islands induced by parfait politics.

As O'Neill recounts, Udall, eager to do the best thing possible for new president John F. Kennedy, dispatched two consultants to the Virgin Islands to weigh possibilities for the new governor to be appointed. On February 13, 1961, one of the consultants, Maurice Rosenblatt, sent a memorandum to Udall warning of the potential to "damage and destroy the tradition, character and physical beauty of the towns." Of the four appointees being considered, Rosenblatt warned particularly against Ralph Paiewonsky, a Democratic party insider and Virgin Islands entrepreneur extraordinaire. "With Paiewonsky as governor," Rosenblatt wrote, "the Virgin Islands would once again become a happy pirate kingdom rivaling the days of Sir Henry Morgan, Bluebeard, and Blackbeard."[4]

That is precisely what happened. Paiewonsky was appointed and the Virgin Islands were transformed. The islands likely would have changed anyway, but under Paiewonsky the transformation was swift and intense, without meaningful effort by Interior to safeguard "tradition, character and physical beauty of the towns." On one front, industrial pollution was introduced. Paiewonsky's government welcomed Harvey Aluminum, a California corporation owned by a big contributor to the Democratic party. Likewise, tax exemptions and other concessions attracted Hess Oil to build a refinery at a choice site. On another front came hotels, more hotels, condominiums, and vacation houses for wealthy part-time residents. Entrepreneurs, investors, and developers preempted beaches, building sites, and old waterfront warehouses. Tracts of former U.S. government property acquired by the Virgin Islands in the mid-1960s were parceled off for sale or lease to insiders. Federal funds for sewage-disposal systems and urban renewal were lost, while public recreation areas were turned into commercial building developments.[5]

The implicit island qualities that Rosenblatt, the consultant, had hoped to protect were thoroughly ignored. Meanwhile, VIPs were wined, dined, and honored. Mrs. Lyndon B. Johnson was appointed a trustee of the College of the Virgin Islands, and Mrs. Hubert H. Humphrey became a director of Caneel Bay Plantation, Laurance Rockefeller's resort on St. John. Two irascible wheelhorses in the House of Representatives, Wayne Aspinall and Michael J. Kirwan, had their names bestowed on a junior high school (Aspinall) and a housing project (Kirwan) for no reason other than their seniority in a Democratic Congress.[6]

Three days before leaving office, Udall approved giving 110 acres of Mangrove Lagoon, a choice wetland owned by the federal government, for airport construction—just where Paiewonsky wanted it. Paiewonsky and Udall were too late to make it stick, however; Walter J. Hickel, who followed Udall as secretary, later revoked the gift.[7]

Another example of Interior's operations was treated in *The Hudson River*, by Robert H. Boyle. It relates the successful struggle in the 1960s of a citizen group, the Hudson River Preservation Conference, to block construction of a power plant proposed by Consolidated Edison at Storm King.[8] Governor Nelson Rockefeller was solidly behind ConEd; at one point he sarcastically suggested that the people who wanted to save Storm King should go buy the mountain. Laurance Rockefeller, the governor's brother and chairman of the State Council of Parks, also supported the power plant. Then came plans for the Hudson Expressway, which the Rockefellers again supported, Laurance defending it as "compatible development." The project required approval by the Department of the Interior. "Such an expressway in the highly scenic and significant corridor along the Hudson River," wrote Udall, "would seriously impair the values we are all trying to preserve."[9] But the Rockefellers persuaded Udall to switch gears and allow the U.S. Army Corps of Engineers to grant a dredge-and-fill permit—an action definitely not in keeping with the "conservation crusaders" image projected by Interior.

"I allowed Laurance Rockefeller to hornswoggle me," Udall conceded willingly when I went to talk with him in 1987 at his law office in Tucson. "Laurance had done a lot. We had worked together for seven years. He was a 'good guy'—although I increasingly had a lower regard for him. This was something he had worked out and about which he, in effect, said, 'I've done a lot of things for the parks and now I want you to give this your blessing.' I shouldn't have done it, but I'm now talking about the kind of personal relationships you develop."

During the course of this visit we discussed various aspects of history. A favorite picture hanging on his wall showed Udall with Robert Frost, William O. Douglas, Earl Warren, and Howard Zahniser (executive director of the Wilderness Society and principal author of the Wilderness Act of 1964). He made it a point to associate with such people, much to his credit. But there were always the pressures, from industry and from politicians speaking on their behalf. For example, where President Eisenhower had turned off the flow of federal dollars to build dams in the West, Kennedy during the election campaign promised to turn it back on. Then it came time to deliver. As Udall told me, Ted Sorenson of the White House insisted that "we have to keep that commitment to the West." Udall supported the Central Arizona Project because the politics of his home state demanded it for his survival.

With seventeen agencies and 55,000 employees under his control, it took Udall two and a half years to get on top of his job as secretary. He recognized his assignment as political and tried to keep everyone happy—environmentalists, senators, congressmen, and governors, particularly those from the West. People like Representative Wayne Aspinall of Colorado, chairman of the House Committee on Interior and Insular Affairs, pressed him not to be too hard on the mining industry. The job of secretary of the interior became a tightrope act. He would make a move founded on strong personal belief, but then someone of importance would demand the contrary.

Congressional Westerners have always felt that they owned Interior, the attitude in Congress being, "if you don't interfere in my backyard, I won't interfere in yours"; besides, urban congressmen, particularly Easterners, know little about public lands and don't have much to gain by learning about them. Because Kennedy rewarded Udall with appointment as secretary, California Democrats got their candidate, James Carr, named under secretary, in part, at least, to protect their state's interest in the continuing tussle with Arizona over the division of water from the Colorado River. Udall told me he regarded Carr as a "lightweight" and was glad to see him head for home after four years.

Congressmen and senators who are close to the winning candidate or hold key committee assignments demand their say in filling jobs above the civil service level. It's a chronically terrible system that gives congressmen improper influence in the executive branch, dividing loyalty and militating against effective government. Udall found that he had to consult Senator Clinton Anderson of New Mexico on almost everything. Anderson would say, "You haven't got anybody from New Mexico. I want somebody in your cabinet." So Udall had to learn not only how the wheels turn at Interior but how to get along with a team of people not of his own choosing.

As time went on, he felt more secure that he had his fingers on all the nerve centers in the department. He was able to appoint his own people and form a team that pulled together. He kept Floyd Dominy, the aggressive dam builder, whom he knew from Arizona and who was favored by Senator Carl Hayden, as director of the Bureau of Reclamation, but he dumped Conrad L. Wirth as director of the National Park Service: "I picked George Hartzog as director. I had to finagle Connie Wirth, sort of push him out the door a little bit early. He wanted to pick his own man to succeed him. I said, 'Make a list of five. I'm going to participate. It isn't your choice.' So I picked George, and George ran a helluva show."

Udall felt that he got caught in the crossfire in two of the big dam fights: at Dinosaur National Monument in the 1950s and Grand Canyon in the 1960s. As a new congressman following the expeditious political approach, he voted for the dams in Dinosaur, though later he had regrets. In the 1960s he felt that the nation had already built all the major hydroelectric dams it needed, and he advocated the National Wild and Scenic Rivers Bill. The coal plants were another matter: "The federal government needed a source of power to pump the water for the Central Arizona Project. I thought of the plant at Page as being tucked away in the gulch. When I first went there after it was finished, there were the big stacks and the pollution wafting around. However, we insisted they have the very best equipment, and in terms of pollution control it is still quite well run."

Udall saw compromise as necessary to progress, as evidenced in the case of the California redwoods. President Johnson's 1964 conservation message proposed eight new national parks. The redwoods in particular were the longtime dream of conservationists. Though about fifty thousand acres of virgin redwoods already were protected in eighteen California state parks, some of the choicest groves were privately owned and vulnerable to imminent logging. In 1963 the Sierra Club published *The Last Redwoods* as part of its appeal, while Udall at the club's biennial wilderness conference pledged his support and the support of the administration in the crusade for the park.

The National Park Service dispatched a team to survey the area. After due study the team strongly recommended that the Redwood Creek watershed, with its abundant great trees, become the core of the new park.[10] The site, however, was owned by three major timber companies, in contrast to another potential site, with only half as much old growth, on Mill Creek that was owned by a relatively small local outfit. The attainable at Mill Creek to Udall became the desirable, manifesting what he called the "art of the possible." He wished, he said, "to pick a park, not a fight," and he recommended an area containing few virgin forests not already protected by state parks. So did Park Service director George B. Hartzog, Jr., who dismissed the Redwood Creek study and recommendation of his own agency as not "professional."[11] That sort of derogation of conscientious performance must make any government employee think twice the next time around. Park advocates clung to the dream of the Redwood Creek watershed, portions of which later were added to the park, but only after some of the best of the trees had been logged.

Udall wanted to spark the conservation crusade, and be recognized for it, but he was pragmatic in the most political sense of the word. Thus on September 26, 1968, he went to dedicate the visitor center at Glen Canyon, the dam that conservationists even now despise above all others. He would be embarrassed by the words he spoke that day, and later would say that they were a mistake on his part, but I believe his statement belongs in the record:

> Before the Glen Canyon Dam was built the river ran through here red with sediment, and the back-country was a no-man's land except for a handful of shepherds and those fortunate few visitors who were able to make their hazardous way through nearly impassable rugged terrain to Rainbow Bridge and other marvels of the side canyons.
>
> Today, thanks to the dam, the Colorado River flows clear, and boaters on jewel-like Lake Powell may float up hidden canyons and

feast their eyes on some of the most fantastic and gorgeous scenery in the world.

We are proud that Glen Canyon Dam was awarded the American Society of Civil Engineers award for the outstanding civil engineering achievement of 1963. And while the Glen Canyon unit furnishes us superb scenery, glorious boating, and excellent fishing, it is also generating hydroelectric power that will pay for construction of the facilities for other basin developments to come. . . .

The $832 million Central Arizona Project will pump water from Lake Havasu on the Colorado River and transport it by aqueduct some three hundred miles to the burgeoning Phoenix-Tucson area, one of the fastest growing sections in the Nation. We are all aware of the fabulous expansion of the sun-drenched area during the past decade and of the prospects for even greater growth in the future. Reclamation has made the past progress possible, and this Reclamation project will help it to continue.[12]

A final page from Interior history under Udall. Joseph L. Sax, a well-known professor of environmental law, titled the first chapter of his book *Defending the Environment* "Fiasco at Hunting Creek." It recorded the sequence of events surrounding developers' efforts to obtain a tract of shallowly submerged land at the southern border of Alexandria, Virginia, which, with dredging and filling, could be expanded into a much larger peninsula of land with a vista of the Potomac and Washington skyline. In short, a marsh fit only for ducks and birds could be transformed into profitable real estate. The developers, facing a few hurdles with local and state governments and the Department of the Interior, hired a law firm in which a principal partner was the nephew of John W. McCormack, Speaker of the House of Representatives. "There is no evidence," wrote Sax, "that Speaker McCormack himself ever became involved in the Hunting Creek matter, but perhaps there is, after all, something in a name."[13] Mystery shrouds the activities of the developers and their law firm between December 1964 and October 10, 1967. As recently as the summer of 1967, though, both the National Park Service and the Fish and Wildlife Service were on record as strongly opposing the landfill on its merits. But in October 1967, out of the clear blue, Dr. Stanley A. Cain, assistant secretary of the interior for parks and wildlife, wrote to the Corps of Engineers, whose approval was necessary for the landfill. Cain was one of Udall's choices for a subcabinet post. He had done good work in natural resources while on the faculty of the University of Tennessee and the University of Michigan, though academic achievement counts for little in the political world. "Half a loaf is better than none," Cain once declared in a speech,[14] which could be translated into "let's yield ground a little at a time instead of all at once." In the Hunting Creek fiasco, Cain advised the Corps of Engineers that Interior had reconsidered its earlier opposition; it now concluded that the proposed landfill would not significantly affect recreation or conservation values, and accordingly was withdrawing objections to the fill permits. But there was no evidence of new studies beyond the work already done by Fish and Wildlife and the Park Service, which Cain conveniently ignored.

During the 1960s, as it happened, the House of Representatives was sparked by a cadre of legislators with strong views on the environment. One of them, Representative Henry Reuss of Wisconsin, conducted hearings in June 1968 through the House Committee on Government Operations. Sax analyzed the hearings: "The principal victim, of course, was Assistant Secretary Cain, whose 'flipflopping' was the subject of much lively discussion and whose indiscreet memorandum, admitting that he had made 'a decision based first on political considerations,' was put triumphantly into the public record."[15]

Cain reported to the hearing that he had been to see Udall about Hunting Creek, and the secretary had told him to handle the issue as he saw fit. But then a letter withdrawing the department's objection arrived on Cain's desk neatly prepared for his signature. Sax learned the letter had been written by Bernard Meyer, a department lawyer, at the behest of Walter "Bill" Pozen, a political fixer in Udall's office. Sax's investigation led him to the following conclusion:

> When the subcommittee report appeared in March 1969, it was unyieldingly critical of the Department of the Interior, charging violation of legal obligations, bad judgment, bad policy, and acquiescence in an unjustified giveaway. The report contained little that had not been revealed in the hearings, but its title left nothing to the imagination—"The Permit for Landfill in Hunting Creek: A Debacle in Conservation." . . . In March 1970 the State of Virginia repealed the 1964 law authorizing disposition of the Hunting Creek lands, and in April 1970, the U.S. Army Corps of Engineers revoked the

landfill permit. Victory at last? Perhaps—but as the man said, "money can always wait."[16]

Money ultimately had its way and Hunting Creek was lost, but not during the tenure at Interior of Walter J. Hickel, Udall's successor. Quite the contrary; on April 3, 1969, almost immediately following the congressional report mentioned above, Secretary Hickel dispatched a letter to the secretary of the army meant to set the Corps of Engineers straight. It included the following: "The filling and subsequent construction of an apartment building at Hunting Creek is not in keeping with the widely publicized goal of this Department to preserve and protect the values of the Potomac River. The Department intends to firmly contest any needless filling of the Potomac or affront to its landscape. . . . The time has come for the government to take a firm stand to protect the fast-vanishing natural shorelines of our nation."[17]

This is surprising language for a man who before coming to Washington was considered an environmental spoiler. Hickel was one of ten children raised on a tenant farm in Kansas. He went to Alaska penniless and made a fortune in construction, real estate, and the biggest and best hotel in Anchorage. As governor of Alaska and interior secretary–designate, he frightened people with pronouncements such as "if you set water standards so high you might hinder industrial development," and "I think we have had a policy of conservation for conservation's sake." Citizens all over the country flooded senators with letters criticizing the appointment, and Hickel received the roughest treatment of any of Nixon's cabinet; he was the last one confirmed.

Hickel proved to be a surprise. He was tough, shrewd, and independent, willing to learn and ready to take responsibility. Once in his office he said to me, "If it's right we'll do it. If it's wrong we won't." The specific case at hand was the proposed construction of a petrochemical plant by the German conglomerate BASF on the South Carolina coast. Despite pressure from a powerful South Carolina congressman, Mendel Rivers, Hickel insisted on heeding and supporting the opposition of South Carolina citizens' groups that ultimately blocked the project, infuriating Rivers. When I interviewed him in November 1969 about proposed oil exploration in Alaska, Hickel spoke of the need to protect the fragile Arctic environment, of safeguarding migration routes of caribou, aesthetic values, ecological research, and areas that should remain as wilderness. In a letter he wrote, "I have dedicated myself to giving the highest priority to improving the total environment in which we live. This will be the basic thrust of my effort."[18]

So far as I can tell, Hickel meant it and did it. He took office January 24, 1969. Three days later a Union Oil Company accident at an off-shore platform in Santa Barbara Channel led to an oil slick. Hickel wrote a new regulation providing for absolute liability, without limitation, for the cost of cleanup for companies responsible for oil spills on the outer continental shelf. He went to the mat with the oil industry there, and again later on the Gulf Coast. He denied the most powerful lobby its license for the pipeline across the Arctic slope. He banned the use of DDT and a number of other chemical poisons by agencies of his department—even while Secretary Earl Butz at Agriculture continued the policy of promoting the worst pesticides and herbicides. With his efforts on behalf of alligators Hickel spotlighted attention on the need to safeguard endangered species. (Once he showed me a letter he was about to mail to the editor of *Sports Illustrated* criticizing that magazine for accepting advertisements for alligator shoes.) Two days before his dismissal he announced his decision to place whales on the endangered species list, despite economic and political pressures.

On June 23, 1969, he met with a delegation of almost a hundred conservationists, representing groups in Tennessee and North Carolina, who had come to protest a highway development scheme proposed for the Great Smoky Mountains National Park by George B. Hartzog, Jr., director of the National Park Service. Hickel gave them a serious reception. "I am impressed by your numbers and the sincerity of your purpose," he declared. He walked around the conference room, shaking hands with every person present. It was touching and impressive. Then he assigned the Park Service to develop a new plan, with an eighteen-month deadline. And the highway scheme died.

At the same time that Vice President Spiro Agnew and others in the Nixon administration were denouncing hippies, Hickel supported Earth Day 1970. He had already established a task force in the department to provide liaison with young people. Hickel wrote President Nixon urging him to declare the Environmental Teach-In on April 22 a national holiday. Upset by the Ohio National Guard's May

4 shooting of Kent State University students protesting the Vietnam War, he wrote Nixon a letter urging the president to listen to the young. The letter somehow reached the press and queered Hickel with the White House. Nevertheless, when thousands of students came to Washington, D.C., for an antiwar rally, he wanted to go to the Lincoln Memorial to be with them. In the end, he settled for talking with them on the phone.

Hickel was in deep trouble but insisted he wanted to exit "with an arrow in the heart rather than a bullet in the back."[19] His firing after twenty-two months in office made him a folk hero. He went to speak at the Harvard Law School, where students cheered his demand that they scrap legalistic jargon and go forth to serve human needs. Hickel might have become a significant influence, even without portfolio, but he returned to Alaska and reverted to type, opposing the 1980 federal legislation establishing new national parks, wildlife refuges, and wilderness areas in Alaska, and supporting the plan to open the Arctic National Wildlife Refuge to oil exploration. He tried twice to run for governor but didn't make it through the primary of his own party, then finally ran as an independent in 1990 and was elected. One of his first stated goals was to open the Arctic refuge.

Hickel's replacement, Rogers C. B. Morton, was a safer player. He came from a wealthy Kentucky family and had graduated from Yale, joined the Chesapeake Bay gentry, and served in Congress before becoming chairman of the Republican National Committee, which certainly qualified him politically. He was the first non-Western secretary of the interior since Ickes, but he had been a member of the House Interior Committee and understood how to approach the issues without making waves.

Morton was essentially mild and gracious, anything but intimidating. He wanted everything to be right and spoke of Nixon as "our first true environmental president." Morton served, unluckily, during the energy crisis induced by the 1973 Arab oil embargo, when the Nixon administration became as mesmerized by growth and alleged energy needs as the Spanish inquisitioners had been by witches. On the one hand, Morton brought on board highly motivated and well-intentioned Nathaniel P. Reed as assistant secretary in charge of parks and wildlife, while, on the other hand, he appointed officials of the American Mining Congress and the petroleum industry to key positions of power. After Nixon resigned, President Gerald R. Ford moved Morton to head the Department of Commerce, where, like the good soldier he was, he dutifully carried on.[20]

President Ford actually had worked as a summer ranger in Yellowstone in his youth. The Park Service tried to make something of it, but Ford showed less taste for conservation and the environment than any president of modern times until Ronald Reagan came along. When thrust into the presidency by the Nixon debacle, Ford talked about national cooperation and conciliation, then chose a divisive and provocative course, naming Stan Hathaway, former Republican governor of Wyoming, with the poorest possible conservation record, as secretary of the interior. The Senate confirmed Hathaway in June 1975, but only after considerable complaint and dissent over his outspoken support of oil development and strip-mining of coal on public lands. Hathaway stayed around for a month, repaired to Bethesda Naval Hospital for "depression brought about by physical exhaustion," and presently resigned to head home to align himself with corporate interests in the public lands of Wyoming.[21] Ford himself, while running against Jimmy Carter in 1976, revisited Yellowstone and tried to spark a positive image. "Being alone with nature strengthens our love for one another and for our country," he told a large crowd—a pleasant sentiment for a president to express. All presidents say something nice about nature, in the appropriate setting at the appropriate time, although for Ford it came too late.

Everything, it was assumed, would be different under Jimmy Carter.[22] Environmentalists had worked for his election and had high expectations. Carter had promised to reorder national priorities. He would start with a reduction in defense spending to slow inflation, and he promised to upgrade environmental concern: "If there is a conflict, I will go for beauty, clean air, water, and landscape." That was promising. He appointed as secretary of the interior Cecil D. Andrus, the Democratic governor of Idaho, who had quite a good record in a conservative state. That too was promising.

But soon after taking office, Carter gave the go-ahead for construction of Interstate Highway 66 at the Virginia gateway to Washington. It shocked environmentalists. I-66 symbolized the trauma of freeways disrupting parks, refuges, farms, and neighborhoods. At first it seemed that Brock Adams, secretary of transportation, had rubber-stamped a decision by his predecessor, William Coleman. But it was Carter's own choice. A memorandum to the president from Stuart E. Eizenstat, his assistant for domestic affairs and policy, dated February 1, 1977, and titled "DOT Decision Memo" subsequently came to light. The memo includes reference to "high-visibility issues." The first of them was I-66: "The proposed reaffirmation of Secretary Coleman's decision is appropriate. This is the end of a long and bitter struggle over I-66. The Coleman choice has upset environmentalists. Early reaffirmation is important to insure that new controversy does not build up."

Instead of dealing the people in with a new start, the idea was to shut them out with old politics. The "decision memo" continued with a reference to a hot highway issue in New York: "Westway— This decision, in a similar case on New York's west side, also deserves early reaffirmation. The highway has considerable political support from Governor Carey, Mayor Beame, and other elected New York officials."

The I-66 case was discussed at length within Interior. Concern was voiced on inevitable effects on federal parklands in Virginia and the District of Columbia.[23] Secretary Andrus was urged to issue a strong statement of concern. A letter was drafted for his signature, but he never signed it.

It was part of the Carter political pattern. In his 1977 energy message he coined a phrase, "the moral equivalent of war." Then he proceeded to define energy goals in terms of coal, nuclear fuel, and synthetic fuel rather than conservation. In July 1980 Carter signed the Energy Security Act, approving the expenditure of $88 billion to encourage private interests, mostly the oil giants, to undertake foolhardy projects they would not consider with their own money. "This is a proud day for America," he proclaimed, predicting that the scope of the synfuels effort would dwarf "the combined programs that led us to the moon and built our entire interstate-highway system." The synfuels folly would also have torn up the public lands of the West; fortunately, however, soon after Carter went, it went too.

It was that way across the board. In *Laying Waste: The Poisoning of America by Toxic Chemicals*, Michael Brown details the abundant failures at the Environmental Protection Agency, including the following: "The administration, despite President Carter's generous campaign pledges to protect the environment, pressed for relaxation of water pollution regulations, with the goal of reducing control costs to industry. When reports grew of resistance within EPA to this policy, the president's press secretary, Jody Powell, informed news reporters that those dissatisfied 'should be aware that their resignations will be gladly accepted at the earliest opportunity and should not be hesitant at all in offering them.' "[24]

Carter's four years are a record of promises unfulfilled. The *Washington Star* reported on June 29, 1977: "As a presidential candidate Jimmy Carter campaigned against major oil company ownership of other energy industries, such as coal and uranium. As president, Carter has changed his mind." On September 25, 1979, despite all his pledges, he signed the bill exempting Tellico Dam on the Little Tennessee River from the Endangered Species Act, though Andrus and environmentalists urged a veto.[25] Carter came to office with the goals of zero nuclear weapons and cutbacks in military spending and the arms trade, then made a nearly 180-degree change in direction. As leaders of the peace movement complained, the budget was so conservative it was hard to tell who really won in 1976. As evidence they could readily cite the MX missile project, a massive five-thousand-mile system of twenty-one-foot-deep trenches Carter was prepared to spread across the West.

Andrus, for his part, came to Washington with a positive reputation born of his first campaign for governor of Idaho in 1969. The central issue of his campaign had been the question of whether there should be open pit mining at the foot of Castle Peak in the beautiful White Cloud Mountains. He argued that irreplaceable natural resources must not be destroyed for temporary economic gain and won an overwhelming victory. His record, however, was mixed. He supported construction of the Teton Dam (which collapsed in 1976, killing a score of people, leaving thousands homeless, and destroying thousands of acres), ignoring pleas by conservationists and warnings by geologists; he opposed the proposal for a Sawtooth National Park and insisted on omitting key timbered tracts in Idaho from protection under provisions of the Wilderness Act. Andrus had begun his career in sawmilling and logging and never lost track of his connections.[26]

Andrus and Carter had a lot in common. Both were personally unassuming and likable, both were former navy men, and both were former governors of backwoods states. Both could straddle the issues and look good doing it. This may explain why from January 1977 to September 1980 the Interior Department approved plans for thirty-three new or expanded major coal operations on public lands in six Western states;[27] why Andrus pressed accelerated oil and gas drilling in ecologically sensitive areas off the coasts of Alaska, California, and New England;[28] and why in May 1977 the secretary announced that he would not try to stop construction of a nuclear power plant on the southeast shore of Lake Michigan, despite inevitable devastating impacts on adjacent Indian Dunes National Lakeshore.[29]

In September 1977 Andrus declared that the government must offer help to Native Americans without destroying their culture; that the nation must seek to compensate for centuries of exploitation or neglect without penalizing the current generation of non-Indians. But the fortunes of Indians declined; their lands became the primary sacrifice areas and Indians the sacrificed people. Alvin H. Josephy, Jr., editor of *American Heritage* and author of works on Indian issues, wrote to me: "From his Georgia perspective Carter equates Indians with blacks and, in a mad sort of way, combining ignorance with dangerous motives, is brushing aside two hundred years of treaties, statutes, court decisions and history." Indian author Vine Deloria was blunter, if possible, asserting that if Carter wanted to do something for Indians, he'd make employment in the Bureau of Indian Affairs a capital offense. Deloria felt there was no sympathy for Indians whatsoever.

Indians, unfortunately, were in the way of corporate profit making.[30] Interior called the Indian heartland of northern New Mexico "the hottest uranium exploitation spot in the U.S." Through generous lease terms Indian-owned uranium resources were opened to conglomerates like Gulf, Mobil, Kerr-McGee, Continental, United Nuclear, and Anaconda. Growing piles of radioactive wastes were discounted in an environmental assessment: "The air quality will not be worse than in most cities or highways."

While it may be unfair to hold a secretary of the interior personally responsible for the handling of particular issues, they serve as telltale signs pointing to a pattern. Lewis Regenstein of Fund for Animals reminded me throughout the Carter-Andrus period of broken pledges to protect whales, of administration help for ivory dealers and trophy hunters, and of more action to dismantle the endangered species list than to protect endangered species.

Andrus nominated Robert Mendelsohn, a San Francisco city coun-
cilman, as assistant secretary for policy, budget, and administration.
The *San Francisco Bay Guardian*, an alternative newspaper, carried
on a campaign against him, alleging improper dealings with the
Coastal Commission and raising enough questions to block Mendelsohn's confirmation by the Senate. Andrus stood behind Mendelsohn and appointed him a special assistant, without need of confirmation. One particular issue Mendelsohn handled involved disputed
parkland along the Georgetown waterfront on the Potomac River in
Washington, D.C. A developer coveted the site for an apartment-
shopping complex. A citizens' group in Georgetown, on the other
hand, fought to protect it as a park open to public access. The National Capital Region of the National Park Service would normally
be in charge of the issue, but responsibility was preempted by the secretary's office, and the park professionals yielded to the politicians,
as some of them are wont to do through Democratic and Republican
administrations alike. The developer consequently won hands-
down. Following the change in administration, Mendelsohn opened
a consulting firm, and the waterfront developer was prominent
among his clients.[31]

I recognize that Andrus had able people who tried hard and did
good work. The Alaska lands legislation of 1980, with all its imperfections, was Andrus's crowning achievement and the best thing to
come out of the Carter administration.[32] But the sleaze pressures are
too powerful and, for some, too tempting. Sleaze is not even, or not
always, a matter of money. It's a source of connections and influence,
a part of the process of staying afloat and getting things done.

In August 1985 I visited Andrus at his home in Boise. He felt more
comfortable in Idaho than in Washington and was preparing to run
for governor once again. Andrus recalled his experience as secretary.
His dealings with members of Congress were much like those Udall
had described: most congressmen were "narrowsighted and selfish."
For the most part, they came to see Andrus only when they had a
constituency problem or when some issue arose in their particular
states.

"They wanted it handled their way, regardless of whether or not it
was good for the resource," Andrus recalled. "There were some
statesmen, but too few. In many instances they were demanding, not
asking. Far too many are there for one purpose: to perpetuate their

own self-perceived image of power. They gauge everything on the idea, 'I must stay here.' They really believe they must stay for the good of the country and do anything to be a member of Congress. That is the driving force."

Governing Idaho clearly would be more fun, even as a Democrat facing a Republican legislature. In 1986 Andrus was elected after a tough campaign, with the help of conservationists, though he gave them no promises. Then he let them down by collaborating with Senator James McClure for a wilderness bill of 1.5 million out of 9 million roadless acres in the national forests of Idaho. But conservationists wanted more, parting company with Andrus and beating the Andrus-McClure proposal in Congress. The issue of wilderness designation in Idaho remained unresolved into 1991.

Ronald Reagan reversed the progressive direction, such as it was, of the Carter years in Washington. As governor of California, Reagan had supported a statewide bond issue to purchase parkland and had approved a bill to protect mountain lions and tule elk, despite opposition from his own Department of Natural Resources. However, he had resisted establishment of a national park to save the last great groves of redwood trees.[33] He is accused in this connection of saying, "When you've seen one redwood tree you've seen them all." Though he denied making the statement, it is consistent with his subsequent simplistic pronouncements as president and his opposition to protecting *anything* for the public estate. Early in his first term Reagan dismissed the idea of conserving energy. It wouldn't work, he asserted, because Americans would be too cold in winter and too hot in summer. In his mind it was logical to place a clutch of antienvironmentalists in charge of the environment—people like Ann Burford Gorsuch at the Environmental Protection Agency, John B. Crowell at Agriculture (a timberman running the national forests and wilderness), and James G. Watt at Interior, plus all the associates and assistants they brought along. Reagan allied himself with the Sagebrush Rebellion, a movement of Western livestock, mining, logging, and real estate interests clamoring for transfer of federal lands to state and private ownership. There were legitimate grievances with bureaucracy, but the Reagan people were less interested in making bureaucracy function properly than in redirecting it to cater to the Sagebrush Rebels.

James G. Watt was ready-made for Reagan. He had earlier worked in Washington for the Chamber of Commerce and the Interior Department, then had established and directed the Mountain States Legal Foundation to fight for free enterprise against the evils of federalism. As secretary he derided environmentalists as "affluent elitists," "extremists," and "fanatics." "They are political activists, a left-wing cult which seeks to bring down the type of government I believe in," he said once.[34] For Watt it was Americanism versus liberalism and socialism. He was all for morality—fundamentalist Christian morality. When he banned the Beach Boys from the 1983 July Fourth festival on the Mall, he showed himself so near the deep end that even the Reagans were embarrassed.

Watt felt victimized by the "news media elite," which tracked him everywhere en masse, always on the lookout for another gaffe.[35] They wanted him fractious and outrageous. He performed and they loved him for it. The media focused on foibles of personality, generously overlooking his record with the Mountain States Legal Foundation and the administration's connections with mining, grazing, logging, and agroindustry. Watt was free to lease the nation's coal to his old Mountain States contributors at prices so far below market they failed to cover the cost to the government of putting on the sale.

The most infamous of these cases, in the Powder River Basin of Wyoming, was exposed by congressional investigating committees who calculated that excessive offerings of federal coal in a soft market, together with irregular if not illegal leasing procedures, cost taxpayers between $60 and $100 million in lost revenues. Less well known was the same kind of giveaway to coal and power companies in the San Juan Basin of northwestern New Mexico, including the Chaco-Bisti region, which is rich in archaeological and paleontological resources. In this case Chaco Culture National Historical Park, charged with preserving the dramatic ruins in Chaco Canyon, was placed at risk. In *The People's Victory over James Watt*, Jeff Radford shows how Watt and others in the administration wheeled and dealed. As public affairs officer for the Bureau of Land Management, Radford saw it from the inside until he quit. He recounts a horror story about the preparation of a required environmental impact statement: BLM managers were pressured or ordered to cite nonexistent land-use plans, to ignore or discount the value of cultural resources, to manipulate coal tonnage figures, and to pretend it would be simple to revegetate mined land in an area where rainfall averages only eight inches a year. Field professionals who failed to provide the right answers were transferred, forced to resign, or fired.[36]

Watt took considerable interest in national parks, though not in preserving their resources.[37] "I will err on the side of public use versus preservation," he told a conference of park concessionaires on March 9, 1981, in Washington, D.C. Then he related to the concessionaires his recent experiences in traveling down the Colorado River through the Grand Canyon. He said he had gone to learn about the phaseout of motors on rubber rafts as proposed by the National Park Service: "The first day was spectacular . . . the second day started to get a little tedious, but the third day I wanted bigger motors to move that raft out. There is no way you could get me on an oar-powered raft on that river—I'll guarantee you that. On the fourth day we were praying for helicopters and they came."[38]

Watt declared himself a champion of "stewardship" and claimed credit for initiating the Park Repair and Improvement Program (PRIP) to correct abundant health and safety hazards in existing parks. The program, however, was begun before he arrived, following a report citing poor conditions of park facilities and multi-billion-dollar maintenance and replacement needs. Watt could not have kept PRIP from happening even if he had wanted to. The PRIP program on the whole was positive, though in a few cases projects were undertaken without adequate review.

The emphasis in Watt's stewardship was entirely on the physical plant, providing for public use rather than resource protection. It did not embrace concerns for water and air quality. And Watt did his best to scuttle land acquisition, whether for new parks or for parks already established.

For Christmas 1982, citizens were asked to support the parks with money. The department issued a catalogue. For $5 you could ensure a canteen for inner-city visitors who lacked their own camping equipment; $300 bought a chain saw; and $30,000 bought a computer "for storage and recovery of ecosystem data." Chevron USA contributed $5000, which led Park Service public relations spokesperson Duncan Morrow, ever loyal, to comment in the *Washington Post* of November 26, 1982: "It fits nicely with his philosophy of involving the private sector in government, relieving some of the burden on the taxpayer."

Nathaniel Reed, an assistant secretary under whom Watt had served during the Ford administration, condensed all the criticism into two sentences: "His insensitivity to the beauty and adventure of the West is appalling. It is as though Secretary Watt can't tell the difference between national parks and industrial parks."[39]

The position of assistant secretary for fish, wildlife, and parks, the secretary's delegate in the chain of command, and a job with considerable authority, has been occupied now and then by individuals who understood something about national parks and cared about them, including Stanley Cain, an ecologist and educator who served under Udall; Leslie Glasgow, former director of the Louisiana Fish and Game Department and a professor of wildlife management, who served under Hickel; Nathaniel Reed, a key player in Florida conservation who served under Morton; and Robert Herbst, director of natural resources in Minnesota, who served under Andrus. Assistant secretaries and other political appointees sometimes are selected by the secretary, but often they are assigned to him as part of patronage, the process of sharing power with those who have power. So far as I can determine, G. Ray Arnett was not chosen by Watt to be assistant secretary for fish, wildlife, and parks; he arrived through more direct Reagan connections. He proved even harsher in dealing with national parks than Watt himself.

Arnett had worked for an oil company in California as a geologist and public relations man before Governor Ronald Reagan appointed him state director of fish and game. He fought California conservationists on issue after issue. He was six feet five, bulky, and didn't look like much of a hunter, but he was always scouting for wild animals to shoot. In 1982, while at an international parks conference in Indonesia, Arnett was eager to get a crack at endangered species of that country, to the embarrassment of the other Americans present. He wanted to allow shooting of mountain lions in Carlsbad Caverns National Park, New Mexico, and to open Western national parks to snowmobiles and Eastern national seashores to dune buggies. He was a wisecracker, adept at one-liners. Environmentalists were "Chicken Little extremists" and "prairie fairies."[40] In 1981 I attended a ceremony dedicating the Grand Canyon as a World Heritage Site. Arnett, the speaker of the day, began with a joke about his country cousin ("If there was a nip in the air, he'd drink it"). Then he helicoptered across the canyon to the North Rim, where his first question to park people was, "What is there to hunt around here?" "Nuclear power is the least damaging and best answer to our energy needs," he said in 1976. "It's ludicrous the way some well-meaning fanatical conservationists are clogging up the system by searching for bylaws to halt progress." Arnett was a hero to the National Rifle Association, which, after he left the government, named him executive vice president at a yearly salary of $150,000. Soon after, though, the NRA had its own internal battle and fired him.[41]

From start to finish, the Reagan years at Interior were a time of repression and intimidation of federal employees. National Park Service people were continually belittled and badgered. In September 1983 Watt put his foot in his mouth with a sick joke (about the makeup of a coal-leasing panel: "We have every kind of mix you can have. I have a black, I have a woman, two Jews, and a cripple. And we have talent") and was forced to resign. His successor, William C. Clark, was a definite improvement. On the other hand, when Arnett left he was replaced as assistant secretary by William P. Horn, who tightened control over personnel and policy even more.

Clark came to Interior as an old Reagan regular. He was chief of staff when Reagan was governor and had been rewarded with an appointment as a California judge. Reagan brought him to Washington to be deputy secretary of state, but he began badly at his confirmation hearing by showing scant awareness of world affairs or world leaders. It was different at Interior; he had more background for it. His grandfather had been a ranger in the Forest Service, and he came from a California ranch family. Clark was quiet, opened to conservationists the door that Watt had closed, calmed things, and kept Interior out of the headlines before the 1984 election. Then he quietly packed his bag, left the hassle behind, and returned to his ranch in California.[42]

Donald Hodel succeeded Clark. Before becoming secretary of the interior Hodel had spent two years as secretary of energy and, before that, had been under secretary of the interior, Watt's number-two man. As administrator of Bonneville Power Administration from 1972 to 1978, Hodel had once charged in a Portland speech (on "Prophets of Shortage") that the environment movement was loaded with Communists. It is hard to forget his role in promoting the nuclear power project of the Washington Public Power Supply System

(WPPSS), which ended in bankruptcy and financial disaster. It only proves that if you make a big enough mistake, no one will notice or hold it against you.

Hodel's big play during his time as secretary was for "balance." He did indeed openly discourage continuance of massive Western irrigation and water-storage projects. He startled everybody by proposing to dismantle and remove the O'Shaughnessy Dam from Hetch Hetchy Valley in Yosemite National Park and restore the valley to the very condition John Muir had fought to preserve. But "balance" meant the pursuit of oil, natural gas, and coal on public lands and the outer continental shelf, which Hodel, like Watt, considered a basic mandate.[43]

"I kiddingly tell people this job has never been a steppingstone to anything," Hodel said near the end of my interview with him in Washington. Secretaries of the interior are easy to forget, and Hodel is no exception, although he deserves some remembrance for his 1987 "Rayban Plan," whereby he proposed a program of "personal protection"—including wider use of hats, sunglasses, and sunscreen lotions—rather than international controls to freeze production of cancer-causing chlorofluorocarbons in the earth's ozone layer.[44]

William Penn Mott had just been appointed director of the national parks, essentially on Clark's initiative and recommendation.[45] Hodel himself chose William Horn as assistant secretary in charge of national parks. Horn, one of the old Watt-Hodel team, went after the Park Service with a vengeance—countermanding Mott's orders, interfering in personnel decisions, changing Mott's recommendations for bonus awards to members of his staff, even changing Mott's efficiency rating of a regional director named Howard Chapman.[46] Horn was in his mid-thirties, half Mott's age, but that didn't stop him. He overruled Mott's order to restrict aircraft over the Grand Canyon and off-road vehicles and hunting in other park units, true to Watt's pledge to favor public use over resource protection.

Horn, too, had bigger fish to fry. He was the driving force in the Interior Department's recommendation to open the Arctic National Wildlife Refuge in Alaska to oil development. He also negotiated deals in secret with several native corporations—entrepreneurial syndicates created by Congress with minimal relevance to the traditional natives—by which the corporations agreed to trade 1 million acres of remote property for rights to 166,000 acres within the Arctic refuge containing potentially enormous oil deposits. As critics, including the state of Alaska, complained, the federal government would be yielding oil deposits so valuable it would have been feasible and advantageous to purchase the million acres with oil revenues. Luckily, congressional approval was necessary and the secret came out. Horn, meanwhile, in June 1988, a few months before Reagan left office, resigned from Interior to join a law firm representing a number of Native American corporations, including one due to receive oil rights in the Arctic Wildlife Refuge.[47]

That is how things have been done in the past. Would they be different under George Bush? As a candidate, Bush said he wanted to be an environmental president, but once in office he showed little desire to change things, at least not at the Department of the Interior. Manuel Lujan, Jr., had given up his seat in Congress after serving twenty years and was ready to return to New Mexico when Bush appointed him secretary. He came on as a folksy follower of the Watt-Hodel line, affable, nonconfrontational, and woefully ill-informed about basic resource questions. He became a handy target for criticism and ridicule; the media referred to him as "the Inferior Secretary," "gaffe-prone," "the Cabinet's weak link," and "one of Bush's dimmer points of light." His mistakes were especially embarrassing because he had served for years as a leading Republican member of the House Interior Committee, which should have left him well informed.[48]

Clearly Lujan was appointed to take orders, not to give them, while Watt-Hodel holdovers at Interior pressed on with the Reagan-era agenda, including commercial use of national parks. Lujan apparently had little or nothing to do with the selection of James M. Ridenour as director of the National Park Service. Though he had never visited the Grand Canyon, Yellowstone, or Yosemite, Ridenour *was* on a first-name basis with Vice President Dan Quayle, for whom he had raised funds as a county finance chairman of the Indiana Republican Party.[49] Ridenour's predecessors—most of them, at least—actually had been to national parks, even had worked in them, and had worked up through the ranks. Ridenour had none of that background. His appointment showed how little national parks counted in the Bush administration's agenda.

4

In all the government the National Park Service is the only bureau with the singular mandate to preserve nature. Nevertheless, the Park Service must justify itself over and over again on the number of visitors to the parks and their contribution to the economy. The body politic considers preservation a bit of a luxury, the special interest of a small but vocal minority. Consequently, director after director of the agency has said something like, "If I must err, it will be on the side of preservation," and then made an accommodation to the contrary, with the promise that "we can repair the damage later." But then, being director of the National Parks Service is a high-risk position, presumably professional yet loaded with political booby traps. More by far have been dismissed than have retired or resigned gracefully, which explains why one seldom hears of a director of the National Park Service standing up to say, "The Smoky Mountains are suffering from acid rain and, by God, something must be done about it!"

Stephen T. Mather, the first director, had great moments as a leader. He built a professional service and had the courage to dare politics and politicians. Early on, for example, he fought a plan of Idaho irrigationists to draw water from the southwest corner of Yellowstone and from Yellowstone Lake. It was one of many incursions he resisted. In a 1920 report titled "A Crisis in National Conservation"

Mather wrote: "Once a small dam is authorized for irrigation or other purposes, other dams will follow. Once a small lake is raised and a small amount of timber is destroyed . . . once start the national parks toward national forest-status, and it will be logically impossible to stop short. One misstep is fatal."[1]

Mather came on the parks scene as a cosmopolitan industrialist known as "the borax king." His family was from New England, but he was born and raised in California. Following graduation from the University of California, Mather worked for five years as a reporter for the *New York Sun.* Then he went to Chicago to do advertising and sales promotion in the borax business, which looked so attractive that he mastered finance and acquired a healthy piece of the borax market. The story has often been told of how, after visiting the national parks in 1914, he complained to Secretary of the Interior Franklin K. Lane (whom he had known as a fellow student at the University of California) about how poorly they were run. Lane challenged him to come to Washington to run the national parks for himself.

Thus Mather, aged forty-seven, a man of accomplishment and influence, arrived at the department in January 1915 as assistant to the secretary. One of the first people he met was Horace M. Albright, twenty-four, a recent graduate of the University of California who had come to work for the department in 1913. Albright became Mather's assistant, protégé, and, when Mather was incapacitated, his stand-in. Their first challenge was to draft the organic act to establish the new bureau to be known as the National Park Service. About a dozen national parks had been established well before this time, starting with Yellowstone, which Congress set aside in 1872, but there was no central administration. The 1916 organic act, properly the National Parks Act, presently was designed to codify the principle, enunciated by Frederick Law Olmsted, that Americans have the right to enjoy public scenery and the government has the responsibility to protect the scenery for them. The systematic protection of scenic resources marked a reversal of the prevalent view of the time that the reserved public domain was meant for commodity production—notably livestock grazing, logging, and mining—and that Yellowstone was all right, in its place, as long as it didn't cost money.

Mather was an aggressive, free-wheeling go-getter and promoter. He was one of a standard type of his time: men of independent wealth and social status, insiders who used their connections in high places for the common good. Members of the Boone and Crockett Club, which Theodore Roosevelt had organized with a cadre of wealthy and influential hunters to advance the cause of conservation, exemplified the breed. So did Gifford Pinchot, who early in life considered a career in social work but turned to forestry as a social movement. While in Washington they would rendezvous at the Cosmos Club, which John Wesley Powell had organized for men of letters and science, conveniently located in those days across Lafayette Park from the White House.

Representative William Kent of California (who joined the Cosmos Club on election to Congress in 1911 and later introduced the 1916 organic act) was another of the elite who used his wealth in support of public causes. He successfully blocked logging and development of a particularly attractive three-hundred-acre redwood grove in Marin County by buying it. Kent discovered he could best save the grove under the Monument Act, which allowed the federal government to accept lands affected by historic or other public interest from private individuals. In accepting the gift, President Theodore Roosevelt proposed to call it the Kent Monument, but Kent insisted that it be named Muir Woods in honor of his friend and wilderness companion John Muir.[2]

One by-product of this effort was the organization in 1917 of the Save-the-Redwoods League, with Kent and Mather among its founders.[3] The league was a private organization oriented to private responsibility and local administration. Its leaders were scientists and scholars, some of them close friends of Herbert Hoover, who decried coercive regulatory bureaucracy. They believed in the lofty obligation to do good for their golden state through moral persuasion and cooperation with redwood lands owners, which explains why the league long rejected proposals for a redwood national park.

Thus in 1921 the Kent-Mather Grove was acquired with funds donated by two of the league's eminent pioneers—so things were done in those days. Mather kept his borax interests and continued to draw a salary and share of the profits, which he dispensed generously on behalf of the national parks. He wined and dined those who counted, entertained influential editors on field trips, and hired an old crony from his newspaper days, Robert Sterling Yard, as publicity chief of the Park Service, with Yard's salary coming from his own funds.

The deliberate intent of these activities was to popularize the parks and to promote visitation as a means of building a public constituency, and thus support in Congress. This approach follows the unwritten law of bureaucratic survival: The more money an agency can spend, or, at least, the more people it serves, the larger its personnel force will become, and consequently the greater its influence and its security in the federal structure. Mather the marketer and promoter held ceremonies to open roads, hotels, and post offices in the parks, while Yard distributed a stream of press releases. They encouraged roads, hotels, concessions, and railroads to bring people to the parks and recognition to the place and purpose of the National Park Service.

Mather enjoyed hiking in the mountains almost every summer, but he sparked construction of highways in the parks and the motorcar invasion. Never missing an opportunity, he kept a big Packard touring car in Los Angeles, license USNPS 1, for use when he went west in the summer. He and Albright foresaw none of the problems of congestion, concrete, and pollution that highways ultimately would bring. They felt they should accommodate the public's desire for travel, and that horses and stagecoaches were more damaging than automobiles. In Yosemite in 1924 there were only 138 miles of rutted wagon road, almost all built by private capital in preautomobile days. In 1924 Mather got a large appropriation from Congress to pave, widen, and improve roads. He promoted the Going-to-the-Sun Highway in Glacier National Park, which was followed in due course by Trail Ridge Road in Rocky Mountain and the Zion–Mount Carmel Highway in Zion.

He worked with the railroads in promoting the parks, exploiting their political connections. Santa Fe and Union Pacific between them invested half a million dollars in national park exhibits at the 1915 San Francisco Exposition. In 1916 the railroads passed out two million copies of park literature.

Concessions became what the Park Service likes to call "supervised monopolies." By the time Mather came along, in Yellowstone alone the facilities included a chain of five hotels and two lunch stations run by the Yellowstone Park Hotel Company; three stagecoach lines; and three systems of permanent camps, each offering overnight lodgings, lunch stations, and transportation to and from the northern and western entrances. Mather thought it was all too much, merged them, and changed the park orientation from stagecoach to motorcar. As Horace Albright wrote to me many years later: "Bringing in the automobile completely changed the operation, getting rid of one hotel, half a dozen permanent camps. You had to be all booked up ahead of time and be available to follow schedules. All that went out the window when we let in the automobiles and the buses. We got rid of a hotel and lots of lodges, fences, corrals, and about four thousand horses. Before, you couldn't go many miles without running into the permanent camps. Now, it's all back again to nature."

For most visitors, going to the parks was more of a resort vacation or excursion than a wilderness experience. Concessions were financed by railroads in Glacier, Zion, Bryce Canyon, Grand Canyon, Yellowstone, and Mount Rainier national parks. The concession in Yosemite was run by the well-established Curry family, including Donald Tressider, who doubled as president of Stanford University. Yosemite was the scene of the fabled firefall, where each summer night the concessionaire's voice at the Camp Curry campfire would bellow, "Let the fire fall," whereupon an assistant atop Glacier Point, 3500 feet above and a mile away, would push a huge bonfire over the edge of the cliff. The firefall and drive-through sequoia tree made Yosemite a bit of a carnival, and so did the bear feeding at Yellowstone. But they fit Mather's strategy of image building—of generating public support to get money from Congress. Concessions in due course would become a major source of grievance, as we shall see later, and in some parks concessionaires have exercised more influence than the administrators in charge.

Toting up the pluses and minuses of Mather's administration is not easy, and maybe not fair. Mather, with Albright's aid, was instrumental in adding Acadia, Bryce Canyon, Grand Canyon, Hawaii Volcanoes, Lassen Volcanic, Mount McKinley, and Zion to the network of national parks. They opened the way for parks in the East, starting with Great Smoky Mountains, Shenandoah, and Mammoth Cave. Throughout the 1920s and 1930s many national forest areas were proposed as national parks, including Olympic and North Cascades, which eventually were designated as parks. With his own money Mather organized the National Conference on State Parks and the National Parks Association (now the National Parks and Conservation Association), with Robert Sterling Yard, his old newspaper colleague, as executive director. Mather defended the national parks from repeated political threats and opposition. In 1919 he resisted and disapproved a five-mile-long cableway for tourists across the Grand Canyon (which Albright favored).[4] In 1925, while on vacation in Glacier, after the Great Northern Railway disregarded his order to dismantle its lumber mill in the park, he led a brigade that exploded the mill with thirteen charges of TNT.

Mather wanted to keep his agency free from politics, and he bluntly told politicians that park personnel would be appointed not on the basis of patronage, like postmasters, but on their merits as resource professionals. He worked to build an organization in his own image: vigorous and aggressive, safeguarding wilderness values as he saw them, and devoted to public service. As his biographer, Robert Shankland, wrote, the National Park Service was "the house that Mather built," and Mather wanted everybody on the parks payroll to love the work. But he was restless, an insomniac who suffered mental problems (then called nervous breakdowns) and was forced to spend time in sanatoriums. He suffered a stroke in late 1928 and officially left his position in January 1929. He died a year later. The *New York Times* editorialized: "His love of nature became his country's good fortune."[5]

Horace Albright was thirty-nine years old when he was sworn in as the second director of the Park Service. He knew every person in his own bureau, from Washington to remote corners in the field. He knew many members of Congress intimately. In 1917, when Mather was stricken for a time, he had served as acting director for a year, building the bureau "by improvising and stubborn persistence." In 1919, at the age of twenty-nine, he became the first civilian superintendent of Yellowstone, replacing the army personnel who had been in charge since 1886. He spent each summer in the park, then returned to Washington to work under Mather the rest of the year. While at Yellowstone he did his share of public relations and politicking, entertaining Presidents Harding and Coolidge, and Hoover before he became president. Though he knew the ropes, Robert Sterling Yard still gave him a few worthy words of written advice to buck up his courage: "Here and there are a few who think the new Director ought to be a rich man, to travel in the wholesale way Mather did, to entertain trail parties, give fine dinners, and associate in general with men of heavy consequence, conferring a super-financial if not super-social aura on the Service. Mather was Mather. The particular creative thing he did with the Park Service no other could have done at the time, nor will any other need to continue. His money was an unnecessary picturesque part in his personality."[6]

Horace Albright was director of the National Park Service for only four years, from 1929 to 1933, yet he made the national park system truly national and broadened its scope to embrace areas of historic as well as natural importance. These extensions started with George Washington's birthplace in Virginia and came to include Civil War battlefields, which the army had administered up to that time. He took on the Forest Service and its commodity-producing allies in toe-to-toe political slugfests. The classic battle was fought over the Grand Tetons, where Albright from his days in nearby Yellowstone had envisioned a major national park; he enlisted the financial support of John D. Rockefeller, Jr., to purchase enough private land in the Jackson Hole Valley to ultimately make it happen.

I first met Horace Albright in the early 1950s. He was still vigorous, and was able to command respect through sheer goodwill. He likely did more to advance the cause of national parks than any other individual, from the very beginning of the parks down to this day, yet he deferred to his mentor; it was always "Mr. Mather." Albright held a positive, optimistic vision, believing that good people by their nature would persevere and, providing they didn't become overzealous or too restrictive, would succeed.

Many people benefited from contacts with him, as is borne out by the testimony of David Condon, a national parks veteran. In 1928 Condon, twenty-four, and his friend Fred, a classmate at Brigham Young University, were taking time out from college to travel north and into Canada. While touring Yellowstone in their Model T Ford, they decided they would like to work there, or in someplace like it, and presented themselves at park headquarters to see the man in charge. Instead they were balked by the administrative assistant, Joe Joffe, who brusquely advised that the park superintendent was too busy. But the superintendent had overheard and called out, "Never mind, Joe. I'm not busy. Send them in!" The students explained that Fred was interested in fisheries work and Condon in natural history and park protection. Superintendent Albright urged them to return to college. "Mr. Condon, you should study geology, botany, zoology—so that you know the plants, animals, and earth history. If you can do that and pass a civil service examination with high enough grades, you can get yourself a job as a park ranger."

"He was kind to us, went out of his way to be helpful. 'I hope you decide to do it,' he said. 'We need young men who are interested in this kind of thing.'" Condon told me this story in 1984 at Vernal, Utah, where he lived in retirement. As a result of the encounter, he returned to school, passed the civil service exam, and began as a seasonal naturalist in Yellowstone in 1931. It was the start of a forty-one-year career in the national parks, including twelve years as chief naturalist in Yellowstone.

Albright resigned on August 10, 1933, to become general manager (and later president) of the U.S. Potash Company. He wanted to get on with a business career, for which he had trained in college, and besides, he was a Republican holdover in a Democratic administration. He left with a message to park personnel:

> In this letter, perhaps one of my last official statements to you, let me urge you to be aggressive and vigorous in the fulfillment of your administrative duties. The National Park Service, from its very beginning, has been an outstanding organization because its leaders, both in Washington and out in the field, worked increasingly and with high public spirit to carry out the noble policies and maintain the lofty ideals of the service as expressed in law and executive pronouncement. Do not let the service become "just another Government bureau"; keep it youthful, vigorous, clean and strong. We are not here simply to protect what we have been given so far; we are here to try to be the future guardians of those areas as well as to sweep our protective arms around the vast lands which may well need us as man and his industrial world expand and encroach on the last bastions of wilderness. Today we are concerned about our natural areas being enjoyed by the people. But we must never forget that all the elements of nature, the rivers, forests, animals, and all the things coexistent with them must survive as well.[7]

Albright bowed out of government, but not out of the parks or the preservation movement. For more than thirty-five years John D. Rockefeller, Jr., and Laurance Rockefeller relied on his advice and judgment in major bequests and purchases to benefit the national parks and other causes. He was on the board of Colonial Williamsburg, the Rockefeller-endowed restoration in Virginia. In 1964, when I was preparing an article about Albright, Edwin Kendrew, vice president for architecture at Williamsburg, told me:

> There were no models in America for reviving an entire segment of the past. Mr. Rockefeller was reticent, cautious, but Horace Albright was able to penetrate with sound advice on principle, policy, and ideals. He supported the architects and other professionals in matters some considered visionary, if not unnecessary. One was the instance of setting the hotel well back from the street. Or he would tell Mr. Rockefeller that detailed research into the shape and substance of original buildings might be costly but was essential. He championed purchase of land not only for restoration but for protection of the area from encroachment. "It will never be any cheaper, you know," he would suggest to Mr. Rockefeller. When it was proposed to intrude on history with modern street lights, he insisted that one concession would only lead to another. "Instead of giving the visitor convenience," he said on one occasion, "we should give him a street map."

Horace Albright lived into his ninety-seventh year. He became a legend in the Park Service, and he continued to advocate and advance the cause of preservation as public policy. This is not to say he was "pure." In the early pioneering years he supported public feeding of grizzly bears at Yellowstone and the "Rock of Ages" singing at Carlsbad Caverns, both more entertainment than conservation. He was criticized during that period for not being preservationist enough by Enos Mills, champion of Rocky Mountain National Park; by Emerson Hough, a two-fisted writer for the *Saturday Evening Post*; and by Robert Sterling Yard, too.

Between 1956 and 1958, while a member and chairman of the National Parks Advisory Board (a group appointed by the secretary of the interior), Albright was the target of an investigation by Representative John E. Moss, a crusading California congressman. Later, at 1964 hearings, Moss documented Albright's involvement in decisions in Death Valley National Monument relating to an exchange of land owned by Furnace Creek Inn for a national park visitor center in return for a guarantee of water rights. In its concluding report the House Committee on Government Operations concluded that Albright had been guilty of conflict of interest as a member of the National Parks Advisory Board since 1952 and reprimanded National Park Service officials for accepting gratuities from Furnace Creek Inn, and officials of the Interior Department for failure to safeguard the water rights. The proposed land exchange was scrapped. Moss charged a "million-dollar land deal," but Horace insisted he was using personal diplomacy for the public welfare. It likely was a case of good intentions and poor judgment.[8]

Into his last years he remembered the past clearly but seemed out of touch with critical issues of the present, let alone the future. In 1974, when he received the Cosmos Club Award (he was then the club's oldest member in terms of age and length of membership) for his long years of civic and conservation leadership, he said:

> Arguments are now being made by some environmentalists that national parks were intended to be wilderness reserves without developments of any kind, and they deplore hotels, lodges, campsites, roads, and other facilities for the enjoyment of the parks by the visiting public. They urge the placement of all facilities outside park boundaries, that no new roads be built, and, wherever possible, existing roads and other facilities be "phased out." Such a view is ridiculous, especially when large parks are considered. . . .
>
> I venture the opinion that many dedicated and high-minded ecologists would be delighted to see the beautiful Ahwahnee Hotel in Yosemite and the famous Old Faithful Inn in Yellowstone demolished. Others would remove El Tovar from the rim of the Grand Canyon along with the adjacent accommodations for camping. They desire the development of tourist accommodations on the perimeter of the park far from the vast overview of the Grand Canyon itself. With nearly a million square miles of wilderness in the park, including the canyon, they begrudge the location of surface structures on only two square miles.[9]

A few excerpts from his notes to me while I was writing for the *Los Angeles Times* and later will show his different sides.

> *June 6, 1978*   I well remember that when I was Director, I spent two weeks in the Great Smokies, riding horseback everywhere, and I remember Gatlinburg. On returning to Knoxville, I remember publicly declaring that Gatlinburg was the ideal national park gateway town, and compared its beauty, serenity, good taste, etc., with gateway towns and cities in the West—Estes Park, Colorado, West

Yellowstone and Gardiner, Montana, etc. A few years later, Gatlin-
burg had "gone over the dam." I could not say anything good about
it. I last saw it in 1961. I feel about it like I do Lake Tahoe—I never
want to see it again.

July 9, 1978   I have always been a train fan. What beautiful trains
we had going to national parks in the 1920s to 1950s. The North
Coast Limited from Chicago to Yellowstone on Northern Pacific; the
Yellowstone Special between Salt Lake City and West Yellowstone;
the pleasant Burlington from Chicago to Cody, Wyoming—all
Yellowstone trains. In the 1920s these trains would deliver to park
entrances over forty thousand happy travelers who toured the park in
open buses—except when raining, canvas tops quickly opened and
the seated passengers were thus protected. Then there were the
Empire Builder and Oriental Limited to Glacier Park; the Grand
Canyon Limited on the Santa Fe from Chicago to Grand Canyon;
Chicago, Milwaukee & St. Paul to near Mount Rainier, etc. With
officers of the Denver & Rio Grande Western I once covered the
entire system, including narrow-gauge high in the southern Rockies;
and in 1947 when my U.S. Potash Company was the second biggest
shipper on the Santa Fe Railway, I was out with the directors and
officers in a special train, inspecting every mile of the system.

July 23, 1978 (on Eureka Valley, California)   Had I known about
it, or had anyone told me about it back in 1933 when I was working
on boundaries for Death Valley National Monument, I most certainly
would have included it—and I could have done it easily. Another
thing about your story—you mentioned the "Saline Salt Tram." My
father supervised the building of that famous tram. He felt there was
no way for him to have a part in what looked like a profitable enterprise, except by undertaking the top supervising job. He did this for a
bare living wage, taking stock in the tram company. I was in college
at the time, and the sacrifices my Dad had to make left him very
little for me—$200 for my room for my freshman year and none
afterwards. Then the tram failed and nobody got anything out of it!

July 23, 1979   The story enclosed revived memories of the Big
Thompson Reclamation Project which contemplated moving water
from the upper Colorado River in a tunnel UNDER Rocky Mountain
National Park at just about the area of the Rockies where the mountains were supreme—their massiveness and power—just where the
Front Range branches off from the main range at Longs Peak. We
opposed the project and refused to permit *surveys* to gather data for

design of the tunnel and other works. Objections on two grounds—invasion of the park by a commercial enterprise with problems of waste disposal from tunnel building, etc., and diversion of Colorado River waters from west of the Continental Divide to areas east of it, when all water originating on the west side would be needed on that side from Colorado to California. Both Director Mather and I succeeded in holding the Big Thompson project in check. When Hoover was president I thought for a while we would be defeated, for the proponents of the project hired a well-known engineer, a classmate of Hoover's at Stanford, to secure permission to make the necessary surveys and design the remaining details of the project. However, I succeeded in my refusal to make any concessions to this engineer, whose name escapes me, and I was never asked any questions from the White House. Along comes the New Deal and Harold L. Ickes. One of the first reclamation projects brought up in the new administration was the Big Thompson. I earnestly recommended against any surveys affecting national park land, and I don't believe Secretary Ickes yielded while I was still there. But before 1933 ended, he authorized the surveys; the project proved feasible and was built with the tunnel under Rocky Mountain Park at its scenic climax. Moral of the tale, don't let any surveys be made in a national park!

June 1, 1984   Since you were in California, we have lost Ansel Adams, as you surely have been advised. He was eighty-two. I knew him from about 1925; was at his wedding in 1928. He was one of the greatest of photographer-artists, but he was erratic at times in his positions on resource conservation. I was not at all pleased with his tirade against Ronald Reagan. It was uncalled for, and certainly hurt himself. His dislike of Reagan was due to the appointment of Watt. He went a lot too far when he said, after the President spent a half hour listening to him, "I hate Reagan." So far as the Park Service and wilderness were concerned, Watt was fair, although I never thought he was a man for secretary of the interior.

I saw Albright last in 1985, at the home of his daughter in Los Angeles. He reminded me that he himself had written an article in the *Saturday Evening Post* titled "The Everlasting Wilderness" in 1928: "That was twenty years before Aldo Leopold's *Sand County Almanac*. If you were to talk about wilderness, Mather was the only one who really identified wilderness as wilderness. In about 1895 John

Muir wrote an article advocating a road from the South Fork of the Kings River to the Middle Fork [in Kings Canyon National Park]. The Park Service never even thought of such a thing. The only people who really did something about wilderness all those years were in the Park Service. They turned down every idea for a tram road, cableway or summer homes, while the Forest Service was encouraging summer homes everywhere."

When Harold L. Ickes came on the scene as secretary of the interior early in 1933 he found Albright serving as director of the National Park Service.[10] The cantankerous Ickes respected people who stood their ground and would not be pushed around. The story is recorded of how Colonel John R. White, superintendent of Sequoia, had occasion to help a Hollywood film company find a suitable mountain location. The producer wanted to reward him with money for his effort, but White declined. Instead of cash, the producer gave White a fine new riding horse. When Ickes found out, he was furious and ordered White to return the horse. But the superintendent retorted that he had done nothing wrong and had no intention of returning the horse. The episode ended there.[11] Albright was another man who refused to be talked down to. He might have lasted with Ickes, but he didn't take the chance, departing in August for the mining business.

The new director, Arno P. Cammerer, lacked the disposition to stand up to Ickes. A native of Nebraska, he had joined the Park Service in its early years and had worked as assistant director under Mather and Albright, both of whom considered him highly competent. Cammerer was refined, inclined to like everybody he met and to respect and defer to his superior. Ickes couldn't understand and took advantage of Cammerer's good nature. The secretary derived pleasure in putting Park Service people down, and Cammerer was the chief victim. Ickes recorded in his diary having a group in one day about a land transaction. "The lawyer of whose desk the papers passed seemed so dumb that I asked him whether his conception of his duties was that of legal robot." But the worst treatment he saved for the director: "I was particularly rough on Cammerer. As usual, he sat by my desk vigorously chewing gum in an openmouthed manner. I asked him who was responsible for his bureau and when he acknowledged that he was, I told him the facts seemed to prove what I had charged him with some time ago, namely, that he is in total ignorance of what goes on in the Park Service."[12]

But there was more by far to Cammerer. He was well respected in Congress and committed to national park projects in the East. Cammerer, in fact, personally traveled over almost all the lands now included in Shenandoah, Great Smoky Mountains, Mammoth Cave, and Isle Royale national parks, and worked hard to push the cause of the Everglades in Florida. He advised the associations, commissions, and state governments on the best methods of securing lands, or securing funds to buy lands, and was instrumental in obtaining funds from private sources. Horace Albright told me that Cammerer had done "the big job of making certain financing for the Great Smokies."[13] Moreover, on February 6, 1930, the governors of North Carolina and Tennessee came to Washington, D.C., to present to Secretary Ray Lyman Wilbur the deeds to 158,799.21 acres of land, which they had acquired to meet the minimum 150,000 acres required under the act of 1926. Governor Henry H. Horton of Tennessee cited Arno B. Cammerer, "unfailing in his cooperation, official and personal, in the enterprise and in his assistance in solving many unforeseen problems that constantly arise in a new project of this magnitude with few precedents to turn to for guidance."[14]

I like even better the story of his meeting with Miss Lucy Morgan, director of the Penland School. Miss Lucy, a gentle wonder woman whom I was privileged to meet in the 1960s, played a key role in organizing the Southern Highland Handicrafts Guild, which helped mountain people to market wood carving, pottery, wrought iron, and weaving during the depression years. In her autobiography, *Gift from the Hills*, she wrote of how she conceived the idea of going to Washington to see the head of the Park Service, whoever he might be. Armed with a letter from the governor of North Carolina, she saw Cammerer, then assistant director. "Not at all what I expected a Washington bureaucrat to be like. He was just as natural and real as someone down under Bailey's Mountain at Penland. I gave him my letters and hoped he wouldn't read them until I was gone, but he did. He asked why I was so interested in the people and the crafts of the mountain region, and I told him I was a mountain girl myself. 'I'm from the sod houses of Nebraska,' he said, and right then won my heart. Mr. Cammerer remained a friend as long as he lived, and he came to Penland often."[15]

Cammerer's greatest gift to the preservation movement was a vision of wilderness restored, an idea that in the late 1980s acquired new credence. Fifty years earlier, in 1938, he delivered a speech calling for establishment of a national park that might not quite measure up to everyone's standards for wilderness, but that, fifty or a hundred years later, with proper protection, would attain a natural condition comparable to the primitive state. Cammerer had the Great Smoky Mountains specifically in mind. As he saw the future, even after the most destructive logging, the flowers, shrubs, and trees would have grown back as if nothing had happened. In another twenty to fifty years even the stumps would have rotted to furnish humus for the plant life to come, so that it would be difficult, even for an ecologist, to ascertain whether a certain area was cut over or not, or that a certain mine had been worked years ago in a given location to the detriment of the park. Such vision among administrators is rare—their focus is on immediacy, political reality, and expediency—but in the Great Smokies and elsewhere Cammerer's vision has been proven a reality.

Ickes didn't care for Cammerer and tried repeatedly to get rid of him. Ultimately he was spared the trouble. In 1939, after seven years as director, Cammerer suffered a heart attack and withdrew from Washington (and Ickes's clutches) to be regional director in Richmond. He died a year later.

In those days, one preservationist followed another, which marks the difference between the old, original order and the new order of modern times. For Cammerer's successor Ickes wanted a preservationist of high principle, regardless of the individual's politics. So, as the fourth director of the National Park Service he appointed Newton B. Drury, a California Republican and classmate of Horace Albright at Berkeley, who had gained prominence as executive director of the Save-the-Redwoods League.

At the University of California Drury was president of the student body, then a lecturer in English literature. He and his younger brother, Aubrey, opened a San Francisco public relations agency with prestigious clients, including the Mark Hopkins Hotel. When the Save-the-Redwoods League was organized in 1919 by Stephen T. Mather, William Kent, Henry Fairfield Osborn, and Madison Grant, they hired Drury as the first executive secretary. His brother succeeded him when he went to Washington as National Park Service director. From 1919 to 1938 the Drury brothers between them assembled thirty redwood state parks comprising 135,000 acres. Newton enrolled members, collected donations for acquisition of virgin redwood forests, and conducted guided tours of the redwood empire, inducing citizens of means to purchase specific groves as living memorials. Guests included John D. Rockefeller, Jr., who gave $2 million to buy the 9000-acre Bull Creek Grove in Humboldt Redwoods State Park, to be known as Rockefeller Forest. In 1928 the league campaigned successfully for passage of the State Park Bond Act, providing for public funds to match private contributions; it was the foundation of California's state park system. From the beginning Drury served as acquisitions officer, putting the new parks together through the terms of four different governors. He continued to fill this role until Ickes brought him to Washington.[16]

In 1940, with war looming on the horizon, the Park Service and other agencies were shipped into cold storage in Chicago to make room for defense agencies. Only a skeleton staff was left in Washington. Though he was outside the main arena, Drury faced a barrage of demands and challenges. The parks were subject to repeated proposals for installation of equipment on mountaintops, for military maneuvers, or for logging and mining. Drury for the most part hung tough. He would answer proposals by saying, "If you can bring a statement from the secretary of your department saying the war absolutely depends on intruding into the national park, we might accede." As a consequence, little damage was done to the parks.

Following the war, however, political pressures intensified. Commercial interests yearned to open Olympic National Park to mining and logging. The Bureau of Reclamation and Army Corps of Engineers discovered potential in parks for power, flood control, and irrigation, and proposed projects in Big Bend, Glacier, Grand Canyon, Kings Canyon, and Mammoth Cave. They demanded access to national monuments, including Saguaro, Organ Pipe Cactus, Death Valley, Joshua Tree, and Glacier Bay. Joshua Tree covered 825,340 acres, but the Park Service agreed to a reduction in its size, and in 1950 Congress excised 289,500 acres, fully one-third of the monument.[17] The heat was on the Park Service.

Ickes, who had chosen Drury, later turned against him over the logging issue in Olympic National Park. After leaving public service

Ickes wrote a column, "Man to Man," in the *New York Post*. In the edition of October 4, 1947, it began: "The lumber interests of the state of Washington, in reaching out to grab 56,000 acres of Olympic National Park, cannot be charged with a statutory crime inasmuch as the Department of the Interior is well beyond the age of consent. And apparently Secretary Krug and Director Drury of the National Park Service were eager to consent."

Ickes recalled in his column President Roosevelt's personal interest in the park. The president had taken a trip to the Olympics and had become so incensed by the regional forester that he ordered Secretary of Agriculture Henry A. Wallace to remove the man. He continued: "President Roosevelt was strong enough to resist the pressures of these same lumber interests. And when they came to Secretary Krug's predecessor during the war [meaning Ickes himself], to argue that it was necessary to lumber the virgin Sitka spruce within the boundaries of the park, that official also resisted, even after it became clear to him that Director Drury was willing to permit the tree-butchers to invade the park under the plea of war necessity. Now the war pressure has been lifted, but Secretary Krug and Director Drury are doing an Alphonse and Gaston act for the benefit of the lumber industry."

Ickes undoubtedly was correct. Conrad L. Wirth, who served under and then succeeded Drury, in his autobiography (*Parks, Politics, and the People*) relates contacts with Henry M. "Scoop" Jackson, who came to Congress as the representative of a district that included the Olympic Peninsula and later served in the Senate. According to Wirth, Jackson fought for extensions of the park boundaries with deep concern and determined effort: "As a matter of fact, Scoop was very upset with Director Drury and me for being too conservative in recommending a boundary line adjustment, and he had a right to be. We were recommending what we thought we could get Congress to approve and not what we felt was really needed."[18]

Drury stuck to his guns in opposing two dams the Bureau of Reclamation wanted to build in Dinosaur National Monument, on the Utah-Colorado border. In June 1950 Secretary Oscar Chapman announced his support for the dams. Drury was given the choice of becoming governor of distant Samoa or a special assistant to the secretary without anything special to do. He chose a third option and resigned.[19] He stood his ground and exited with principle.

"If we are going to succeed in preserving the greatness of the national parks, they must be held inviolate," Drury insisted. "They represent the last stands of primitive America. If we are going to whittle away at them we should recognize, at the very beginning, that all such whittlings are cumulative and that the end result will be mediocrity."[20] In the long run his view at Dinosaur prevailed: the dams were never built.

Governor Earl Warren of California, his old classmate, forthwith appointed Drury director of California's Division of Beaches and Parks, which he had been instrumental in establishing years before. Thanks to him, the system embraces natural areas, beach parks, and historic areas, including the homes of Jack London and Will Rogers and the San Simeon castle of William Randolph Hearst. He retired at the mandatory age of seventy, but that same year his brother died, so Newton Drury resumed his post as executive secretary of the Save-the-Redwoods League, later serving as president and chairman until his death early in 1979.

At a dinner in Eureka, California, on June 16, 1968, commemorating the fiftieth anniversary of the founding of the Save-the-Redwoods League, Horace Albright paid tribute to his old friend and classmate: "Newton B. Drury is indeed one of the outstanding conservationists of all time. While he has not written essays or books as did Henry David Thoreau, Ralph Waldo Emerson, John Burroughs, or other naturalists, he is a naturalist in every fiber of his body. He could have written extensively, but he dedicated his life to saving and protecting segments of America's heritage of primitive and unspoiled features of our natural environment—not by words alone but by deeds. He belongs to the rare species of preservationists, a group considerably higher than the resource conservationists."[21]

Drury was succeeded by Arthur Demaray, who was nearing retirement after a long career dating from the very beginning of the Park Service with Mather. Demaray served eighteen months in ceremonial farewell while Conrad L. Wirth waited and prepared himself in the wings. The National Park Service of that period needed all the goodwill and public support it could find. Appropriations had been cut during World War II, while the volume of visitors to the national parks soared (a record 42.5 million in 1952, twice as high as in the first postwar year of 1946). The emphasis now was on the cold war and the Marshall Plan. It was a difficult time, years before the environmental upsurge of the 1960s and early 1970s.

"Connie" Wirth's father had been director of city parks in Minneapolis. Wirth himself joined the Park Service in 1931 and had been in charge of the extensive CCC activity in national parks and state parks. Wirth had the ability to involve prominent citizens of means, like Paul Mellon, who funded a major survey of the nation's seacoasts and the acquisition of Cape Hatteras, the first national seashore; and Laurance Rockefeller, who, in carrying on his father's work, funded acquisition of the national park in the Virgin Islands.

The park conditions Wirth faced when he became director called for drastic measures, and the ten-year program called Mission 66, which Wirth conceived to restore the national park system to a standard the American people expected of it, was initiated. Mission 66, unfortunately, is remembered today mostly for its minuses. Roland H. Wauer, a preservationist in the Park Service, summed up the criticism in a speech to the Southwest Studies Summer Institute ("Are the National Parks in Peril?") at Colorado Springs on July 20, 1981: "From Mission 66 to the present, visitor comforts, facilities, and enjoyment have been placed in higher priority than the protection and perpetuation of the resources and natural systems for which the parks were established and the purposes for which visitors come to the parks."[22] In fairness, the pluses of Mission 66 are significant, too. During its first seven years, more money was made available to acquire private properties within the parks ("inholdings") than in all the preceding years. The "visitor center" came to the fore as a focal point for visitors to obtain information and guidance (although visitor centers have earned their share of criticism). A number of new parks were established, including Cape Cod, Padre Island, and Point Reyes national seashores. Mission 66 did a lot of good and bad building: roads, parking areas, picnic areas, utility systems, employee residences, comfort stations, marinas, and training centers. Wirth defended construction of the Clingman's Dome Tower, a monumental uglification in the Great Smoky Mountains, and the Tioga Pass Road in Yosemite, which facilitates motoring at the expense of the backcountry through which it passes. Canyon Village in Yellowstone, intended as a model for commercially developed lodgings for the entire park system, may be the worst of all; it proved faulty in design and construction, an urbanized tourist ghetto landscaped largely with black asphalt.

However, Wirth did resist development at Flamingo, at the tip of the Florida peninsula in the Everglades, until he was overridden by political pressure, and he successfully stalled road construction in the Smokies. As he once explained his view: "To one person, climbing the Teton peaks is an inspiring experience, while to another driving along the Snake River and looking up at the mountains holds the same appeal. My basic philosophy has been that parks are for people —for people to use and enjoy, but not with the right to destroy."[23]

Wirth got along with Congress while upholding park principles as he saw them; he didn't give away the store. Senator Harry F. Byrd of Virginia, one of the most conservative men in Congress, was his close friend and supporter. During the early stages of Mission 66 Wirth was invited to make an unprecedented presentation on parks to President Eisenhower's cabinet and won some strong support. In 1980, more than fifteen years after retiring, he endeavored to set the record straight with *Parks, Politics, and the People,* but the book proved to be a disjointed ramble that only skimmed the surface.

Wirth intended to stay until Mission 66 was completed in 1966, the fiftieth anniversary year of the establishment of the National Park Service, but that was not to be his fortune. Once the Kennedy administration took over in 1961, Wirth became a holdover; even worse, he was out of step with the new crowd. There is a time to stay and a time to go, but a public official who has been around a long time forgets that rule.

Jim Faber, Stewart L. Udall's first public information director at Interior, years later told me, "It took us two or three years to get rid of Wirth, but we did." Udall, when I interviewed him at Phoenix in 1985, explained why and how:

> I was discontented for two or three reasons that Connie never
> understood. He had run his own show. He wanted to be left alone to
> run his own show. He was a veteran, older than me, old enough to be
> my father. He didn't take direction well from the top. Mission 66
> was his program, but essentially dealt with better management—
> visitor centers, roads, and different things. Connie was a good man
> and a good manager, but when we got into this whole expansion
> program, a park director had to go to the Cape Cods and Sleeping

Bears in Michigan and be a politician and help sell the park. Connie couldn't do it. He set Sleeping Bear Dunes back for years. He went to an angry citizens meeting, tried to reason with them, and then told them, "Well, there's going to be a national lakeshore, whether you people like it or not." And he stomped out. [Udall had a tough time himself when he tried to sell the idea of a prairie park in Kansas.]

John Carver was just horrified. He and Connie were always fighting because Connie didn't like anybody looking over his shoulder, and here we were in this new era. So the minute he hinted he was thinking of going, why I encouraged him and got my own park director. George Hartzog was more my type.

John and Connie fought almost every step of the way. John was also inclined to be blunt and not diplomatic. The Yosemite episode was clumsy on John's part. I had to smooth that over.

John Carver, the eighth assistant secretary, and the man to whom Wirth reported during his twelve years as director, was by all odds the toughest. Carver was not a conservationist, then or thereafter. In his book Wirth describes Carver: "He was a lawyer by profession and very opinionated, dictatorial, and demanding at times. If he didn't get just what he wanted, he would flare up and become very critical, and then he would cool off."[24]

It all came to a boil in the "Yosemite episode" at the annual Superintendents' Conference on October 14, 1963, at which Wirth was prepared to announce his retirement. It was billed as the "Conference of Challenges," and Carver unloaded a heavy one, more criticism than challenge, which found its way into the media almost as it was delivered—unquestionably by design; it was one of those orchestrations that set up the victim to dangle in the wind. Carver declared:

> When all else fails, the Park Service seems always to fall back upon mysticism, its own private mystique. Listen to this sentence: "The primary qualification of the Division Chief position, and most of the subordinate positions . . . is that the employees be . . . imbued with the strong convictions as to the 'rightness' of National Park Service philosophy, policy, and purpose, and who have demonstrated enthusiasm and ability to promote effectively the achievement of National Park Service goals."
>
> This has the mystic, quasi-religious sound of a manual for the Hitler Youth Movement. Such nonsense is simply intolerable. The National Park Service is a bureau of the Department of the Interior,

which is a Department of the United States government's executive branch—it isn't a religion, and it should not be thought of as such.[25]

Wirth's retirement was announced four days later, on October 18. The insiders in the media were ready. Under the headline "Park Service Faces Big Changes in Realignment," William M. Blair, of the *New York Times*, reported on October 17: "Kennedy Administration officials have chafed for some time over the semi-autonomous status assumed by the Park Service. The conflict has deepened since Secretary of the Interior Stewart L. Udall created the Bureau of Outdoor Recreation last year to serve as the focal point within the Government to coordinate the activities of Federal and state agencies in the expanding outdoor program."

The Interior Department news release of October 18 announcing Wirth's retirement quoted Udall's tribute at Yosemite: "Connie Wirth has won a place on the highest honor roll of those who have done the most to preserve a rich outdoor legacy for the American people." However, conveniently coupled to the news release was a copy of a report by the National Academy of Sciences calling for changes in administering Park Service research.[26] This led the *Washington Post* to editorialize that "more criticism was heaped on the National Park Service yesterday as word of the retirement of its director, Conrad L. Wirth, became official." The academy report became "the latest critical blast," although the Park Service had requested the review.

An article by Willard Clopton in the *Post* of October 18 reflected the shallowness of media expertise on resource issues and agencies:

> Among the projects to which he [Wirth] has objected have been the construction of interstate roadways along the shore of the Potomac and Anacostia rivers, erection of high-rise apartment buildings on the fringe of Rock Creek Park and the use of express buses along the George Washington Memorial Parkway in Virginia.
>
> He [Carver] reminded the superintendents that the national parks were created by Congress for the public, whose right to enjoy them should not be abridged by bureaucrats.
>
> As an example of "thoughtless" actions sometimes taken, he cited a man who wanted to take flash photographs of a national monument but was refused because of an alleged fire hazard. Similarly "pointless," he said, has been the issuance of tickets to Post Office mail

truck drivers who used Memorial Bridge in violation of the Park Service's no-trucks policy.

Carver panned Wirth for taking tough stands that should have been praised and supported. Udall was smoother. In the news release of October 18 that announced the change in National Park Service leadership, the secretary paid tribute to Wirth and placed him "on the highest honor roll." But the idea behind it was, "Close the door on your way out, Connie."

Conrad Wirth was the last director associated with Mather or Albright. Thus ended the old order.

5

Directors of the New Age–Innocence Lost

In 1971 the Friends of the Earth (FOE) criticized George B. Hartzog, Jr., director of the National Park Service, and then called for his dismissal. So did a number of other conservation groups. This cheered some people in the National Park Service, but by no means all. Hugo H. Huntzinger, a field employee, wrote a letter of protest that appeared in the October 1971 issue of *Not Man Apart*, the FOE periodical: "To pretend that we still live in the Nineteenth Century with a population of some 50 million is untenable in today's world. Director Hartzog understood this early in the game and, if for no other reason, has my respect for moving the National Park Service into the Twentieth Century. I too miss the simple unsophisticated Park Service of years past; but, just as innocent youth is lost, so must it be for a maturing organization (it is up to groups like FOE to keep us on our toes so that middle age spread and complacency do not develop)."

Huntzinger had a point. Things were definitely different now that innocent youth was past. The slogan became "Parks are for people." Hartzog was just the man for it, a "people person." The *Current Biography Yearbook* of 1970 referred to him as follows: "On Capitol Hill he is reportedly highly respected, although some leading conservationists consider him too much of a 'wheeler-dealer.'" I remember Hartzog as breezy, tireless, overweight, a hard drinker and heavy smoker, puffing cigarettes in between big cigars, a super salesman for new parks and highways who spent considerable time cultivating politicians.

During Hartzog's nine years as director, seventy-eight new areas, totaling 2,694,000 acres, were added to the national park system. He made it possible for Park Service people to find jobs and promotions. But the outlook in the ranks toward preservation and park purpose changed considerably along the way.

David Condon, the longtime Yellowstone naturalist I interviewed in 1984 (see chapter 4), illustrates the contrast between the old and the new. He recalled the age when almost all of Yellowstone's visitors came during a short summer period of four months and the park was wild for the other eight. Now, with snowmobiling and skiing as established activities during the lengthy winter, the park gets no chance to rest. There is no rest for the animals or the birds. The swans along the Madison River and the Canada geese have become semi-domesticated. Buffalo, elk, and mule deer wintering in the geyser basins are semidomestic, too, because they can't go anywhere but right where they are, with people all around them. The park concessionaire and commercial tourist interests don't recognize any problem in this circumstance—it's good business for them—while park personnel are willing to accept it. "Our goal," said Condon,

> was to stimulate you to see more and enjoy things more, to comprehend beauty and significance. Well, now, none of that. On my last summer trip I went to the information desk at Old Faithful. The man on duty happened to be the district naturalist, the top supervisor. I asked how we could get to Riverside Geyser since they eliminated the road. You used to be able to drive to a parking area, from which you could watch Riverside Geyser. "What do you want to go to Riverside Geyser for? You've seen Old Faithful, haven't you? When you've seen one geyser you've seen them all." I could not believe it, but that's what he said—and this was the head district naturalist at the station. If I had been superintendent, I would have fired that SOB. In winter when you get to Old Faithful a bunch of snowmobiles are parked where automobiles are parked in summer. Then they go roaring around, ten times louder than chain saws. Most don't slow down to see whether there's a geyser or hot spring. They get to Old Faithful, watch it squirt, and zoom off.

Hartzog was a ship's captain steering a course into new waters with little personal grasp of natural values. He began his career as a government lawyer, worked in concessions, then was assistant superintendent in two national parks (Rocky Mountain and Great Smoky Mountains) and superintendent of Jefferson National Expansion Memorial in St. Louis, in charge of building a huge stainless steel arch— a monumental marvel of boosterism, mid-America's answer to the Eiffel Tower. In August 1962 he left the Park Service to become executive director of Downtown St. Louis, Inc., a business-promotion organization, which Udall convinced him to quit with a promise to appoint him director of the Park Service.[1]

John McPhee profiled Hartzog in a *New Yorker* article titled "Ranger" (September 11, 1971), though Hartzog was never a ranger. He wrote of Hartzog's central staff of twelve—his high command— without providing much information about their training or goals. The article said that of the seven Park Service directors, Hartzog was the second to come up from ranger, without identifying the first (I can't find one in the records). However, McPhee told a revealing story of Hartzog's approach to green space. Office buildings were coming down on the Mall in Washington, which the Park Service administered. "The last thing we need in downtown Washington is more grass," Hartzog complained. "We've got grass coming out of our ears in this city, and in summer we let it turn brown. We're up to our noses in horticulturists who don't know enough not to water grass when it gets hot. We need more vistas like a Buick needs a fifth hole." It was consistent with his attitude toward preservation.

I remember the 1966 wilderness hearing in the Great Smoky Mountains. Elbert Cox, a regional director, read carefully and without digression from an uninspired statement that offered nothing new or consequential in wilderness philosophy or protection. The director had already made a commitment to local politicians for a multi-million-dollar transmountain road across the park. When conservationists complained, Hartzog said that hikers on the Appalachian Trail had been well considered; they were to be spared by a new tunnel constructed just below the mountaintop. There had been no public hearings, no public notice. The Park Service was proposing a road plan to solve seasonal traffic jams, plus corridors for additional inner loops. The *New York Times* editorialized: "The Park Service has put forward a road-building project that transgresses the spirit of the Wilderness Act and that would bring heavy automobile traffic streaming through the very area that needs to be protected. The proposal for this transmountain road reflects weariness rather than foresight and clear thinking."[2]

Hartzog resisted wilderness all through his tenure. On April 7, 1967, at the Sierra Club Biennial Wilderness Conference in San Francisco, he warned that applying the criteria of the Wilderness Act "would jeopardize the whole national park concept." He echoed the sentiments of Forest Service chief Edward P. Cliff, who shared the program with him, about "purity" in classified wilderness: "If we are to preserve the integrity of national park wilderness, we dare not lower its standard or compromise its integrity by the inclusion of areas that express in less than the highest terms the definition of national park wilderness."[3] Thus, by the end of 1970, six years after passage of the act, only two areas (within Craters of the Moon National Monument in Idaho and Petrified Forest National Park in Arizona) comprising less than 94,000 acres had been added to the wilderness system.

In the North Cascades, where a new national park was established in 1968, Director Hartzog embraced the idea of a series of trams to place visitors swiftly into the heart of the alpine zone. The idea was justified on the grounds that tramways cause less damage than roads.[4] But experience has shown that with a tramway comes a concession, snack bar, restaurant, and overnight lodge; the need to keep the concession profitable then brings a cocktail lounge and souvenir shop, as well as electric power, water lines, sewage disposal, employee quarters, and bulldozers, until the integrity of the resource is thoroughly disrupted. Fortunately his idea went nowhere, though I wished at the time that he or someone in the Park Service had emphasized protection of a wild, fragile resource as the best approach, with limited use by those who prepare themselves properly and make their way with difficult access. The very character and purpose of wilderness limits its development, while increased use undermines the values for which an area has been set aside—but this point was never made.

Hartzog was quoted in the *Washington Post* of August 5, 1969: "My experience in government leads me to believe that generally 'uniformity' is a synonym for 'mediocrity.'" He said he wanted to attract "highly motivated" people and "encourage, recognize and reward" their initiative. He wanted to promote "an attitude of constructive inquiry, a receptivity to change and a determination to find better ways of doing our job." He endeavored to make much the same point in a book of reminiscences, *Battling for the National Parks*, which he published in 1988. It was largely anecdotal, good-old-boy talk, with some good pokes at the Reagan administration. He wrote of how well he handled personnel: "And there were absolutely *no repercussions*, even if the employee was wrong in perception or reality, and especially if the employee was right!"[5] The following evidence strongly indicates the contrary:

1. In August 1970 four seasonal rangers resigned at Mesa Verde National Park after the Park Service threatened to fire them for informing park visitors about the massive strip-mining project on public lands at nearby Black Mesa and its effects on the Indian inhabitants in the area.[6]

2. In Glacier National Park fourteen seasonal employees, all members of a trail crew, signed a letter criticizing construction in a fragile alpine meadow of a walkway designed to accommodate crowds where they felt crowds did not belong. Three days later they were advised they would not be rehired the following year. Only protest from Montana conservationists brought reversal of the punitive recrimination.[7]

3. Riley McClelland in the same park was assigned by his superiors to work as a specialist in resource protection. When, however, he urged environmental review of the proposed walkway and other questionable developments in the park, he was ordered transferred. He stood his ground and came to an interview with the director. "I hear you are capable and intelligent but you are an opinionated, self-centered individual," Hartzog said for openers.[8] McClelland responded that his objective could hardly be self-serving, considering he had subjected himself and his family to ostracism and harassment at Glacier. He was dismissed but pursued his case. Eight years later he was ordered reinstated with back pay.[9]

4. In Grand Teton National Park a ranger, Bernard Shanks, was assigned to study domestic stock grazing within the park. He concluded that several permittees, including Senator Clifford Hansen, had acquired grazing rights illegally and that a key winter range of moose, elk, and deer was subject to serious environmental change

as a result of heavy stock usage. The chief ranger directed Shanks to lay off, and the superintendent disavowed his findings; the grazing continued and Shanks quit the Park Service.[10]

5. In October 1971 Hartzog decided to consolidate the Eastern Service Center in Washington, D.C., with the Western Service Center in San Francisco, and shift the operation to Denver. The decree gave 660 employees—planners, engineers, architects, landscape architects, and other professionals—one month to transfer and ten days to decide if they wanted to go. They could not be assured of holding their present grades and, on arrival at Denver, might be subject to a reduction in force.[11] John Cramer, government affairs columnist for the *Washington Daily News*, called the Park Service "the government's rottenest employer" (October 19, 1971).

As an example of how well he stood behind his employees, Hartzog cited the particular case of Roger Allin, superintendent of Everglades National Park, who took a lot of political heat for efforts to ensure the flow of water to the park. "Roger did a superb job," wrote Hartzog. Nevertheless, he continued, Senator Spessard Holland, who had helped to establish the park, demanded, "Move this guy Allin out of the Everglades." "I allowed as how important he [Holland] was to the park, but declined to move Allin, saying to the senator that Allin was doing exactly what I had asked him to do."[12]

In 1985 I interviewed Roger Allin on tape and recorded the following:

"Was it George who decided it was time for you to leave the Everglades?"

"Oh yes, there's no question about that. He'd been at me for about six months and finally told me to come up to Washington; he wanted to talk to me. When I came he said, 'I'm just telling you eyeball-to-eyeball that you're coming up here.' I think I had done his job. I had done a good job, was recognized as a competent manager, and wanted to stay—very, very badly. But he told me that was where I was going to pick up my paycheck, and so I went."

Allin went further: "He had a magnificent command of the language, was enormously talented and persuasive, but didn't have much concern really for the people working under him. I think that his grandmother, if she wasn't sold down the river, was fortunate. He was an absolute master administrator and I had the highest admiration for him, but I didn't think much of him as a person."[13]

I'm not sure he *was* a master administrator. He could be charming, disarming, and persuasive, but he was difficult to pin down. His own people were on guard, unable to act because they didn't know what he really wanted. Hartzog was careful about the people around him. Through reorganization and reshuffling, the cast of characters became composed of lawyers, planners, and professional managers, all of whom had little background in the parks or natural resources. Hartzog could say, "Our national parklands, after almost one hundred years, remain unimpaired for our continuing benefit and enjoyment," and the snowmobiler and skier in Yellowstone, on seeing bison and elk warming themselves around the geysers, would agree. So would his close associates. In March 1972 I checked on his central staff, the "directorate," eleven in number: director, deputy director, three associate directors, one deputy associate director, and five assistant directors. The deputy director, Thomas F. Flynn, Jr., was a lawyer with twelve years in the Park Service, all in Washington, and no field experience. One associate was a landscape architect who had worked in Washington and regional offices. Another was in the Park Service two years, after having served in the Bureau of Indian Affairs without any background in resource protection. The third, Stanley A. Hulett, was recruited by Hartzog only the year before, after working for Representative Don H. Clausen of California, an opponent of the Redwood National Park. (Hulett later became a timber industry lobbyist in California and returned to Washington as one of James G. Watt's right-hand men.) The only two of the twelve who had been rangers or had worked in a national park at all were the deputy associate director and the assistant director for park management.[14]

Rangers were concerned about the advent of a new type of office-oriented "manager." The word went out from above that there were too many rangers; people with a "broader view" were needed to interpret parks. Those in offices would be classed as "professionals," while those in the outdoors would be "technicians," reduced to the lowest possible federal grade levels, in reduced numbers, with diminished time and reduced training for duties in the backcountry. It was all in keeping with the new order beyond the age of innocence.

Hartzog was dismissed after Nixon's reelection in 1972. He insisted he was fired for denying Bebe Rebozo, President Nixon's close friend, access to a Park Service dock in south Florida.[15] But there was more to it than that. His mistakes were catching up with him. In

1971 Hartzog granted a right-of-way across Gettysburg Battlefield to Thomas R. Ottenstein, a businessman in suburban Washington, in return for three acres conveyed to the National Park Service, at the same time giving clearance for the construction of a three-hundred-foot tower that was subsequently widely denounced as an "environmental insult." The state of Pennsylvania entered legal action to stop what Governor Milton J. Shapp called "the second battle of Gettysburg."[16] Hartzog offered an alibi about being out of town, not knowing what he was signing.[17] The consensus was that he was too independent, too inclined to make end runs around superiors in the Interior Department. "George Hartzog can walk through an assistant secretary easier that I can step over a three-legged stool," Rogers Morton once told me. From the Nixon standpoint he was an overripe melon held over from the Kennedy-Johnson administration.

Conservation groups had little faith in Hartzog. The *Alaska Conservation Review* editorialized:

> George Hartzog, the crafty director of the National Park Service, junketed through Alaska with Senator Alan Bible, pausing long enough to give an audience to Fairbanks conservationists. He said he was down on the automobile and searching for better ways to make the parks accessible to all Americans. . . . The Park Service has been making overtures to conservationists in Alaska over the past year, seeking support for master plans and feeling out the reactions to development and other management practices. Unfortunately, there is very little give and take. Our meetings with various Park Service officials have amounted to them coming to ask our opinions and, instead of listening, telling us what they intend to do.[18]

In November 1971 the bulletin of the local Sierra Club chapter in Washington, D.C., complained of the impact of an impending ultra-freeway system on national memorials. "How would you like to visit Washington and find the Tidal Basin bare of cherry trees? Or view the Lincoln and Jefferson Memorials through a haze of automobile fumes and not be able to reach them across a six-lane depressed highway? . . . When the director of the National Park Service was asked for specific information, a vague reply was given that they were 'seeking to find a design to restore as much of the aesthetic values for the benefit of the visitor as possible.' How can a plan be agreed to if the details are not worked out? And how can hundred-year-old elms and cherry trees be 'restored'?"

Larry Williams, executive director of the Oregon Environmental Council, complained in a letter to Morton dated June 14, 1972: "Mr. Hartzog has been counterproductive to the long-range goals of the National Park Service. . . . He has made it virtually impossible for the citizens to participate in the master plan for Crater Lake National Park."

George Alderson, legislative director for Friends of the Earth, said in a letter to Secretary Morton dated June 6, 1972:

> The National Park Service is going downhill fast, and taking the national parks with it. Ever since George Hartzog was appointed director, there has been a trend away from protection of the parks. Instead of working with us, Mr. Hartzog is constantly working against us, and against the public interest in the national parks.
>
> Mr. Hartzog has made political deals involving the giveaway of lands in the National Park System for totally incompatible purposes—such as the Alexandria waterfront high-rise development, the use of national memorial grounds in Washington, D.C., for freeways, and the deletion of Dry Mesa from Arches National Monument (Utah).
>
> Mr. Hartzog is seeking to abolish park rangers, and turn the management over to mere administrators. Mr. Hartzog, himself never a ranger, is prime evidence that this will hurt the parks. The National Park Service should be staffed and run by professionals who understand ecology, and who will put their love for the land above political wheeling and dealing.
>
> The use of transfers as a reprisal technique also discourages park employees from trying to save the parks. If a park naturalist, like the one at Glacier National Park [Riley McClelland] earlier this spring, warns against practices and developments that will hurt the park, he can be transferred to Omaha the next day. The reprisal technique is hurting the parks, and is breaking down the esprit de corps that has always made the National Park Service a great agency.

I received many letters, signed and unsigned, from individuals in the National Park Service expressing bitterness and disillusionment; for example: "We are so busy creating new platitudes and giving lip service to lofty goals that it becomes difficult to notice that we are being molded into first class hypocrites and the slightest inclination to voice concern for traditional values brands one as a rigid malcontent not flexible enough to hold a position in the *New Thrust*. Those who show concern for ideas that are being left behind are made to feel like soldiers in a guerilla army who must meet in secret and discuss their convictions only with a trusted few—with irreparable damage to career ambition the inevitable result of exposure."

In 1975 the Justice Department investigated Hartzog and a former Interior Department lawyer, Bernard R. Meyer, for possible conflict of interest. The previous fall they had become lawyers for Landmark, operator of tourmobile buses in Washington, less than two years after leaving the department. They had met with Interior Department officials in efforts to negotiate a new twenty-year contract for the firm. They resigned as Landmark's lawyers and as lawyers for MCA, the parent company. "I don't see what else I could have done besides practice law," Hartzog was quoted as saying (*Washington Post*, August 3, 1975), and the legal area he knew best, as he said, was the federal parks.

He was involved in real estate as well. He was a 20 percent partner (with Gerald Halpin, a prominent developer in northern Virginia with Democratic party connections) of a multi-million-dollar real estate deal at Harpers Ferry, West Virginia. The plan called for construction of a two-hundred-room hotel and 120 townhouses on forty acres of cliffside property being considered for acquisition as an addition to Harpers Ferry National Historical Park. The plan proposed exactly what the Park Service was trying to prevent: commercial development along the Potomac River. The feasibility of construction on the steep hillside covered with rock outcroppings was dubious, but it might have resulted in a substantial increase in the property value.

The *Hagerstown Morning Herald* of August 8, 1979, reported that Hartzog dropped out of the deal after receiving a pointed letter from Park Service Director William Whalen: "We would strongly recommend that you withdraw the application so that rumors and gossip will be stopped . . . you would be ill-advised to pursue this action in the context of our expressed desire to acquire that property." Hartzog had claimed he knew nothing of the Park Service interest in the land when he purchased it, but Whalen wrote: "I would like to point out that the authorized boundary of the park was authorized in 1974 and was public knowledge throughout the community prior to your in-

volvement. I would also like to point out that the legislation that expanded the boundary in 1974 was based on studies that were generated as early as 1971 and completed early in 1973."

But "Big George," as he was called, remained the hero who had ush-
ered in the new age. On May 11, 1985, the George B. Hartzog, Jr., Visitor Center was dedicated at Jefferson National Expansion Memorial
in St. Louis, bearing an inscription: "A forceful and inspiring leader
who specialized in crisis and favored bold strategies, Hartzog was one
of the great builders of the National Park System."

Who would take Hartzog's place? In December 1972 Secretary Morton announced he had just the man. "I have selected Ron Walker because he is a dedicated person of unusual talent and ability." Morton
actually hadn't selected Walker at all, and didn't want him. The
choice was all Richard Nixon's. But government officials play word
games, winning points for news releases and public statements that
cover the truth with veneer and make their actions look efficient and
proper.

I met Ron Walker at the beginning of his tenure as director. Walter
Hickel telephoned me on his behalf from Alaska, mentioning that
Walker had worked for him for a time at Interior and done a good job
and that he would need help. Then Walker called and we arranged to
meet. We talked then and often thereafter, through his dismissal and
beyond.

Walker came to the Park Service from the White House, where he
worked as Nixon's chief advance man; he organized the president's
trip to China and a dozen summits with heads of state. He was also
involved in countering anti–Vietnam War protests, principally at a
rally in Charlotte, North Carolina, an action that later was linked
with the Watergate scandal. Following the 1972 Nixon landslide,
Walker and his wife had just returned from a three-week vacation in
Ireland when Robert Haldeman and John Ehrlichman, Nixon's principal aides, called him in.

The two had been in Florida with the president on Bebe Rebozo's
boat. While passing the keys in Biscayne National Monument,
Nixon told them he wanted to get rid of Hartzog because he was too
independent and too interested in pushing his own programs. He had
been director nearly ten years, and it was time for a change. Nixon
wanted his second term to concentrate on the domestic side of gov-

ernment, and he was determined to clear the deck by appointing new people to subcabinet and bureau chief positions. Ehrlichman and Haldeman protested that Hartzog had too much support in Congress. Besides, they didn't have a replacement. "I have my replacement," Nixon told them. "It's going to be Ron Walker."

"They all indicated later, Bebe and everybody else," Walker related to me, "that you could have knocked them off the houseboat with a feather. I looked at them [Haldeman and Ehrlichman] and said, 'You've got to be kidding. I don't know anything about running the National Park Service.'" He had been on a couple of trips to parks with the president but never professed to know anything about them, or about conservation issues.

Haldeman and Ehrlichman gave him the night to think it over. He awoke in the morning remembering the unwritten rule—never say no to the president—and decided to try. The appointment was badly received almost everywhere. Secretary Morton didn't like the appointment because it was rightfully his to make. Assistant Secretary Nathaniel P. Reed didn't like it because suddenly a man from the White House was being imposed on him to run one of his bureaus. But Haldeman, Ehrlichman, and Attorney General John Mitchell, Nixon's close henchman, came to his swearing-in ceremony at Interior, and their presence carried a message. When he went to testify before his first congressional hearings Walker was unprepared and inarticulate, and the Democrats in control took him apart.

Walker tried to catch up. He visited parks; he floated the Colorado River, climbed in the Grand Tetons, sat around campfires with rangers, and talked with visitors. He felt that his performance improved at the next round of congressional hearings, but he was still given a tough time by Democrats who didn't like Nixon. It wasn't much easier at Interior, where he was regarded as either an alien or an enemy. "Nat Reed for the first eighteen months was scared to death of me, though he had no reason to be. He might have thought I was a spy for the White House, but all the White House cared about was that I do a good job."[19]

Reed had various problems of his own. He wanted the cooperation of environmentalists but grew testy whenever they challenged him on an issue. He became tied to a position on grizzly bears in Yellowstone that led to expulsion from the park of John and Frank Craighead, the foremost research scientists studying grizzlies.[20] In 1972 the National Parks and Conservation Association learned that during a four-day period in April a military unit from Fort Campbell, Kentucky, conducted maneuvers in Great Smoky Mountains National Park. At the height of the spring flowering season the soldiers bushwacked through the heart of the park. Anthony Wayne Smith, president of the NPCA, wrote a letter of protest to Secretary Morton. The response, dated August 25, 1972, came from Curtis Bohlen, a deputy assistant secretary who worked directly under Reed: "The anti-military implications of your July 25 letter are most disturbing. In these times when it is chic in some circles to jeer at our country's Armed Forces we want to make it plain that we cannot tolerate any bias against U.S. servicemen in the operation of the National Park System."

Walker, for his part, liked the parks and wanted to get on as a parks person. In mid-January 1974, before a meeting of Park Service historians and archaeologists, he said, "When you get down to the bottom line, it says preservation. . . . The time has come for a major effort to upgrade the preservation of the historic resources of the National Park System. We must understand that, consistent with the 1916 Organic Act, our first duty above all others, is preservation. If we do not 'preserve,' certainly this or later generations cannot 'use.'"[21]

He respected conservation groups and wanted to relate openly with them. On May 24, 1974, Walker and half a dozen of his top staff attended the first of what became known as the unity meetings. The meeting was held at the Cosmos Club with representatives of major citizens' organizations. Subsequent meetings were scheduled regularly at Park Service headquarters, giving both sides a chance to express themselves on proposed new park areas, funding, concessions, wilderness reviews, grizzly bears, and off-road vehicles; they definitely served a useful purpose.

But the Nixon connection and his inexperience in parks doomed Walker. He made a mistake by promoting a hokey television series called "Sierra," which was filmed during its brief, unhappy life by Universal Studios in Yosemite National Park. The filming created problems of its own (see chapter 10); in addition, however, Universal was a subsidiary of MCA, a Hollywood conglomerate that had lately acquired the Yosemite Park and Curry Company, the old park concession. MCA came into the park business like gangbusters; there were plans to attract convention business, build an aerial tramway from the valley floor to Glacier Point overlook, and replace low-cost accommodations with luxury units.[22] MCA sought to influence the Nixon administration to get its point across—just when the Park Service was working on a master plan aimed at *reducing* facilities in Yosemite Valley.

Democrats in Congress picked up on the Yosemite fiasco, joining it with a brouhaha over a system for reserving campgrounds in the parks. As Walker recalled it when I talked with him in Washington in 1985: "The first year American Express operated the reservations system for us in six parks with about 1300 campsites. The second year I said I wanted it expanded and we added Everglades and Acadia, which took us up to 2000 or 2300 campsites. I really had very little to do with it. I said to concessions operation, 'Look, you guys handle those activities. If you've got problems, then I want to be involved.' It was part of my management style. I said, 'Guys, I'm not going to tell you how to do it. Goddamn it, it's your park, you run it. If you've got problems, then you call me and I'll do what I can for you. Let me run interference for you.'"

But American Express sold its reservation system, the Park Service opened the contract for bids, and a firm headed by someone Walker had met at college was awarded the contract and performed poorly. Walker:

> I had no forum at the time to say anything, but it's twelve years after the fact and I don't give a shit now. This guy had become a friend when I was a freshman at the University of Arizona and he was in his second year of pharmacy school. If you read the accounts of [Senator Howard] Metzenbaum [of Ohio], you'd have thought we were roommates in the same fraternity. I graduate, go into the military, go overseas, come back, settle in California. There was a large alumni group from the University of Arizona, which is when I meet Don Middleton. Don Middleton in the meantime is connected with this company out of Los Angeles and came in and said, "We're going to bid on that reservation system." I said, "Fine, great." Metzenbaum said later I had forced that contract.
>
> That reservation system, when you look back at it, basically was a bureaucratic screwup. I never had one thing to do with awarding the contract, except in the final briefings. John Cook and Stan Albright [associate directors] said, "These people have the system we need.

We feel they're the best." I said, "Fine, as long as you feel they're best." Ticketron in the meantime was pissed off they didn't get it and got a large lobbying operation going. Ticketron had a major installation in Ohio where Metzenbaum is from.

Walker is right: Park Service officials saw disaster on its way but didn't bother to warn him. Congressional critics intent on nailing Walker scarcely looked further. I recall that on other issues he was given poor data. Russell Dickenson, who served as deputy director under Walker and later would become director, years later told me:

> I berated myself when he began to fall on hard times. I said to my closest associates, "I wish I had been just a little bit smarter, maybe a little more forceful with Ron. Maybe I could have kept him out of trouble." I felt some of the blame attached to me because I was supposed to be the old pro there to help him.
>
> I paid a high price before one of those committees on December 23, 1974, with about a sixteen-hour day testifying in Ron's absence. It was over the reservations system and concessioner relationships. There was a whole litany by this time: MCA, the paint on the rocks, the number of bars in Yosemite, just on and on. Ron was in Denver by design; he had ducked the hearing and they were threatening to subpoena him back. As a matter of fact, I got him on the phone first and said, "Get your ass back here." It was obvious these were issues conveniently at hand to attack Walker. They wanted to blast him and they did.[23]

Meanwhile, Walker, because of his relationship to the president and his travels, was being called to Watergate hearings with grand juries and special prosecutors. He was trying to run the Park Service in the mornings and spending his afternoons with attorneys or in front of grand juries. His questionable activity in the antiwar confrontation at Charlotte, North Carolina, became a focal point, but he won a trial before a jury on all nineteen counts, and the special prosecutor dropped the charges.

Once Nixon resigned, Walker became a sitting duck. He was in his office when a fellow on the secretary's staff came down and said, "I hate to do this, but you gotta go." Walker replied, "Fine, you'll have my letter on your desk this afternoon." On September 11, 1974, Morton announced Walker's resignation, paying tribute to Walker's leadership and innovative programs, and expressing appropriate regret.[24]

Just before Christmas, Democrats in Congress took one final shot, at the House hearing referred to above by Dickenson. As Walker recalled it:

> They beat up on me so bad that all I wanted to do was get out of town. I was a wet noodle. I couldn't go out and look for a job with all this stuff hanging over my head. Everybody was saying, "Jesus, he's the guy who had that reservation system." Besides, anybody who'd had anything to do with Nixon—.
>
> That's the story of my resignation. I have never seen Nat Reed. I did not see Rogers C. B. Morton again. I was very supportive and helpful to Gary Everhardt and to Bill Whalen [two successors]. I did not go back and assert myself. I never called for a favor, never have gone to a VIP house. I have gone to some alumni meetings. When I first came back here they asked me to come to a Christmas party at Hains Point [headquarters of the National Capital Region] and I went. Some young man who had too much to drink came up to me and was really obnoxious. My wife doesn't know why, with my hot personality, I didn't punch his lights out. He took me on and said, "Oh, you're that Nixon guy," and all that kind of stuff. I said, "Hey, pal, this is Christmas, time for good cheer."[25]

Walker managed to survive, even prosper, in the world after government. A decade later he was in charge of the Republican party convention that nominated Ronald Reagan, and then of the inauguration in Washington that followed. He might have had a top job in the administration, but he preferred to run an executive search consulting firm.[26]

After Walker, the time was plainly at hand to choose a director from within. The logical choice was Russell Dickenson, the deputy director, who had come up through the ranks and wanted the job. Reed, the assistant secretary, favored Jack Anderson, the superintendent of Yellowstone, who had a considerably mixed record, which included banishing the Craigheads from their grizzly research in the park and welcoming the snowmobile invasion. Anderson didn't want it but recommended his neighboring superintendent, Gary Everhardt, of Grand Teton.

The appointment surprised everyone, including Everhardt. He was a down-home North Carolinian who had started his career as an engineer on the Blue Ridge Parkway, worked in regional offices, and met George Hartzog, who became Everhardt's mentor. Hartzog had moved him up the ladder as assistant superintendent under Jack Anderson at Yellowstone. From there he went to the Tetons. In 1985, eight years after he was fired as director, he reviewed his appointment: "I had never worked in the Washington office. To reach down and get somebody from within the ranks, as in my case, shows a certain amount of naïvete. It's not like being out in Wyoming with a local conservation community. It's as different as night and day."[27]

As director, Everhardt let the unity meetings slide. He faced his share of problems. One involved the concessionaires, who were being absorbed by corporate conglomerates, leading to congressional inquiries of presumed sweetheart deals. On another front Everhardt felt badgered by William Turnage, the business manager of Ansel Adams, the famous photographer and conservationist. Turnage had his own ideas on how the Park Service should be run; he wanted a hand in running it and deciding who should be in the top spots.

One problem, however, Everhardt created for himself. The deputy director he inherited, Russell Dickenson, was plainly disappointed at not getting the top job and wanted to return to a position in the field. Everhardt was more than willing; he allowed Dickenson to choose his spot (as regional director in the Northwest), which meant he could pick his own right-hand man. Despite protests from inside and outside the agency, Everhardt insisted on appointing William J. Briggle, superintendent of Glacier National Park, a man feared and disliked as a heavy-handed authoritarian. There were people in the field after Briggle's hide, and their chance came after Jimmy Carter became president and Cecil Andrus was appointed secretary of the interior. The Andrus team asked for and received a lot of input on key positions, including director of the Park Service. Briggle's enemies went after Everhardt as well.

"I never have, to this day, known exactly why I got fired," Everhardt said when I talked with him in 1985. The word came when Everhardt was visiting Puerto Rico and the Virgin Islands, meeting with a group of Canadian parks officials.

> We exchanged meetings every two years; it was our turn and they wanted to see island parks. I received a message asking me to return to Washington right away—thankfully the meeting was about to

conclude. A few days after my return I was asked to come to the assistant secretary's office. "We want to make a change," [Assistant Secretary Robert L.] Herbst said, "and there are many things we want to do." They were nice about it, but still I was shocked. "You're a young guy with twenty years ahead and you've done a good job. Take a week off and let us know what you'd like to do." He certainly was gracious about that. Briggle got his word the next day. They sent us to an office in northern Virginia where we stayed for about six months with nothing to do.

During their six-month exile Everhardt and Briggle stewed in their own juices, with nothing to do except pick up their paychecks. Finally they got their orders: Briggle to be superintendent of Mount Rainier National Park in Washington, and Everhardt to be superintendent of the Blue Ridge Parkway, his dream job.

For William J. Whalen, the next director, his new appointment was just another upbeat milestone in a storybook life. He had known only success and could not imagine anything else coming his way. He was raised in a small western Pennsylvania town (where his father was mayor), had graduated from college (in less than three years), and was married, with one child and another on the way, by the time he was twenty. He taught high school history and government, then became a guidance counselor and guidance director of a rural county school system. In the early 1960s he joined the Job Corps in the Great Smoky Mountains, counseling and helping young people in the outdoors. It was a job that combined everything he loved. And it was only the beginning.

Presently he went to Washington with his wife and four children; he transferred to the Park Service, where he became another Hartzog protégé. Whalen helped establish a training program to condition new rangers to the problems of the increasingly urbanized parks. The program was designed to attune them to the masses beginning to visit the parks, as compared with the more traditional middle-class visitors, and to teach them to relate to nonconformist, outdoors-oriented young people. The program was based, appropriately, in the National Capital Region, whose clientele comprised largely African-American inner-city Washington. Russell Dickenson, the regional director (before becoming deputy director under Walker), thought highly of Whalen and expanded his responsibility to cover interpretive programs, concerts at Wolf Trap Farm for the Performing Arts, and protest demonstrations before the White House—a singular opportunity for a very young man.

In the summer of 1971 Yosemite erupted in the first riot in the park's history. A crowd of young people established a counterculture enclave with pot-smoking, singing, and sex, disturbing family campers and driving off rangers with stones and bottles. More than a hundred law enforcement officers equipped with mace, ropes, and nightsticks were summoned to gain control. Director Hartzog dispatched Whalen, the wunderkind, to find a new approach. He showed that more could be accomplished by substituting twenty-five unarmed young interpreters for the armed police. The park established a youth campground, separate from family campers, and initiated the shuttle bus system and a variety of activities. Whalen played a major role in turning the young nonconformists from enemies into allies. His recognition and reward came in late 1972 with his appointment as the first superintendent of the newly established Golden Gate National Recreation Area in San Francisco.

Arriving in his new position as a thirty-three-year-old, Whalen couldn't imagine anything but success ahead, even without staff, secretary, or typewriter. The key to making the park work, he felt, was citizen involvement. His training as a rural guidance counselor and his work with defiant young people who refused to reckon with old rules and rote enabled Whalen to effectively involve citizens in park policy. Many resource professionals spend their careers sheltered from the public they serve. Their isolation begins with professional training at land-grant forestry schools; they shudder whenever they are required to go forth and heed the people. But Whalen, perhaps because of his different background, was able to establish a meaningful citizens' advisory commission and to conduct useful public meetings.

We spent several hours one Sunday in San Francisco in mid-December 1984 reviewing his career. He already was three years out of the National Park Service. Whalen came to my hotel, and for lunch we went to the Greens, the wonderful Buddhist restaurant at Fort Mason on the waterfront. It was my choice—I consider it the most fitting of the eating places in any national park—but I didn't realize Whalen's role in putting it there. He explained how it happened.

As the park was being established he brought together a group of strong supporters and asked for their counsel in turning Fort Mason, the old military post that the Park Service had inherited, into a center for the arts, environment, and education. He recalled these two key points of advice:

> First, establish a center independent of the Park Service. Let the Park Service provide broad guidelines but stay the hell out of day-to-day business—meaning that if there were to be theater groups the Park Service shouldn't be saying what the hell plays should be staged.
>
> Second, if we were going to involve nonprofit groups, if they were a little controversial, and anti-administration and anti-this, we should still accept them, allowing for broad interests.
>
> Those were good words of advice. Working with our citizens' advisory commission, we held a series of public meetings and established the coordination center, now flourishing with marvelous groups ranging from the Greens to the Oceanic Society, Friends of the River, Save the Tuolumne, just marvelous groups.

In the process, one of the groups he befriended was the Zen Center, which initiated the restaurant idea. By that time he was back in Washington as director. A Zen spokesman called him and said, "We have a little problem here." Their proposal differed sharply from the typical park concession restaurant—either a fast-food operation like Big Mac or a strictly sit-down place serving chicken and apple pie. The Park Service was thinking of standard fare, the Zens of opening an elegant vegetarian restaurant. "I was able to convince my colleagues that, since San Francisco is a little different city and the clientele different from what we might see in national parks, we ought to allow the Zens to open their vegetarian restaurant. I told them to let the marketplace determine whether vegetarian food should be there. From the first week it opened, reservations for Friday and Saturday nights were backed up three months in advance. Five years later it's just booming, one of the in-places in San Francisco." With the Buddhist food and service, plus the setting on the water, the Greens for me is one of the classiest places in town.

Whalen was elated when Assistant Secretary Herbst called with the tidings that he'd been chosen as director. But it wasn't that simple. Whalen was part of a package deal, with Ira Hutchison as deputy director and Howard Chapman as number-three man, associate director for operations. Hutchison was really a new man in the agency. He had worked in the National Capital Region and was more a specialist in therapeutic recreation than in wildlands conservation, but he was African-American and the Carter administration was committed to advancing blacks. Chapman was an old hand who had come up through the ranger ranks to be superintendent of Grand Teton National Park and then regional director in the Far West. But Chapman backed out; the truth is, he didn't think much of Whalen.[28]

Hutchison made a good appearance and took his important position seriously, but he lacked both background and administrative skill. Whalen, however, faced larger problems, both personal and professional. Two months after being appointed director in May 1977 he fell into a deep depression. He couldn't make a decision on anything. People would brief him on a lake in the northeast section of a park, and five minutes later he couldn't remember whether it was northeast or southwest, whether it was a lake or a river. He thought he was suffering from some dread disease and was scared to death; he couldn't even discuss it with his wife. It went on and worsened—he couldn't balance his checkbook, couldn't add figures. I recall during that period that he and I were on a television program together, the "MacNeil-Lehrer Report" on public television, discussing park issues. We met at the studio beforehand, but he barely spoke, looking blankly into space. He said little of consequence during the program. His body was in the chair, but his spirit was somewhere else, though I had no idea then of what was wrong.

Finally, he found help from a physician who treated him successfully for clinical depression. He was able to function again, but he had lost about nine months. Whalen felt that it would take a long time to regenerate direction and enthusiasm, and that his ineffectiveness and isolation hurt him immensely in the eyes of his superiors, the conservation community, and many others.

Whalen faced another problem. Earlier, when it had become known that Everhardt was to be fired as director, William Turnage endeavored to promote his own candidate, Larry Moss, a California state official, formerly of the Sierra Club staff, for the position. Whalen had known Turnage in Yosemite and again in San Francisco. In fact, Turnage had told him that if Moss was appointed, Whalen probably would be tapped as one of his principal aides. Whalen's decision to apply for the job himself infuriated Turnage. Then, near the end of his first week on the job, Turnage and Ansel Adams called on the new director.

> I thought that was a very nice thing. They talked to me about their views of the national parks and how things needed to be changed and that the way to change them would be to hire Bill [Turnage] himself as associate director for operations, the number-three man. We already had the deputy director—Ira was in place—and so they wanted Bill as associate and knew that I had the freedom to make the selection.
>
> I rather politely and, I thought, sensitively, told them I just couldn't do that. Ira and I were both thought of as outsiders, even though we were from within the organization. To fill the pivotal operations job, the sort of super chief ranger, with someone totally from the outside who had never worked for the Park Service would just undo everybody. I didn't think the assistant secretary's office or anybody in authority would go along with it, and I couldn't go along with it. I wanted someone who had grown up with the Park Service, was a traditional park man, and understood the park people well.
>
> Turnage was very angry. He wouldn't listen and told me I was not a very strong leader. About six weeks later he wrote me the most blistering letter, telling me in four pages how dumb I was, how I lacked backbone, and how something was going to happen in the Park Service if he didn't come in as the associate director, but still asking for the job in the last paragraph. I thought, "That sonofabitch, this letter doesn't even deserve an answer."

Perhaps it didn't, but Turnage subsequently became executive director of the Wilderness Society, where he spent considerable energy on national parks affairs, including an effort to get rid of Whalen. More about this later.

Once he got rolling, Whalen wanted the Park Service to concern itself with what he called "real environmental issues of the day." He wanted to upgrade monitoring of external threats—from power plants, poor forestry practices, and acid rain—influences causing long-term damage. Unfortunately, he concentrated on air quality, principally the visibility aspects, and overlooked impacts on park ecosystems, leading to internal criticism of "superficial gimmickry."

The critics might have been right. It was hard to tell from the outside, and perhaps from the inside, too, for that matter, as the story of the 1980 "State of the Parks" report demonstrates. Prior to that study, the National Parks and Conservation Association and the Conservation Foundation, both private nonprofit organizations, had conducted and published surveys on threats to park resources from incompatible uses of adjacent lands ("NPCA Adjacent Lands Survey: No Park Is an Island," April 1979; and "Federal Resource Lands and Their Neighbors," Conservation Foundation, December 1979). Those reports stirred concern among members and staff of the House Interior Committee.

"I drafted a fairly lengthy letter for signature jointly by Chairman Phil Burton and Ranking Minority Member Keith Sibelius requesting a 'State of the Parks' report from Director Whalen," Clay Peters, a member of the committee staff and former Park Service career professional, recalled in a letter to me in 1990. "The Park Service people ignored the letter, and dragged their feet so completely that a short time before the response from them was due, they hadn't even started to do anything. For the extension of time we gave them we demanded a much more thorough effort. When the report finally surfaced in May 1980, I had strong conversations with Dick Curry [assistant to Whalen] about the great opportunity it presented to Whalen to come on like gangbusters and also, if he handled it right, to look like a highly committed director. There was no interest at all, which didn't surprise me."

The "State of the Parks," which was based on a questionnaire sent by the Park Service to every field unit, was published as a report to Congress. It showed that all the parks were in trouble and conditions were worsening.[29] When it was all over, however, more attention was paid by the agency itself to fixing facilities than to serious threats to natural and cultural resources. The leadership dodged the tough ones.

Whalen, unlike his predecessors and successors, at least avoided proclaiming that the parks were "in better condition than ever." Early in his tenure he mocked conservationists and their "mossback" allies in the Park Service, but I observed that in time he tried to forge a working relationship with the environmental community. I recall his difficulty in getting his outfit to take strong stands. Though he thought the Colorado River flowing through the Grand Canyon should be better zoned and the use of motor-powered rafts reduced, the Park Service mounted only a weak effort to get its message across.

Whalen again:

I always felt the National Park Service holds a place in America where we are regarded as the "people who do it right"—that if it's embraced by the National Park Service it must be a good operation. I believed the American people expected us to speak on problems on our borders and threats to the parks.

But the structure, of the National Park Service as part of the Interior Department, doesn't allow the director of the agency to speak out. The voice becomes muted moving through the bureaucracy and the position subject to tradeoffs with other departments and bureaus. You finally come out with a mediocre statement that "We wish it weren't happening, but we realize we can't be dependent on somebody for oil; so, therefore, if you want to develop an oil shale program next to the park, why, go ahead, it's okay." Somebody ought to stand and say, "Hell no, it isn't all right. It's going to do this, this, and that to the park," then let them make the political decision, knowing full well the park's going to get screwed in the process.

Of course, Whalen himself, handicapped by inexperience and ambition to succeed, failed to speak:

With the Park Service being a bureau of Interior, such warnings are not allowed to come to light. I'm not criticizing anybody like Cecil Andrus, the secretary when I was there; it's just the way it is. He assuredly made better environmental decisions than his successor [James G. Watt], but he's still part of a political structure that must consider a wide variety of factors in the decision-making process, whereas the Park Service should be able to speak up on its own specific condition.

By the nature of the political process, the Park Service has a lot of visibility in congressional districts. Secretaries and assistant secretaries want to concentrate power in their offices. You don't see the Stephen Mathers and Horace Albrights with the courage to speak out. It has nothing to do with individuals. They'll do nothing to rock the boat; you've got guys holding on, trying to walk the narrow line to protect the title, whether cardinal or bishop. I saw it over and over, sitting with the regional directors and pleading, "Please take risks. I'll back you whenever I can." I mean, I was so goddamn frustrated that these guys didn't want to get out of line on issues.

But Whalen was not an insider. He had worked *under* Howard Chapman and Russell Dickenson, regional directors many years his senior both in service and age. He didn't help himself by bringing back Robert Binnewies, a former Park Service employee, as superintendent of Yosemite after he had spent several years in private conservation work. That, as both Binnewies and Whalen later recognized, "was like the pope bringing back the bishop after he was screwing a harlot somewhere." Whalen also brought in Nancy Garrett, a government professional, to take charge of Park Service administration; but she proved overbearing almost to the point of farce and became known as "the dragon lady."

Superintendents were disturbed by what they took to be erratic actions. In California it had long been planned that state parks in the redwood country and the Redwood National Park would come under combined administration; Whalen, however, without warning or consultation, at the last moment made a personal decision against it. An older, more experienced hand likely would have been more cautious, for better or for worse, and touched all the bases.

Whalen made his share of mistakes, but he was willing to explore original twentieth-century ideas. He felt the Park Service might find some way to recognize individuals with significant humanitarian, cultural, and educational achievements. At meetings of the regional directors he mentioned the names of Martin Luther King, Jonas Salk, and Elvis Presley. Laughter greeted Elvis's name, but Whalen believed that in due course Presley's effect on music and entertainment would be considered seriously.

One day he telephoned Coretta Scott King and arranged to visit her in Atlanta to discuss the possibility of a national site commemorating her husband's life and work. At their first meeting she responded with caution and reluctance. Whalen realized Mrs. King was not about to yield the interpretation of her husband's career to the white outfit called National Park Service, but he remembered someone mentioning that Lady Bird Johnson had reacted much the same way regarding memorializing her husband. He telephoned Mrs. Johnson to solicit her interest and was surprised to learn that the two women had never met. Nevertheless, Mrs. Johnson invited Whalen to bring Mrs. King to Texas to see the Lyndon Johnson Historic Site and visit the Johnson ranch. He and Mrs. King flew to Texas, first for a dinner in Austin:

> Then the next morning we flew to Pedernales country, spending a
> delightful day with Mrs. Johnson and her daughter Lucy. We're

sitting around this big kitchen table—Mrs. King and her sister-in-law, Martin's sister, talking about those civil rights days, the marches, the feelings they had as individuals, the daughter and wife of a president expressing their feelings when the Civil Rights Act was passed—the women's side of history that had gone on around their husbands. It was just a gracious, wonderful day and I think Mrs. Johnson was captivated by Mrs. King. Flying back, Mrs. King said, "You've certainly done a good job with the Johnson site in Texas. How do we go about it in Atlanta?"

Jesus, there was a lot of jealousy in the Department of the Interior. But I was spurred on and cheered by [Under Secretary] Jim Joseph. He did a lot to help. The bill passed Congress, but not until after I had left and returned to San Francisco. I got a call from a friend who said, "Listen, I was talking to Mrs. King. She was at the White House with Carter. They're going to have a bill-signing ceremony and the president asked who to invite. She put you at the top of the list. So they're going to invite you back, but don't say I said anything." A couple of days later I got a call from [official of the Interior Department; name withheld at Whalen's request]. He told me about the ceremony and said, "Bill, I added your name to the list. I insisted your name be added to the list."

That's how things are done in the New Age.

Whalen's undoing came about as a result of a controversy over concessions. The concessionaires talked long and loud about free enterprise—while they were operating under a socialist system that gave them a preferential right of renewal, despite abundantly mediocre service, and which allowed contracts of up to thirty years that were simply renewed year after year. Whalen wanted to shake them up and require them to improve service in order to keep their contracts. Because Yellowstone was a particular disgrace, Congress had lately allocated funds to buy out the concession and take control of the facilities. The other concessionaires, led by Don Hummel of Glacier National Park, the chairman of their association, were edgy; they sensed they were now a handy target following the reservations investigation and suspected the Yellowstone takeover might be only the first move against them.

On October 18, 1979, the concessionaires were meeting at Wahweap Lodge in Glen Canyon National Recreation Area. Hummel introduced Allan Howe, a former congressman from Utah who had served on the Interior Committee, as the new Washington representative of the Conference of National Park Concessioners. Whalen felt they were laying down the gauntlet, trying to block his efforts to upgrade standards. He took it personally and was angry: "I let them know so—probably due to youth and to lack of wisdom that comes from being around for a long time, being able to keep quiet and save my anger for a better time. I told them if they were going to play hardball and go political on this whole issue on the Hill, then I would be equally as hard-nosed and go to the nation's press and let them know what the hell these people were doing under the cloak of anonymity, without many people knowing what the hell was going on. Unbeknownst to me at the time, they taped this whole soliloquy of mine, which probably served me right. I've heard Don Hummel say that as a result of the tape he got rid of me. It's probably true."

The transcript of the tape was circulated. Representative Morris Udall, chairman of the House Interior Committee and an old political ally of Hummel, wrote Interior Secretary Andrus on January 29, 1980, that he was "outraged" and "personally offended" at the suggestion that any group should not be free to express its views to Congress and employ any spokesman it might choose. "I strongly urge that the Department review Mr. Whalen's performance. I think you will find you can do far better in this key position which has usually been held by sensitive, outstanding conservationists."[30]

At the same time, Turnage, Whalen's nemesis from the Wilderness Society, was also after him. Turnage and Ansel Adams came to Washington and expressed their grievance to Morris Udall and Cecil Andrus. Shortly before his dismissal Whalen was in New Orleans for a meeting of the Secretary's Advisory Board on National Parks. Andrus came to speak to the board for the first time. It went well and Whalen returned to Washington feeling upbeat.

I thought everything was going fine. A week later, early in the morning, my secretary said, "The secretary would like to see you in his office. Would you go up?" It must have been around nine-thirty or ten. I saw Herbst sitting there, looking kind of funny, looking real bad. I thought, "God, I hope he's not ill. They're going to tell me something about poor Bob's health being bad." I hadn't thought of being fired; I felt rather secure at the time.

Andrus didn't beat around the bush. He came right to the point. "Look, Bill, we'd like to replace you as director of the National Park

Service. You've been working too hard, you're tired and need a rest and a break, and we'd like you to take another job in the Park Service. You can have any job you want, any regional director's job, anything. We'll just make the announcement that you're leaving for personal and health reasons."

I went out of there thinking, "That's what he said, but I know all these other guys are after my ass. What's the real truth?" It could have been a totally humanitarian act on the part of Andrus, or it could have been the other thing. Reflecting on it today, it was probably both.

I did not have real rapport with the secretary. The way things were set up, the assistant secretary was the operator for parks, wildlife, and BOR [Bureau of Outdoor Recreation]. We were never encouraged by the assistant secretary to go to the secretary's office, and I sensed that his crowd would not be happy if I had gone around them.

I was remiss in not trying to develop some sort of personal relationship with Andrus. I had the utmost respect for him, and still do today. But you can look back and wish for a helluva lot of things. It didn't help that people would come in and tell the secretary how bad a guy I was; if he's not hearing anything good and enough people say bad of you, you're going to be in a little bit of trouble.

Hartzog and I had our problems over some things he wanted to do in behalf of his clients, but I don't think he was vindictive. He was not part of the group that tried to get rid of me. It was the concessionaires under the leadership of Don Hummel, and Bill Turnage, with the help of Ansel, and I imagine Ansel was used a little bit in the process.

When I visited Andrus at Boise in August 1985, I wanted to review his dismissal of the two Park Service directors. He told me how he looked for people who had the proper professional credentials. As governor, he had determined that professional training and background were absolute musts for important resource positions. But he was vague on park matters. He thought, incorrectly, that Bill Whalen had wanted Ira Hutchison as deputy director. He was unfamiliar with Everhardt, whom he called "Eberhart," adding, "I didn't know him very well. I believe he was not a professional park man. Wasn't he the Republican appointee?"

As for Whalen: "The man had an illness that we were not aware of. And he was not aware of the severity of it. It was unfair to him and his family to put him through the strain. He resented very deeply what I did. His feelings were hurt, but I guess he admitted to himself that he was ill. When I saw him down in San Francisco some months later, he said, 'I didn't ever think I'd be saying this to you, but I do thank you. It was the best thing you did for me.'"

As a career employee, Whalen had employment rights. The Golden Gate superintendency was open, so he opted to return to San Francisco. He took the position with the idea of looking for another job, a course of action his superiors understood and accepted. In due course he left the government and became a private consultant. "Russ up in the Seattle area [Russell Dickenson, Northwest Region director] was one of the biggest middle-of-the-roaders who didn't want to stick their necks out. I like and respect Russ, but that's an example of how things go. On the outside now, I look at entrepreneurs living by their goddamn wits, taking risks every day. They have no tenure; if one of them doesn't make it, the only person he can blame is himself."

Superintendents of the big parks, the mainstays of the Park Service, were not sorry to see Whalen go. On his departure they wanted a restoration of traditional leadership—there were even hints of a superintendents' strike, unheard of in history. After considerable searching and consulting, Andrus summoned a group of superintendents and regional directors, numbering between eighteen and twenty-five. "The next director is in this room," he told them, "and I want you to decide who it will be."[31] They chose Russell Dickenson.

On May 1, 1980, Andrus announced the appointment with another of those rosy press releases: "In his thirty-three years with the National Park Service, Russ Dickenson has demonstrated all the qualities that are most needed today to lead that outstanding organization. He has solid experience in both urban and rural parks. He's an 'old pro' who can be expected to inspire confidence among coworkers and those concerned with the future of the great National Park System."

After it was all over, Andrus wasn't so sure. "Russ was enthusiastic at first," Andrus recalled when he was back in Boise, "but was a very cautious person. Maybe that's why he survived thirty years in the Park Service. But the other regional directors went out of their way to keep their word to me—to work with him and not bite him in the back, and to make him look good. I was disappointed in him after the change in administration, when things he said were totally different from what he and I had discussed. He could not have been expressing his own belief. Had it been me, I would have just said, 'No thanks.' I was disappointed that he didn't have what it took."

Andrus was referring to happenings in the Reagan days, the unhappiest of times, when national parks were at the mercy of a merciless antipark, antigovernment crowd running the government. I think, had I been given the choice, I would have followed Andrus's prescribed behavior, told the Reaganites off, and departed with a blast. Dickenson felt otherwise, and perhaps he was right. "I swallowed such pride as I might have had," he recalled in one of our many conversations, "as long as I could protect the operational capability of the parks—which is why I felt we did about as well as we could."[32] Dickenson was a Southwesterner, from Texas and Arizona, who had come up through the ranks in various Western parks, had twice been a regional director, and had virtually run the whole Park Service under Ron Walker. On May 15, 1980, at his installation he quipped about being "the living embodiment of the principal of recycling," but pledged a strong voice against threats to the parks and promised to instill confidence and pride. Dickenson had wanted to be director when Walker was fired. He felt qualified and deserving, and was thus disappointed that he didn't get it. He stayed and helped Everhardt, then departed for Seattle and was quite satisfied. Whalen telephoned in 1977 and said he would not apply for the job if Dickenson wanted it. "Be my guest, friend, because I have no interest," was the response. Dickenson recalled it all with mellowness of a sort: "Changing directors is just part of the political mentality. It's 'Cast the bastards out and we're the victors and to the victors belong the spoils.' That's what made my retention during the first Reagan administration all the more remarkable. I was ready to go and felt my days were numbered. I'd known and worked with Watt in an earlier time, but when his appointment was announced I had no belief or inclination that I would be asked to stay."[33]

Watt wanted a professional parks director and (according to Dickenson) fought opposition within the administration to retain a Democratic holdover. Dickenson, for his part, worked against a budget-cutting binge to maintain funding for operational capability in the field. "Look, we understand we have to make choices, we have to give and take, but let's not compromise visitor service and park protection at the park level. That's number one."

Watt had his own ideas about parks. He shut off dialogue with conservationists and opened the door to concessionaires, promising them that if he erred, it would be on the side of public use, certainly not on preservation. On January 26, 1982, Watt directed Dickenson to evaluate park managers based on the money their parks produced. In the name of life, health, and safety, he endorsed the Park Repair and Improvement Program (PRIP). Watt was saying he wasn't going to get rid of the parks, he was going to improve them with big bucks for maintenance and construction. It sounded like a good idea, but money flowed without anyone deciding where it would do the most good or what the environmental consequences of a project would be. Spending became an end in itself. Jack Hughes, a veteran ranger at Olympic National Park, told me: "We flew outhouses out of the backcountry and outhouses into the backcountry. The outhouses were built here of heavy lumber at high cost, then moved by plane at high cost, which means the air resistance was *humongous*. Then they were set in the wrong places."[34] Meanwhile, funding for park protection, land acquisition, and historical preservation was slashed, though park people and conservationists considered these things imperative.

Dickenson at times appeared a too-willing partner to Watt's schemes. In September 1981 he attended a conference at Jackson, Wyoming, conducted by the National Parks and Conservation Association. The crowd in attendance was astonished to hear him say that morale and sense of mission in the ranks were high, when it was obvious that sheer distress prevailed. His support of funding maintenance backlogs rather than land acquisition was poorly received; Joseph Sax criticized him sharply from the floor, and others were ready to do the same.[35]

On the other hand, Dickenson felt he was holding his outfit together in the hostile Reagan environment. Watt laid down an edict one morning that he didn't want any kind of exchange with environmental groups. It was the very day of a scheduled unity meeting. Dickenson canceled the meeting, but complaints voiced through Congress and the media forced Watt to back down. Assistant Secretary Arnett was even worse than Watt. He saw the Park Service as a crowd of tree-huggers who needed constant harassment and spanking. On March 17, 1982, he issued a humiliating order that all policy or budget information and/or responses to questions from Congress, the Office of Management and Budget, and other government or non-government entities must be cleared through Arnett's office first, and that no advance copies could be sent to anyone prior to Arnett's review and approval.

That order was relayed to Park Service personnel by Dickenson's newly appointed deputy director, Mary Lou Grier.[36] She had worked at Interior during the Nixon days, then had owned and managed a shopping center, apartment house, service station, contracting firm, and concrete company, and lately had worked for a Republican congressman at his home office in Texas. As the direct liaison of the administration, she prevented the Park Service from taking a strong stand against the proposed nuclear power dump site at the edge of Canyonlands National Park in Utah and frustrated Jack Stark, the superintendent of Grand Teton, in his efforts to cope with the Bureau of Reclamation's plans to upgrade the dam at Jackson Lake.

"Every operating principle established throughout our working lifetimes was challenged," Dickenson recalled.

> We spent a lot of our working hours trying to defend the past and what we were doing—things tested through trial and error—as making good sense. We were subject to constant end-running. People seeking redress of grievances would no longer come to the bureaucracy, but found a willing listener in an Arnett, or Ric Davidge, or Watt. So they would go spill, or unload, and we would catch it coming back the other way.
>
> "The bureaucracy is overbearing, the government is overbloated, spending the taxpayers' dollars unwisely"—all of these were biases of the administration, like the president was still running against the government. It's incomprehensible when you sit in a director's seat and are expected to criticize the very apparatus you're in charge of.[37]

A GS-15 appointment, even if not a superintendent, had to be cleared first by the assistant secretary. The Alaska regional director and deputy director and the superintendent of Glacier Bay National Park were summarily removed, though by all accounts they were performing efficiently in the public interest.

"Sometimes you can win, though," Dickenson continued. "For each of the four years I served under the Republican administration, Cal Black [one of the chief park foes in southern Utah] tried to get [Park Superintendent] Pete Parry out of Canyonlands. The secretary called me in and discussed it. I defended Pete Parry in the strongest terms. You fight to the death for a guy like that. I said, 'If you're going to get rid of Parry, get rid of me, too.' I don't know how he responded to Black, but the secretary dropped the issue."

Dickenson faced a tough challenge in dealing with A-76, a little-used directive from the Office of Management and Budget requiring all departments of government to contract work deemed prudent and cost-effective to private enterprise.[38] In 1982 OMB ordered all agencies to decide by 1987 which jobs could be eliminated. In 1983 Watt set a mid-1984 deadline for national park administrators. He wanted them to put selected maintenance, garbage collection, construction, road repair, and service jobs out to bid or defend their reasons not to.

It was part of the shift to privatize public service—to turn national parks over to states or contract them out to private enterprise, along with prisons, hospitals, schools, garbage collection, and public safety. It's a system that doesn't improve efficiency, doesn't save public funds, and benefits only the private entrepreneur. The mere threat is a blow to pride in public service. Dickenson recalled:

> I remember going to one hearing where Senator McClure [of Idaho, chairman of the Senate Committee on Energy and Natural Resources] gave me holy hell because I wasn't supporting A-76. It really took me aback because I had been walking a very narrow precipice between the kind of pressure I was getting from within the administration and deep concerns based on what I was hearing from people in the field. I kept telling that to everybody, including the secretary.
>
> They'd call me up and chew my ass every so often—that I wasn't following party lines. Within the government bureaucracy they're committed to a thing called "goal setting." They have these little goals and objectives, most of them set numerically. "You meet them, or else; we can get a new boy." You're supposed to have so many parks converted to A-76 by such-and-such a date. We regularly fell behind—that's why I got chewed out. I gave every logical explanation for not moving more rapidly. I was whipsawed in two different directions—catching holy hell from my good people in the field who

looked on me as their protector and defender. I was trying to do my best in dealing with the departmental apparatus without falling on my sword. . . .

My greatest disappointment was the constant bickering and challenge over administrative minutia. I found things very debilitating at times. Maybe the best thing I did was simply being there. It ensured some continuity and stability. I tried to maintain a standard of professionalism that influenced peers and associates. I think we retained the public's confidence. I can't claim that for myself, but perhaps I provided the leadership for that to happen.

The trouble was that Dickenson went around the country making cheery speeches about high morale, the end to park expansion, and the PRIP program. "Your national parks and historic sites have never looked better," he told the Rotary Club of Hagerstown, Maryland, on August 15, 1984. "Morale has never been higher," he told the Association of National Park Rangers in mid-October 1984 at Acadia National Park, when every ranger present knew otherwise.

In any event, the *Los Angeles Times* summed up the visible issues in an editorial of November 26, 1984. The editorial, "Shuffle in the Parks," commented on Dickenson's retirement:

> Dickenson was thrust into the uncomfortable position of carrying out the new policies of the Reagan Administration and, at the same time, buffering the Park Service and its professional ranger corps from the political vicissitudes and outright nastiness at times of his boss, Interior Secretary James G. Watt.
>
> Some critics thought that Dickenson could have used a little more Smokey-the-Bear gruffness in dealing with Watt on important policy issues. Perhaps he could have—and lost his job on the spot. What Dickenson did was battle like a good general in behalf of his troops, preventing a major purge of veteran park personnel to unwanted jobs in the Siberia of other Interior agencies.

Late in 1984 Dickenson met with Interior Secretary William C. Clark to discuss his departure and possible successor. Clark raised the name of William Penn Mott. The idea was unlikely, considering that Mott was seventy-four years of age, but appealing because Mott was widely known and respected in the parks field. He had been a successful director of California state parks under Governor Ronald

Reagan (when Clark had been the governor's chief of staff) and was endowed with enthusiasm and energy belying his years.

Mott approached his appointment in March 1985 with confidence. "If President Reagan can run the country at age 74," he said, "I can run his National Park System at age 75." He recalled his productive relationship with Reagan in California, where they agreed the parks would be administered without interference. "You handle the parks, I'll handle the politics," Mott frequently quoted Reagan as saying.[39]

In discussions with Donald Hodel, who succeeded Clark as interior secretary, Mott made it clear that he expected the same arrangement with the federal government. His self-assurance and optimism stimulated good feeling, the sense of a shift away from the harsh, myopic mind-set of the Watt crowd. "When in doubt," Mott vowed, as others had before him, "we must err on the side of preservation. Should we subsequently find ourselves wrong, we can always provide for more use." He reopened doors that Watt had closed. Speaking in June 1985 to a conservation assembly at Yellowstone, Mott sought support for his new twelve-point plan. The plan was meant for the Park Service, but he wanted the agency to reach out, with such subheadings as: "Effectively share our understanding of critical resource issues with our public(s)"; "Increase public understanding of the role and function of the National Park Service"; and "Expand the role and involvement of citizen groups at all levels in the National Park Service."

It read well on paper, but little changed. "We're coming up with new ways of doing things. We're action-oriented now," Mott would say, always enthusiastic. "Everybody is excited about the way things are going on here." He felt that his directives were read, believed, and followed to the letter. In an interview with me in 1986 he said: "We're telling our interpreters they have a responsibility to talk about environmental issues. We're asking them to understand acid rain, gene pools, biotic diversity. The average public reads about these things, but doesn't really know what they're about. Up to this point our interpreters have been told, 'Don't talk about anything except national parks.' But we're part of a total, interrelated, interdependent world and we've got to talk about all those things."[40]

He said much the same thing when we appeared together on a panel at the Yosemite Centennial Symposium in Concord, California, in October 1990. He still believed interpreters were instructed to brief the public on real issues, and that they were doing so.

But most personnel hunkered down. Despite Mott's best intentions, there was very little citizen involvement, little taking the preservation message to the people and asking their support on critical resource issues. In a message to the ranks (published in the *Courier*, the Park Service house organ, in November 1986), Mott exhorted the cause of activism. He identified two types of managers: "passive" and "assertive." Of the former, he wrote: "Such managers travel the road of least resistance. They unflaggingly follow the rules; rarely question decisions handed down; are careful to stay within the mainstream of opinion; and deliver assignments and handle responsibilities in a satisfactory manner. . . . They do little to provide the kind of support, leadership, and creative initiative necessary for an organization to continually grow and develop." His plea brought scant assertiveness in the cause of preservation. Park administrators are trained in technical fields, in which they feel safe. There is no reward for risk taking.

Mott traveled tirelessly; he went wherever he was asked. A biologist in one of the parks said to me, "I tried to talk to him about the issues here, but I don't think he knew where he was." He advocated his own pet causes, like day-care centers in national parks. He grew defensive against criticism; at a conference of superintendents at Yellowstone in June 1988 he insisted the parks were in better condition than ever.[41]

Worst of all, the seeming improvement in attitude around the Interior Department was all illusion. Mott was undermined from the very beginning by his superiors. Assistant Secretary William P. Horn had ideas of his own on how the national parks should be run, and by whom. Mott wanted to ban aircraft from flying over the Grand Canyon but was overruled. Then Horn ordered a major reorganization of personnel, without Mott's knowledge or approval. One of the changes would have forced the early retirement of Howard Chapman, Western Region director, by downgrading his annual job evaluation from excellent to unsatisfactory. Chapman, whom I observed over the years as a cautious administrator, felt constrained to strike back. He asserted publicly that the move was made against him for resisting the A-76 order for private contracting of park work and for taking environmental positions, and that political appointees were "dis-

membering the professional capability of the National Park Service."
When Chapman retired later, on his own timetable, he left as a
hero.[42]

Mott, however, was just getting his second wind. He outlasted the
pesky Horn, who left the government in June 1988, and remained un-
fazed and optimistic. He was a rare bright light shining through the
darkness of the Reagan days. The national parks were hurt, all of
them, but Dickenson and Mott kept the parks and the Park Service
from being thoroughly debased.

Once the Bush administration took hold, however, Mott was
dumped. He didn't want to go, and he wept in the farewell meeting
with close associates after hearing them pay tribute to his sense of
humanity and purpose; and some of them wept, too. Mott was replaced by James M. Ridenour, who had served as director of natural
resources in his native state of Indiana. The new director's knowledge
of national parks was negligible—he had never been to the Grand
Canyon, Yellowstone, or Yosemite—but, as Republican finance
chairman in Tippecanoe County, Indiana, he had raised campaign
funds for Vice President Dan Quayle.[43] Ridenour actually was hoping
for a regional field position with the Fish and Wildlife Service, but he
came up with a bigger plum out of the plum book. During his first
year as director he operated cautiously and close to the vest. "He listens well and asks good questions," reported a park superintendent.
It was on-the-job training time. He continued to be cautious after his
training was over.

Mott's deputy director, Denis Galvin, was dumped too, by Watt-
Hodel holdovers at the Interior Department, and dispatched to a minor research position. But the complaints of environmental groups
echoed in Congress and Galvin was returned to the "Hall of Heroes"
at Park Service headquarters as associate director for planning and
development.[44] Galvin might do the planning, but partisan politics
was plainly in control of policy and program.

6

Perplexity of a Park Superintendent

In the summer of 1980, after a pack trip in the Yellowstone high country, I met Park Superintendent John Townsley, who had offered to spend a couple of days with me. He took me around and shared a few secrets. For example, he showed where he had torn down a number of buildings and expressed the desire to eliminate more, specifically those occupied by Hamilton Stores, the entrenched park concession. Running Yellowstone is sometimes considered the second most important job in the National Park Service—second only to the director in Washington. Thus Townsley was a kingpin in his own right. He was a huge fellow, at least six feet three or four, and weighty in the wrong places, with his belt below the equator. At first glance he looked more like a barkeeper than an administrator of a national park. Some of his personnel grumbled about his preoccupation with politics, but Townsley had grown up in the parks, as the son of a ranger, and from all my contacts with him I felt that he had the right instincts, and that he cared deeply about Yellowstone.

We overnighted at a patrol cabin, accessible by an administrative road and definitely off the beaten path. The evening was mild and Townsley grilled elk steaks outdoors. We sat under the stars exchanging views on issues and policies. "Wouldn't this be a great place," I suggested, "for a seminar or small meeting, of about twenty people?" The superintendent did not agree. "Twenty would make too big a crowd. Eight or ten might be right. But our people would want to meet at a hotel in Las Vegas or Atlanta or Miami."

The point was well taken. The higher a parks person rises on the ladder, the less he or she knows about the smell and feel of resources, and the more acclimated he or she becomes to meeting in city hotels and to their conveniences. I've been with experts on wilderness, actual decision makers, who hadn't camped in years and would perish if left on their own in the wild. Many park superintendents scarcely know their own parks except for the highway, visitor center, and concession facilities.

Early in the 1970s a group of citizens in North Carolina and Tennessee decided to hike en masse to protest a proposed road that would intrude into the lovely Cataloochee Valley of Great Smoky Mountains National Park. The park superintendent, Vincent Ellis, a courtly silver-haired gentleman, agreed to meet with the group to explain the park's plans. He was following orders, from the regional and Washington offices, designed strictly to accommodate the local congressman, Roy Taylor, who held the key post of chairman of the parks subcommittee in the House. Ellis came to the appointed rendezvous with entourage and maps. When he was through explaining things, the superintendent said, "Okay, now let's get in the cars to drive around and see where the new road would go." When members of the group insisted they wanted to walk, Ellis was taken aback. "But you won't see *nearly* as much." But the citizens hiked anyway, and the Park Service people did too, for a change.[1]

When Ellis retired in 1975 he was succeeded as superintendent by Boyd Evison, who had quite different ideas. Instead of building new roads, he closed old roads, turning them into what he called "quiet walkways." Instead of garbage cans at scenic overlooks along park roads, facilities that spawn waste and ugliness, he shifted litter-collection stations to park exits, where visitors were urged to deposit their trash. He set a model for his own staff by picking up litter where he found it.

Evison's behavior rubbed some people the wrong way. Park personnel didn't like the idea of traveling in the backcountry by shank's mare where they formerly had driven over "administrative roads," or of using hand tools instead of power machines. More serious, a handful of politically privileged North Carolinians balked and squawked when Evison closed a cozy fishing retreat maintained with public funds for their private benefit. They were mostly local businessmen and boosters, "civic leaders" interested in the park to the extent that it benefited their communities, and they had direct lines of communication to their congressman and governor.[2] Then, in 1977, Evison engaged a team of professional hunters to undertake a test project aimed at reducing the number of wild boars uprooting and destroying vegetation in the park.[3] Local shooters protested loudly; they had been hunting boars in and around the park, legally and otherwise, for years. The Interior Department came down on the side of the hunters and ordered the project halted. Evison for his part was removed. He survived and later advanced elsewhere, but the message to park superintendents was clear.

There now are more than three hundred park superintendents, including the kingpins of large and popular parks like Yellowstone, Yosemite, Glacier, Grand Canyon, Sequoia–Kings Canyon, Great Smoky Mountains, and Shenandoah, and lesser nabobs in charge of seashores, small monuments, and historic sites. A few, but not many, superintendents get out to hoof the trails in their parks or to pursue serious cultural studies. Generally they're too busy with paperwork and politics. They've been chosen for advancement not for their outdoor skills but for their indoor skills. They attend Rotary meetings in town and meet with concessionaires and park planners; they answer phone calls from the regional office, Washington office, congressional office, governor's office, newspaper office, and pestiferous citizen conservationists. Despite their assigned responsibility and authority, they are often told what to do. More and more they decide less and less on their own. As personnel lose touch with the park resource and make more money, their lives and life-styles change. Superintendents grow heavier and paunchier. They acquire a rhetoric with more verbiage and less substance. They opt for convenience and time saving. Many become paper tigers or shadowboxers; even when they care, they know the other guy has the power behind the punch.

Park superintendents walk on eggs. Each one knows that a congressman with clout, even a little, can bring him down; or a congressional aide maneuvering and manipulating in the name of the boss; or an assistant to an assistant secretary in the Interior Department; or a regional director sensitive to political winds and whims who reckons the best way to steer the boat is to avoid rocking it.

Congressmen know very little about national parks or what they're meant for. To most congressmen, parks are pure pork and plums. In the 1960s Julia Butler Hanson of Washington State became chairman of the House appropriations subcommittee controlling the national parks budget. When she visited Glacier Bay in Alaska she told the park superintendent, Robert Howe, that he ought to build roofs over all the lodge walkways so that visitors wouldn't get wet—which is certainly one way to avoid experiencing a rain forest. She also wrote into the budget funding for a reconstruction of Fort Vancouver National Historic Site in her own district, where her son, as it happened, became the curator.

Don Gillespie did a good job as superintendent at Fort Vancouver from 1972 to 1978 and so was promoted to Utah state coordinator, somewhat like a subregional director. But in 1986 Robert K. Weidner, a legislative aide to Senator Jake Garn, threatened to get rid of Gillespie for his outspoken opposition to paving the Burr Trail, a dirt road crossing Capitol Reef National Park and Glen Canyon National Recreation Area, a project favored by the commercial interests of southern Utah. Gillespie faced Weidner and bluntly told him he was a horse's ass and that he, Gillespie, had no intention of altering his view. But soon afterward Congress eliminated funding for Mr. Gillespie's position, and he retired.[4]

To cite another case, John Chapman went to Glacier Bay in 1979 as a promising young superintendent. He aspired to do great things, things worthy of a natural preserve of mountain ranges rising over fifteen thousand feet, with deep fjords, tidewater glaciers, seabird nesting colonies, grizzly bears, and humpback whales in their summer migration. Glacier Bay has become popular with cruise ships that sail north from Vancouver, Seattle, and San Francisco. They stop at Alaskan ports, but Glacier Bay is the high point of the cruise, especially for whale watching. A sharp and inexplicable decline in whale numbers became Chapman's ill fortune. When studies indicated that ship noises had a possible negative impact on whale feeding,[5] restricting cruise ships appeared to be the logical course of action, which Chapman proceeded to follow. He was supported by the regional director, John Cook. But the cruise industry complained, and the tourism industry complained; members of the Alaska congressional delegation listened, and they complained. Cook and

Chapman both were removed. Cook fared better by far, surfacing as park superintendent in the Great Smoky Mountains, while Chapman was dispatched to shuffle papers in a regional office.

Chapman was succeeded in 1983 by Mike Tollefson, another promising young superintendent. He still faced the challenge of cruise ship regulations and knew he must proceed with caution. As he told me in 1985, the resource management specialist, the chief ranger, an Interior Department attorney from Anchorage, and he sat down and drafted the regulations. After initial approval from Washington, the regulations were published in the *Federal Register*. The park held public meetings and took public comment, incorporating improvements into a new draft. Then the regulations went for final approval to the regional office and eventually back to Washington. There were many hurdles along the way, both within the Department of the Interior and in the Office of Management and Budget. OMB held the regulations for several months, then expressed reservations that may or may not have reflected industry influence. Consequently the park was unable to institute its regulations until virtually the start of the whale season. Tollefson in two years learned that the regulatory process could be stopped anywhere at levels of authority above him and, by the same token, started elsewhere than at the park.[6]

While regulatory processes have grown ever more complicated, the early park superintendents faced their share of handicaps in getting things done—particularly if they meant to preserve and protect. Sequoia–Kings Canyon, in the heart of the Sierra Nevada range of California, represents a classic case.

Sequoia, the second oldest national park, after Yellowstone, was established in 1890 (five days before Yosemite) to preserve giant sequoia trees, the largest living things, in large degree thanks to the efforts of John Muir singing the praises of "giants grouped in pure temple groves." The central feature (then as now) was Giant Forest, including the General Sherman Tree, the largest tree on earth in terms of bulk (272 feet tall and at least 32 feet in diameter at the base). The smaller General Grant Grove, containing several of the very largest trees, was set aside in the Yosemite Act as part of what was then named General Grant National Park. Fifty years later, in 1940, after a struggle with power and irrigation interests, lumbermen, hunters, and ranchers, Kings Canyon National Park was established, including General Grant National Park. The two parks, stretching sixty-five miles from north to south, protect as a single unit an unbroken wilderness of granite peaks, gorges, rockbound glacial lakes, flowering alpine meadows, and virgin forests.

Early park administrators didn't know any better when they constructed the first cabins to serve tourists in 1899 and the original Giant Forest road in 1903. But Superintendent John R. White expressed serious concern in the early 1920s, and in 1930 he brought the matter to a head by refusing to authorize major improvements. He suggested developing a completely new tourist lodge at a less sensitive site elsewhere in the park, thus beginning a process that has never ended, not to this day.

White was by all odds one of the legendary park superintendents.[7] Born in England, he left home at sixteen to join the Greeks fighting the Turks in Macedonia, then worked in the Klondike gold fields, enlisted in the U.S. Army in the Philippines, and headed back to Europe as a pilot in World War I. He thought he would try his hand as a park ranger, but Stephen T. Mather made him superintendent of Sequoia and Kings Canyon national parks, where he served from 1920 to 1947, with two years out, 1938–40, when he was regional director.

Though lacking a college degree and formal training in natural resource administration, "Colonel White" was a vigorous preservationist. On February 10, 1936, he delivered a telling speech before a conference of national park superintendents in Washington, D.C., on the subject of "Atmosphere in the National Parks":

> We should boldly ask ourselves whether we want the national parks to duplicate the features and entertainment of other resorts, or whether we want them to stand for something distinct and, we hope, better in our national life.
>
> We are a restless people, mechanically minded, and proud of doing constructive work. Our factories, railroads, roads, and buildings are admired by the world. We have in the parks a host of technicians, each anxious to leave his mark. But in all this energy and ambition there is danger, unless all plans are subordinated to that atmosphere which, though unseen, is no less surely felt by all who visit those eternal masterpieces of the Great Architect which we little men are temporarily protecting.[8]

But no matter how hard he tried, White was unable to close and move the developments in Giant Forest. The park concessionaire objected and White was overruled in Washington. He did, however, gain something of a compromise: development henceforth would be limited and anything new would be located elsewhere. Removing all facilities, in fact, became the official policy and goal of the agency. Elaborate plans were drawn for lodgings and housekeeping cabins elsewhere. Finally, in the late 1960s, long after White was gone, the campgrounds were closed and the post office, gas station, and visitor center were moved; not the lodgings, however. In 1968, when I was in the park, there was much talk of closing the facility, but the concessionaire had pleaded for "temporary construction," which was granted, with temporary due to last a long, long time.

When I returned to the park in June 1985, nearly twenty years later, the motel facility was still there, and more besides. Between 1963 and 1983 a total of ninety-seven modern motel units and numerous other improvements were added. In the winter of 1982–83 officials of the Park Service negotiated with the concessionaire, Guest Services, Inc. (GSI). The park superintendent, Boyd Evison (formerly of the Great Smoky Mountains), later told me that Director Russell Dickenson had promised to come down hard for the closure and move.[9] GSI was represented in the negotiations by its general counsel, George B. Hartzog, Jr., a former director of the National Park Service. The park superintendent and staff were stunned, for the concession got virtually everything it wanted. The concessionaire was permitted to replace fifty old units with fifty new ones, on the condition that they be movable, ready for transport to the new site by 1988; Hartzog succeeded, moreover, in getting agreement that closing could be delayed until 1990.[10]

On that 1985 visit I observed that the Park Service had built a wooden fence around the General Sherman Tree to protect it. Standing behind it reminded me that sequoias, for all their size and bulk, rise from shallow roots, that foot and vehicle traffic compact the soil, reducing percolation and the availability of moisture to the tree. This isn't the only way human use has inhibited sequoia growth. Though natural fires scarify seed cones and prepare the seedbed, fire has long been suppressed in the vicinity of buildings. How could fire be tolerated with tourist facilities at hand? Or spoil the setting with charred bark?

I also observed, in the new development area, what Park Service people call with grim humor "K-Mart West," the complete embodiment of a catch-all supermarket designed to fit the basic commercial highway strip anywhere in America. I can't imagine any superintendent being proud of it in his park.

A park superintendent may shadowbox with the politicians, but he at least can be tough on the people who work under him. Sometimes it's like the army: you just can't have the job you like. In 1986, at Badlands National Park in South Dakota, Lloyd Kortge, the chief ranger, recalled the start of his career almost twenty years before. He had just completed "intake" training and was assigned to Glacier National Park in Montana. It was winter when he arrived. Kortge spent the first month at park headquarters reading manuals. He was assigned as a subdistrict ranger on the North Fork. It was wild country, which pleased Kortge. Presently he was summoned to meet the park superintendent for the first time. It was William J. Briggle, a man tough enough to eat new rangers for breakfast.

"So, you're going to North Fork," said Briggle, unsmiling. "What do you think of that?"

"Oh, I think it's great! I'm looking forward to it."

Briggle's face reddened. He was taken aback. He glared at Kortge, wordless, then looked the new man in the eye. "Well, you're *not* going."

So Kortge was assigned spitefully to the east side of the park, while other rangers at some expense were shifted from one point to another till the North Fork job was filled.

Later, Briggle was superintendent of Mount Rainier National Park in Washington State. He had mellowed to some degree but was still a taskmaster who would lecture a seasonal ranger on how to tie a tie and was always "Mr. Briggle," never just plain Bill. Though he thought he knew what was going on at all times, whenever he headed from park headquarters at Longmire to the visitor complex at Paradise Valley, thirteen miles away, the word preceded him. "The ghost is walking. Make sure everything's clean," was the warning phone message. Or, "Straighten your hats. Polish your shoes. The ghost walks."

Briggle was moody. In some ways he was like his mentor, George B. Hartzog, Jr. They were scramblers in a hurry to succeed, measuring success by the authority they acquired. Both liked to push buttons, even when the buttons were people. They respected power and demanded loyalty. Briggle came to Glacier with a directive from Hartzog to clean house. Kenneth Beck, the park administrative officer, later testified that he was ordered to give one employee so many assignments that he couldn't possibly complete them and would resign. Beck refused and was transferred. "Every transfer of staff personnel from Glacier during my tenure under Briggle," Beck subsequently declared, "was through either coercion, subterfuge, intimidation, artifice, or some other manner in direct conflict with the Civil Service Commission regulations, departmental manual, and the National Park Service transfer and promotion plan."[11]

Canyonlands would be different, a real wilderness park in southern Utah, its enthusiasts predicted during the 1960s, when the legislation to establish it advanced through Congress. The trouble was they never reckoned with the power elite in the neighboring town of Moab. Edward Abbey has immortalized those folks, and I would hardly try to improve on his characterizations.[12] Simply stated, they never accepted the park, neither in the beginning nor at any time since, except as a source of tourist revenue. They wanted roads and considered a park without extensive motorized access a federal rip-off, if not a communist conspiracy. The *Salt Lake Tribune* of December 9, 1977, reported on a hearing conducted by William Whalen soon after he became director of the National Park Service. The article quoted Ray Tibbets, a county commissioner: "You could put a six-lane highway down the center of that park and there would still be more wild area left than a backpacker could see in a lifetime. I feel the Park Service is being infiltrated by the worst kind of environmentalists—people trying to lock up these areas. Let's put the parks back on a business basis."

By the mid-1980s many of the same crowd were pushing for construction of a proposed nuclear waste site less than a mile from the park boundary. It was one of nine sites being considered under the 1982 Nuclear Waste Policy Act. The proponents included former uranium miners who figured that once there was a place to dump the waste, the price of ore would rise and they could work their claims. With hope in their hearts they picketed a hearing carrying signs proclaiming, "Tree huggers are buggers" and "Shoot the No-Nuke Pukes."

I relate these episodes to underscore the hazards of park superintending. It isn't easy under the best of circumstances, but on the Utah frontier it becomes a challenge worthy of a Zane Grey or Louis L'Amour Western thriller.

Actually, as early as the 1930s, plans were being considered for one vast park in that area, to be known as Escalante. It would have been the marvel of the planet, covering 4.5 million acres where the Anasazi of prehistory cultivated crops and hunted game with atal-atals and spears until drought forced them to leave, and where the Mormons saw rock formations as natural temples, cathedrals, pulpits, and landings for angels. It was tough, remote country, unyielding to either settlers or ranchers. In the 1950s, however, prospectors arrived to search for uranium. Then Glen Canyon was drowned beneath the waters of Lake Powell, and the grand Escalante vision was shattered for all time.

Also in the 1950s, Bates Wilson, superintendent of Arches National Monument, looked down from a small plane and saw arches, spires, canyons, crevasses, and rainbow-colored fins. On his own initiative Wilson explored by jeep, horse, and foot, and campaigned for a new national park. The establishment of Canyonlands National Park in 1964 was a high point for the Great Society, even though it covered only a fraction of the original Escalante concept. Bates Wilson was another legendary superintendent. Born in Silver City, New Mexico, Wilson ran pack trips as a teenager, worked in Arches as early as 1949, and served as superintendent of both Canyonlands and Arches until he retired in 1972. He smoked, drank, swore, got out on the grounds, and tried to understand miners and ranchers. He was a local Will Rogers of the color country, and a hero of Abbey's *Desert Solitaire*. He retired to a hay ranch, where he died in 1983 at the age of seventy-one. After his death the Utah legislature adopted a memorial resolution in tribute to his "charm, grace and wit."

I met Bates Wilson but never traveled with him. In October 1985, however, I hiked and camped with the park superintendent of that time, Pete Parry. He joined three of my friends from Salt Lake—Rich, Gary, and Garn—and me for two days in the wild desert of the Needles district. We camped at Devils Kitchen and hiked wonderful trails in Chesler Park to Druid Arch and Squaw Flats, passing ancient rock walls erected by Indians along the way. While the autumn desert has no oaks and maples, the cottonwood leaves had turned yellow before the high red rock walls, while brilliant red leaves of squaw-bush and subdued brownish Gambel oak spread here and there across the ground. In potholes I saw tiny snails, shrimp, and little algaelike plants growing where water is very temporary. The desert had a magic mood; even when nobody was around I didn't feel alone, and I imagined that I could see as well as feel the wind.

Pete Parry came with us for a purpose. He wanted to explain the critical damage implicit in the proposed nuclear dump. For one thing, railcars and trucks would haul radioactive waste to the dump both day and night. The superintendent talked about the impacts on visitor experience, the values of primitiveness, solitude, and silence, the spectacular night vistas that would be destroyed by searchlights, the inevitable increase in noise, degradation of air quality, and loss of endangered species.

It wasn't easy for him to speak. Russell Dickenson, who succeeded Whalen as director, later told me how he had defended Parry from Interior Department officials when they wanted him removed.[13] Parry was prevented from testifying at public hearings.[14] At a hearing held October 12, 1984, Deputy Director Mary Lou Grier (imposed on the Park Service by Interior Secretary James G. Watt) talked about studies, monitoring, cooperation between agencies, everything but park principles: "We intend to continue to participate fully in the EA [environmental assessment] process and, following our review of those documents and data presented, will press any concerns we may have."[15] Robert Redford, the actor and a resident of Utah, told the same hearing: "The thought of combining a national park and a nuclear repository is, to me, an absurdity."[16] The park superintendent would have said the same, if only he could. Of the 4.5 million acres once envisioned for Escalante National Park, Canyonlands protects only 337,570 acres. Southern Utah, for all its beauty, remains a tough country. Rocks, plants, and fossils have been stripped by souvenir hunters. But, of course, poaching is an old tradition; a few of the defiant and adventurous locals make picnic outings of their hunts for decorated Anasazi pots, which command high prices.[17] In 1980 David B. Madsen, Utah's state archaeologist, reported that of twenty-five thousand known archaeological sites in the state, 90 percent had been disturbed in one way or another. In 1984 Madsen said that conditions were worse than ever. The Archaeological Resource Protection Act of 1979 sets high fines (and even provides rewards), but he complained there hadn't been an arrest in five years. So goes life and law on the last frontier.

Over the years I've known many park superintendents closely and have shared diverse pleasure and pain and frustration with them. Off-hand, I can't imagine a superintendent more continually in hot water over hard issues than Roger Allin. He served as superintendent of Everglades National Park and Lake Mead National Recreation Area, and was removed from both, subsequently ending his career as superintendent of Olympic National Park, where he was embattled and embroiled all the way through his tenure.

In March 1985 I visited Roger Allin at Whidbey Island, Washington, where he lived in retirement. He spoke frankly (but then he always did):

> When you've bitten off more than you can chew, with too many issues at a time, your problem is getting support from above, where the politics lie. But they can't take the heat upstairs.
>
> Superintendents don't want to risk transfer, so they duck the tough issues. Many take the safe course, saying "This is a big problem, but I would just as soon minimize as confront it." I just don't believe in that kind of administration. If I had looked to my personal comforts and to my family, maybe my decisions weren't so smart. But I had to live with myself and my family supported me.
>
> When I came here to the Northwest, John Rutter, the regional director, said, "You kick any sleeping dogs, you're on the way again." I had just a few more years and thought I could live with that for a while. But it's just not in my character. After about a year I started kicking a dog or two. I was assured that I wouldn't be transferred, but he really made it difficult for me.

I knew Roger well. He started his career as a fisheries biologist for the Fish and Wildlife Service in Alaska. In the mid-1960s he switched to the National Park Service in the Southwest regional office. His boss, the regional director, was Dan Beard (son of Dan Beard, the Boy Scout leader), the first superintendent of the Everglades from 1947 to 1958 and then superintendent of Olympic National Park for two years before working in the upper echelons in Washington. Beard wanted to be Park Service director, but he was concerned more with resource preservation than with politics and was passed over in favor of Hartzog. Nevertheless, although Allin had never worked in a national park, Beard cited his biology background and in 1966 successfully pushed him as superintendent of the Everglades.

It was a hot time in south Florida. Allin took on the Army Corps of Engineers and the Florida Flood Control District, which had been starving the park of water with diversionary canals. Then the Port Authority began construction of a major jetport near the edge of the park and Allin took that on, too. Powerful interests and individuals, including Senator Spessard Holland, complained, and Hartzog transferred Allin to Washington.[18] He resisted the transfer, but Hartzog told Allin his paycheck would be delivered to Washington and nowhere else, so he went, immediately campaigning to return to the field.

"I hate the Washington idea," he told me at Whidbey Island. "I don't like being that close to people you've got to bow and scrape to if they're a bunch of bums, and in Washington you've got to scrape to a lot of bums. Yes, promotions and so forth, but you can't make decisions in Washington—there are too many strings attached to everything. It's no fun."

Allin was in Washington for a year, then moved to Lake Mead National Recreation Area, which covers almost 1.5 million acres of deserts, canyons, and plateaus spread across Arizona and Nevada from Grand Canyon National Park almost to the edge of Las Vegas, with two massive reservoirs—Lake Mead, behind Hoover Dam, and Lake Mohave, behind Davis Dam. He followed a superintendent who had been there more than fifteen years, which is long enough to settle in cozily. Part of the superintendent's responsibility was to cater to Senator Alan Bible of Nevada, who chaired two key subcommittees, one dealing with parks legislation and the other with the parks' budget. He was a fishing friend and ally of Director Hartzog.

I knew Bible in Washington as very pleasant, but not a man to cross. Allin waded in nonetheless. In my files I have a letter dated August 11, 1970, from Vernon Bostick, a Nevada conservationist: "About a year ago I gave the National Park Service hell for not enforcing anti-litter laws and for permitting Las Vegas sewage to pollute Lake Mead. We are still polluting Lake Mead, but the new superintendent of Lake Mead National Recreation Area is not complacent about it. This is a change. After stalling for two years with a high-priced study the proposed solution was to stop polluting Lake Mead by polluting Lake Mohave instead. The superintendent [Allin] told the consulting engineers that the Park Service would not permit the degradation of Lake Mohave."

That was only one of the issues Allin faced. Within two years he received word that he was being removed again. On October 16, 1970, he wrote Hartzog that he had faced up to unacceptable conditions too long ignored:

> We have attempted to cause repair and improvement of deteriorating concession facilities and remedy the shabby public service provided. We have made strong effort to reduce the heretofore unchecked highway and boat accident rate. We have attempted to control the increasing use of this area for drug and drinking parties by juveniles.
>
> It is not possible to be successful in these tasks if at the same time we attempt to avoid all adverse reaction. On the other hand, in my opinion we have gained a great deal of public support by creating within the community a new respect for the Park Service as an agency actively concerned with total public welfare, at times despite the views of some who prefer the old days and old ways.

His transfer initially would have sent him to a regional office; after repeated pleas he went to Olympic National Park instead. In reviewing Roger's short tenure at Lake Mead, Vernon Bostick wrote to me on March 7, 1971:

> Allin is willing to take a stand for what he knows is right and can't be budged from it. We started to put up a fight for him, but the Park Service headed this off by offering him a better job. Roger Allin is ahead; the Northwest is ahead; conservationists in the Southwest lost a real champion.
>
> Roger Allin opposed the recommendations of the Boyle report which would stop pollution of Lake Mead by dumping Las Vegas sewage into Lake Mohave after tertiary treatment. I have a letter from the "acting" superintendent indicating he now goes along with the Boyle recommendations.
>
> Allin recognizes that the various companies offering float trips through the Grand Canyon were overdoing it. He wanted to put a ceiling on the number of people who could be accommodated each year. Naturally the companies don't want any such restrictions on expanding their business.
>
> I paddled my canoe up the Colorado River from Pierce's Ferry at the head of Lake Mead to Emory Falls in the inner gorge. Roger Allin is right. What has happened to this stretch of wild river in one decade is almost unbelievable. Toilet paper doesn't stay buried in

shifting sands. Colorado River float trips are for ten days or longer, so instead of bringing their garbage out with them, the raft companies bury it. Coyotes soon dig it up. The Grand Canyon was an unspoiled wilderness ten years ago, but it is getting to be a mess.

The idea that wilderness has a limited carrying capacity for recreation is just beginning to be recognized. When this capacity is exceeded, the quality of the recreation resource deteriorates just as the range resource deteriorates when grazing capacity is exceeded. Roger Allin wanted to preserve the quality of the trips offered by limiting the number to a fixed yearly quota.

Roger Allin opposed the building of a huge coal burning electric generating plant in Arrow Canyon outside the boundaries of Lake Mead National Recreation Area. The Bureau of Reclamation favors the generating plant. It was probably the Dam Bureau that had the muscle to force Roger Allin's transfer.

Maybe so, but who can tell? The transferee may be the last to know. While I was at Whidbey Island I asked Allin if he had ever been able to pinpoint the precise cause of his move, but he could not. Pollution was very bad in the Lake Mead National Recreation Area, but tackling the pollution problem meant taking on the Las Vegas power structure. Concessions were universally substandard. One of the people on Senator Bible's staff controlled one of the worst concessions Allin had run into anywhere. The sewage from the concession was disposed of in fifty-five-gallon drums in the sand; the restrooms had holes bored through the men's and women's facilities so there was no privacy; the whole thing was junk. Allin tried to upgrade it, but the concessionaire sat across from him and said that Allin didn't have the horsepower, the political clout. The energy business, safety, concessions, the Las Vegas Wash sewage—Allin couldn't identify the final straw; it was a little of everything. He created a few problems of his own by tackling too many things at one time.

At Olympic, for six years starting in 1971, Roger showed he hadn't learned and hadn't changed. Again he tackled too many things at one time: private inholdings in the park, commercial concessions, shelters in the backcountry, and pleasant living perks for park personnel.

He believed it was right to purchase and remove intrusive structures to improve the park's integrity and sustain its purpose, but he often saw these inholdings converted into living quarters for seasonal naturalists or seasonal rangers instead of being destroyed. After all, they need someplace to live; but Lake Crescent remained ringed with structures.

This arrangement offered a great opportunity for a professional person, coming as a seasonal naturalist, to have a lovely lakefront summer place for the whole family. Allin did not want the seasonal personnel to consider the facilities as theirs, year in and year out. He felt it wasn't compatible with the purpose of acquiring the property—that is, to restore the area to natural condition—or the reason for establishing Olympic National Park in the first place. But when Allin directed demolition of a number of the buildings he created animosity among the staff.

In my observation the seasonal rangers and naturalists as a breed generally love the parks in a personal way. They like to exercise minds and bodies in the outdoors; they enjoy serving the public—not all, but most. Only a few, however, concern themselves with environmental issues facing the parks or society. They like to wear white hats, but not to be involved. The same is true of permanent employees.

Roger Allin was involved all the way. He may at times have rushed in where angels would have tread cautiously, but his summation is right as rain, reaching to the core of why national parks are in deep trouble: "Rarely do you run into the kind of Everglades challenge, where the entire park and reason for its existence are threatened. That becomes a national issue. The usual thing is the nibbling away process, a little attrition at a time: a boundary revision, timber use, mining intrusion, concession, inholding, even public use activity, undermining the integrity of the park, watering down the entire system to the point of meaningless rhetoric. A park superintendent must either fight these minor battles and find a local constituency to support him or we've watered down the entire system to the point of meaningless rhetoric."

Yes, a park superintendent ought to be a courageous risk taker and a good communicator reaching out to caring citizens of conscience, and by so doing set an example for park personnel. As I mentioned in chapter 5, William Penn Mott wanted superintendents to be assertive and involved with real issues, rather than travelers down the road of least resistance. But the system scarcely allows assertiveness and risk taking.

7

We opened another beer and Jack Hughes explained why he wanted only to be a ranger, without any higher ambition. He was like a friend of mine in Minnesota, a college graduate, cultivated and well read, who wanted only to be a rural letter carrier, which is how he spent his working career, fulfilled and free of envy.

Jack Hughes is a ranger's ranger, a throwback to early days—self-sufficient and self-possessed, conditioned to the out-of-doors, and outspoken for what he believes to be right. In the early 1970s he established the Professional Rangers Organization and then the Glacier Defense Fund when Riley McClelland was dismissed by William J. Briggle. Over the years various superiors tried to get rid of Jack, but he understood his rights under the civil service and how to exercise them. Besides, he was too valuable in the Olympic backcountry.

"The satisfaction in being a field ranger is that I can do things I couldn't do otherwise," said Jack. It was the fall of 1984. We were lounging at a work center in the park on a Saturday evening. It was his kind of hangout, unadorned and close to the park. He knew others who had gone to work in the Washington office pledging to represent the ranger division. They were going to change things—so they thought before they were swallowed whole by the bureaucratic system. In the field Jack felt personally fulfilled.

He could help people to enjoy the area, rescue them when necessary, and try to prevent them from getting into trouble. His gross salary as a GS-9 at the highest grade was $27,000 a year, but he was raised in the depression, never expected to make that much, and thought it was a lot of money. Jack was fit to hike thirty mountain miles in a day, planned to ski a thousand miles during the year, felt good about himself and his work, and whenever William Briggle, the deputy regional director, might walk into the room he felt no obligation to stand.

It isn't all that easy. Rangers as a breed look great in their uniforms, like Jack Armstrong, the all-American boy, or Jill Armstrong, the all-American girl. But a close-up reveals their share of frustration and weakness. As, for example, the ranger who announced his resignation in the midst of a campfire talk. As reported in the *Monterey* (California) *Peninsula Herald* of August 25, 1979, visitors to Pinnacles National Monument were gathered at a primitive amphitheater to learn about nature. They were in for a surprise. Larry Wells, thirty-six, a full-time employee who had worked in four national parks, said he probably would be fired for what he was about to reveal if he hadn't already turned in his resignation. Visitors would soon note a marked deterioration in the parks; the National Park Service was politicized; he was quitting because of mounting frustrations and because "I'm an idealist and I really care." He said he was sorry to see the Park Service play Mr. Nice Guy. "It indicates to me that management doesn't really believe in its own work."

Generally, rangers keep a neat appearance, follow orders, and stay out of trouble. Some know a great deal about their particular parks, while others know precious little. For example, Richard C. Porter, economics professor at the University of Michigan, wrote to me in 1977 and 1978 about his frequent visits to Yellowstone: "We were often warned at the ranger stations of 'bad trails,' which were, in fact, excellently maintained. Most rangers are almost useless in helping plan a trip—they seem never to have walked anywhere in the park." The bear advice the rangers gave, wrote Professor Porter, was elaborate and contradictory: "Play dead, climb a tree, stand still, back up slowly, raise your hands, keep on going, put everything up in the bear bag, even the clothes you cook in."

To cite another revealing case, in 1985 I was in Denali, passing free time one afternoon in reading the draft master plan for that park. I was struck by a particular statement: "A past solution in many parks has been to relocate problem bears. However, this concept has flaws." I spent that evening with the superintendent, Robert Cunningham, and asked him to explain. Cunningham reminded me that ten years before he had been a ranger in Yellowstone, then gave this charming confession: "We subdistrict rangers relocated bears all over hell. In fact, we used to trade bears while passing each other in the morning. 'You take my bear and I'll take your bear.' We were carrying out the policy set down by the biologist, Glen Cole, though we didn't agree with it. Field managers were telling Cole, 'As soon as you close those damn dumps, we'll be dealing with bears.' Sure as hell, I had bears in Madison campground the first damn night."

The early rangers were more independent, on their own, without higher authorities giving orders and looking over their shoulders. They were essentially self-trained and self-sufficient. Park rangers came on the scene after 1916, the year the National Park Service was born, replacing soldiers, who had protected the parks in dutiful military fashion since the mid-1880s. Congressmen wanted to exercise political control over these positions, but Stephen T. Mather, the first director of the National Park Service, defied the precedents of patronage and insisted on building a professional corps. Those rangers had little technical training, but they could do almost any job required in the field. Curiously, even while patrolling against poachers, they carried out the government's holy war against predators. In Yellowstone alone, between 1904, when figures were first kept, and 1935, a total of 4352 coyotes were officially reported trapped, shot, or poisoned. Cougars and wolves were shot on sight, practically exterminating the species. Eliminating the "bad" animals so the "good" ones could make it was considered a conservation mission. So it wasn't all "better then."[1]

Early rangers loved their work. Wayne Replogle, normally a collegiate athletic coach in Kansas, worked as a seasonal ranger in Yellowstone for at least fifty summers. Back when there were bear feedings in the park, at Canyon and Old Faithful, he would sit and hold a rifle in case a bear decided to go for the audience; it never happened, but he conveyed a sense of security. He was one of the first rangers to use a motorcycle on patrol. He said he enjoyed being a park ranger so much it was almost criminal for the Park Service to pay him. He died on July 4, 1976, and all the flags in Yellowstone were flown at half-mast.

Walter "Scotty" Chapman worked as a ranger in Yellowstone for almost half a century, from 1930 to 1976, when he retired to a small ranch outside Gardiner, on the north boundary of the park. I visited Scotty and his wife, Louise, in July 1986 and stayed overnight with them. Scotty recalled being raised in a cabin at the foot of Mount Rushmore, in South Dakota, while his father worked in the Black Hills gold mines. It was shortly before the mountain was carved by Gutzon Borglum. Rushmore was a wild place, and young Scotty and other kids climbed over granite rocks and watched the remnant herd of native elk. When the Four Faces were completed, a beautiful mountain had been desecrated. To finish it off, the elk were slaughtered and barbecued at the dedication. That little narrative made me realize how each succeeding generation accepts less and less of the real thing because it has no way of understanding what has been lost.

Scotty attended Colorado State University, taking basic forestry courses, rudimentary for park work, before starting his career in Yellowstone. He was assistant chief ranger from 1942 on, but more comfortable as a field man than in the office. He was never one who could spend the whole season writing letters, but in the field he was sure of himself—a good packer and skier, and he always had the horses, which he liked.

In the 1920s and 1930s, Scotty recalled, park men were imbued with basic preservation values. When park foresters proposed building roads through the backcountry for fire protection or some other purpose, the chief ranger and assistant chief strongly resisted and battled them down. Actually, many who came from forestry schools were too deeply indoctrinated with management and manipulation techniques to be good park men. Yellowstone spray programs as recently as the 1950s followed the Forest Service design and caused considerable damage. During the spruce budworm spray program, an airplane lost power while making a pass on the Douglas fir in the Mammoth area; the pilot dumped the whole load on an eagle's nest, and neither eagle nor osprey has been seen there since.

But again, each generation doesn't know what it's missing—it's as though eagle and osprey were never present. But the Chapmans remembered, which explains why they deeded the land on which they lived, a private parcel between the national park and national forest, to the Nature Conservancy. In their lifetime the frontier world had turned upside down. When it came time to turn in, Scotty led me to a little bunkhouse away from the main house. "Scotty," I inquired, "whatever should I do if I see a grizzly coming in the front door?" "Hug him—I haven't seen a grizzly through here in five years."

Jack Hughes was like a second-generation Scotty Chapman. At the time we talked on the Olympic Peninsula Jack was fifty-two, tall and gangly, still riding the high of an athletic life. He had been a cross-country and marathon runner at the University of Colorado but had given up running for long-distance skiing. He had been married; currently, however, he was living alone in simple accommodations in Port Angeles, the old logging town at the edge of the national park. He had started his career at Yellowstone but had long been at Olympic, watching superintendents and other rangers come and go. In 1976 he was seriously injured in a helicopter crash on a mountain rescue mission. Jack suffered four broken vertebrae, luckily without severing the spinal cord, and a Seattle surgeon restored his spine with bone grafts and steel rods. I would never have known; he seemed more agile than most men half his age.

I first met Jack in 1970, the year he established the Professional Rangers Organization. He and a few others were concerned about a move designed by the Washington office under Director George B. Hartzog, Jr., to phase out rangers, or at least to reclassify them as technicians at lower grades. In a bold letter published in the August 1970 issue of *Courier*, the in-house journal, Hughes wrote:

> Early rangers were uneducated men of great skill in outdoor work. They knew the area and could get around it under all conditions. Men of this skill are rare today. By 1930 rangers were recruited from forestry schools, or "Ranger Factories." At least two types of career followed for these new rangers. One group went very quickly into offices and became in amazingly short time chief rangers and superintendents. Many of the latter were sent to offices *because* they were not good with the field work. Thus, *not* measuring up to the job for which one was hired could predispose one to becoming a supervisor of those who did!
>
> The office group gained control of parks, regions and key staff jobs in Washington. Having never spent long enough in a field job or even an area to know that work, they had small regard for the standards of the working field ranger. This group encouraged new men to move often—two years or less per area was not uncommon. Now this

"second generation" of managers is again selling short the skill and knowledge needed by a modern ranger for field work. Instead of encouraging top men to stay in field level jobs long enough to learn them and the areas in-depth, people are being pushed into offices and transfers.

The Professional Rangers Organization showed promise for a time, but it was too militant for most in the ranks. They wanted something safer, and in due course established the Association of National Park Rangers, keeping it closely tied to management. Its efforts have been directed toward such goals as improving the uniform allowance and standards for field equipment, with scant emphasis on the principles of preservation or challenge to authority.

We talked about the Olympics. Barely a century ago, when the entire Olympic Peninsula was still a wilderness, a park without a capital *p*, and without any protection, loggers, miners, and land speculators picked off the best parts of it. Gifford Pinchot, chief of federal forestry, complained that nearly every acre "passed promptly and fraudulently into the hands of lumbermen."[2] The very quality of the Olympic rain forests, with their immense trees—western hemlock, cedar, Sitka spruce, and, above all, Douglas fir—nurtured by the heaviest rainfall in the country and mild temperatures, has been their undoing and has made the Olympic Peninsula a conservation battlefield.

In 1897 the Olympic Forest Reserve of almost 2.2 million acres was established by presidential proclamation. That began the battle. The reserve subsequently was reduced in size, but President Theodore Roosevelt in 1909 proclaimed Mount Olympus National Monument to preserve the primeval forests, along with the steep, snowy peaks and glaciers at higher elevations, and the Olympic (or Roosevelt) elk. Once TR left office, however, the monument was reduced until only half remained, virtually none in timber. Thus the campaign shifted to the idea of a national park. Interior Secretary Harold L. Ickes became an aggressive spokesman, with the strong support of President Franklin D. Roosevelt. Establishing the national park in 1938, however, did not end the conflict; during World War II the old foes demanded that the park be opened to mining and logging, and they have never quit.

Rangers who care have been let down by their own leadership. Directors were willing to transfer the precious lush rain forests to Forest Service administration for certain logging. The Park Service itself during the 1950s and 1960s authorized extensive and questionable logging of wind-blown timber and timber around camping areas for "safety" and "access." It agreed in 1977 to construction of logging roads *inside* the boundary and juggled boundaries to permit access to state-owned timberlands, even through an area the Park Service had recommended for classification as wilderness.

Jack Hughes called Olympic a "jinxed national park." But all the parks have been jinxed in one way or another. Olympic in particular is a park of tragedy, lovely but fractured, protected on paper only. Logging trucks dominate the roads of the Olympic Peninsula. The rain forests, drenched in moisture and magic, are mere fragments at most.[3]

But administrators carry on. While James G. Watt was interior secretary the park received an injection of funding from the PRIP. The object, as Hughes saw it at ground level, was to get the money out without deciding where it would do the most good or what the environmental consequences might be. Spending became an end in itself. People involved in PRIP were given awards which more or less said, "They did a good job because they were able to spend that money."

Rangers tend to become cynical or opportunistic or disillusioned or absorbed with minutia; some become renegades in the ranks. They often are unprepared by their training for what they find on the job. In college they are taught technical subjects related to "resource management," focused on facts and numbers, on rules and regulations rather than history or culture. They acquire the distinctive jargon of the trained resource professional, so their frame of reference and their friendships are directed inward, not toward the community around them. They become isolated from local people, most of whom earn less than they do. Unlike Jack Hughes, the typical ranger in the field is passing *through* to the next assignment in a year or two, hopefully with promotion and raise.

In the old days the ranger was an all-around expert. Now there are different kinds of experts—in resource management, law enforcement, and interpretation. Only a small portion of rangers are permanent, full-time employees. Most are seasonals who work during the peak visitor periods; but then there are permanent seasonals and long-term seasonals who work nine or ten months a year. Some will say they don't really want to work full time for the government so they can speak freely, but they are also cautious to be sure they are rehired.

Rangers are apt to feel the hostility of local antagonists. Antipark people can make it plenty hot. In 1980, for instance, major new national parks were established in Alaska, to the displeasure of much of the population. Alaska residents, at least the vocal ones, resented the advent of restrictions and regulations. I don't recall anyone getting hurt, but for some time rangers were subject to abuse and threats.

Ranger Rick (as we shall call him) was subject to intensive threats. For his own safety he and his family were moved out of Shenandoah National Park, in Virginia, in the dark of night. He committed the unpardonable sin—shooting a mountain man's hunting dogs.

This happened on November 28, 1977. Ranger Rick came on duty at 6:00 A.M. to cover the Fork Mountain Road area. Rick monitored a CB radio channel used exclusively by hunting clubs in the Rapidan River area in legal hunts outside the park and illegal hunts outside and inside. More than a hundred loose dogs had already been captured in the park during the year; sixty-four wearing tags were returned to their owners; the others were sent to the dog warden.[4]

Shenandoah National Park, to set the stage, lies seventy miles southwest of Washington, D.C., on the crest of the Blue Ridge Mountains.[5] When the park was authorized in 1926, every acre was privately owned, by about 450 families clustered in crossroads communities and hill farms. Portions of the country were still lovely. Herbert Hoover was so fond of the area that he built a lodge on the Rapidan River where he could break away from Washington to fish the quiet pools and riffles. In those days Congress refused to appropriate funds to acquire parkland; that responsibility was delegated to the states that cared enough. In the case of Shenandoah, it took Virginia nine years to purchase the land and relocate the people. Even so, the boundary is irregular and unrelated to topographic or ecological features; it varies in width from a little more than seventeen miles down to the toss of maybe two beer cans. The park is mostly surrounded by private lands, except for a few state-designated wildlife areas; fingers of private land reach almost to the crest. And even after all the years, the scars of resentment remain raw and sore. When the Park Service took control in 1935 there were no bears—they had all been hunted and killed; there were no wild turkeys, bobcats, or white-tailed deer, and few small mammals. The land was eroded as a consequence of poor farming practices. Since then, virtually all the vegetation and wildlife have come back.

Ranger Rick picked up a transmission, "Big George, men in green are everywhere in the park, checking guns and issuing permits." He heard hunters in a steady stream of conversation say they had released dogs between Bear Church Rocks and Fork Mountain and were after bears. He called the dispatcher requesting that state game wardens be summoned, and contacted another ranger to say, "Dogs have been intentionally set loose to hunt the Rapidan/park area and are pursuing game in the area of Camp Hoover." He heard a pack of baying hounds and saw the small black bear they were chasing. He fired buckshot from his shotgun and his .38 service revolver and dispatched three blue tick hounds. One had no tag, the other two had tags identifying their owner.

Ranger Rick later wrote to me at great length. Recognizing that killing another man's bear dogs can be very serious business, his decision to dispatch the animals was based on the knowledge that 1 / organized hunt groups had deliberately and illegally committed their dogs to hunting bear in the state-administered Rapidan Wildlife Area and the park; 2 / the hunters were pursuing bears in front of the dogs and had successfully killed one and tried to get shots at two others; 3 / no effort was made at any time to head off the dogs; in fact, just the opposite actions were taking place, and dogs were deliberately led onto bear sign; 4 / at least one hunter was in the park hunting bear pursued by these dogs; 5 / four distinct chases took place on park lands; 6 / he had observed a bear being pursued by some of these dogs in a fully baying, close chase; 7 / firearms were the only means available to end this chase because tranquilizing equipment was not available; and 8 / efforts to have the state game warden alleviate these activities had brought negative results.

He continued to feel he had acted responsibly, even though in doing so he had brought down the wrath of hunters on the park and its personnel. He felt it was apparent that the hunters had deliberately chosen to violate federal and state regulations and to exploit the protection given to wildlife.

"Shooting Incident Outrages County," read the headline in the *Madison County Eagle* of December 8, 1977. It quoted Superintendent Robert R. Jacobsen as admitting the ranger's action but refusing to release the ranger's name for fear of reprisal. The congressman of the district, J. Kenneth Robison, wrote the park superintendent to remind him that, notwithstanding regulations prohibiting hunting in national parks, good hunting dogs hold the very highest respect and affection of their owners, and "the death or disablement of an experienced hunting dog is the matter of highest concern to a sportsman."[6]

Wayne Dean, one of the Madison County hunters, was quoted in the *Richmond Times-Dispatch*: "You have to know how the government came in here and created the park and how they moved people out to little plots of land and a bunch of stick houses. Then when something like this happens, you know the feelings are going to run deep and there's going to be a lot of angry people. There isn't one man in 500 who would just shoot a dog like that. Those dogs were doing what they're trained to do. A dog isn't going to stop tracking a bear just because he's about to enter the park. There's something wrong with a man like that."[7]

Threats against Ranger Rick and his family intensified. He was directed to say nothing and was spirited to the West for his own safety. After being assigned to another park, Rick wrote me further. He had been told to keep mum on the details, but he felt that the rangers' side of the mess—what they are forced to ignore—should be recognized and dealt with. He feared the continuation of a public relations approach to soothe the "good neighbors" of the park.

Precisely this approach had fostered the confrontation. Rangers were fully authorized to shoot miscreant dogs. There was no written statement from the superintendent or chief ranger to the contrary, yet the unofficial word, with a hand cupped to the side of the mouth and whispered breath, was "shoot dogs if justified, but don't get caught." Written policy suggested tranquilizing a dog with a dart gun and returning it to the owner, but *not* to issue a ticket. Any hunting dog observed hunting in the park, whether once or fifty times, would be caught, impounded, and returned to the owner. But no tickets.

When Rick delivered his report to the superintendent he recommended that Jacobsen release it to the press. He wanted the public to know *why* a park ranger had to shoot three fine hunting dogs; otherwise the incident would be distorted to make the Park Service the

villain of the piece. Rick felt the park had a responsibility to seek support from all its supporters rather than meekly soothe and pacify the
antipark fringe in Madison County.

But Rick's report did not tell it all. It did not say that a game warden
had chosen not to pursue the illegal use of dogs on adjacent state land,
thus causing the park's problems; nor that a county deputy sheriff
was a member of the hunting group; nor that the same deputy led the
cry against Rick with death threats which required the superintendent to transfer Rick from the park. Thus, concluded Ranger Rick, "I
believe my removal was to protect me, but I hate to see the park cave
in to such methods."

Getting along with local interests is one thing; appeasement, or caving in, is another. To the ranger who joins the Park Service full of idealism, chronic caving in can be downright disillusioning. This leads
me to the case of Bernard Shanks, the ranger who tried to take on a
United States senator.

Shanks grew up in rural south-central Illinois, planning to become
a teacher until a high school biology teacher sensed his interest in
birds and advised him to try for a summer job in the parks. So in 1959,
at the age of nineteen, he went to work in Yellowstone. He had read
about pioneers on the frontier wilderness but couldn't imagine anything as wild as what he saw from his fire lookout fifteen miles from
the nearest road. The country was alive with elk, buffalo, deer, peli-
cans, and signs of grizzly bears where they had torn up the Pelican
Creek Cabin. That was the summer of the earthquake at Hebgen
Lake, a few miles outside the park, and even atop a ten-thousand-foot
mountain everything shook. Shanks presently switched to the university closest to Yellowstone, Montana State at Bozeman, and set
his sights on becoming a ranger.

He took up mountain climbing while he was still in college, then
started smoke-jumping for the Forest Service so he would have fire
experience. In summers he smoke-jumped in Alaska, and he worked
two winters for the Park Service in Arizona. One day in Alaska he
took the train from Fairbanks to visit Mount McKinley. A friendly,
matronly woman sitting across the aisle turned out to be Margaret
Murie, a singular personality who has touched and influenced
many lives. "Mardy" Murie was born in Seattle in 1902; her parents
moved to Alaska, where she became the first woman graduate of the

University of Alaska. In 1923 she married Olaus Murie, an honored field biologist and wilderness advocate; since his death in 1963 she has continued the activity they both shared, even into her late eighties. During the trainboard conversation she expressed interest in Shanks and his work; he couldn't have been more fascinated if he had met John Muir. Once at McKinley Station Shanks met Adolph Murie, the brother of Olaus and a biologist of distinction in his own right, who he would see again, at great length, in the Grand Tetons.

In 1965 Shanks became a permanent ranger in Grand Teton National Park in western Wyoming, scarcely realizing that he had moved into a hot spot. The striking Teton range, narrow and jagged and high, and the valley at its foot called Jackson Hole comprise one of the beauty spots of the West that has somehow survived, albeit imperfectly, through a history of strife.[8]

The Tetons might once have been set aside as part of a great national preserve, joined with Yellowstone, which lies only a few miles to the north, but the influence of commercial users, notably stockmen, was too great. In 1929 a portion of the area was designated Grand Teton National Park, with dimensions clearly inadequate. To compensate for it, President Franklin D. Roosevelt in 1943 proclaimed Jackson Hole National Monument from various parcels of private, state, and federal land. (With the advice of Horace Albright, John D. Rockefeller, Jr., in 1926 established the Snake River Land Company to quietly purchase key tracts. When it became known, park foes called it a connivance of the federal government and Eastern capital. But the Rockefeller gift ultimately added 32,170 acres of protected land.)

The Roosevelt proclamation stirred powerful political opposition from ranchers, loggers, hunters, and the U.S. Forest Service. Many of the locals felt Jackson Hole was meant for growing cattle and hunting elk, principally by them. They trotted out Wallace Beery, the movie star, a Jackson habitué, to ride across the monument with a rifle in his arms as a gesture of defiance to park rangers. Wyoming brought legal action to nullify the proclamation. When that failed, Representative (later Senator) Frank Barrett successfully amended every appropriations bill from 1944 to 1948 to forbid any expenditure for administration or protection of the new monument. Finally, in 1950, a compromise bill combined park and monument, transferring certain tracts of the monument to the adjacent national wildlife refuge and providing that Wyoming hunters be deputized in the fall season as rangers.

Grand Teton National Park is an area of violated naturalness. Dams as a rule are not tolerated in national parks, yet Jackson Lake is no longer a natural lake but a reservoir, dammed and controlled by the Bureau of Reclamation to provide water and irrigation to eastern Idaho. Moreover, the reduction of water flow in winter severely affects aquatic life in the lake and Snake River. Elk hunting is an established annual event, though the Park Service does not allow hunting in any other national park, except for subsistence hunting in Alaska. Fish are stocked artificially. Park visitors fly into the Jackson Airport, the only airport within the boundaries of a national park in the lower forty-eight states, and a main-stem highway through the park speeds travelers on their way to and from Yellowstone.

Bern Shanks's first summer in the Tetons was a very busy time. When not involved with the mountain rescue team, he explained to visitors the reasons for park regulations: why their dogs could not run loose, why flowers should not be picked, why wildlife isn't hunted. He felt that a ranger by definition is both protector and educator, that managing a national park is legally simple and ethically straightforward.

Then came fall; he worked on the elk hunt and the disillusionment began. He saw the hunt as a classic example of the endless compromises made by the Park Service. The agency had already paid the price in 1950, when Grand Teton became the first park to allow hunting. Now, each fall, hunters descend on the Tetons, sign a simple form, and become "deputy park rangers." The rationale is that the elk herd is now limited to a winter range less than one-third the size of its range of a century ago and needs to be hunted for its own good. So the shooters wait on the flats east of the Snake River for the elk migrating from the summer range in the high country to the winter range in the sagebrush of the national elk refuge. Of 8000 to 10,000 elk, they kill about 1700 and wound 200, including 450 to 600 elk inside the park.

Shanks worked on ranger patrols that looked for ravens in the morning frost, indicators of spots where wounded elk had slowly bled, sickened, and died. Crippled elk, some with legs shot off, were a daily sight. Coyotes, seldom seen in summer, when they pounced on unsuspecting meadow mice, were changed. Hunters saw them feeding on elk carcasses and mistakenly regarded them as competitors rather than as an efficient scavenger patrol.[9]

Bern shared his apprehensions with Adolph Murie, who had spent many years of field research in both Denali (called McKinley National Park in Murie's time there) and the Tetons. Ade was a scientist and scholar endowed with a clear vision of national parks as they ought to be. Bern would often drop by for coffee at the log cabin at Moose where Ade and his wife, Louise, lived simply—close to the log house of Mardy Murie, where Mardy and Olaus had lived for years. (More about the Muries in a subsequent chapter.)

In winter Bern was assigned to work on revamping grazing permits in the park, which were in a state of disarray. The 1950 compromise legislation by which Jackson Hole National Monument became part of Grand Teton National Park permitted "valid existing grazing" to continue. Shanks spent months researching and compiling grazing records. He found that certain permits had been inherited from the Forest Service and were considered a temporary political price to pay for establishing the park.

But he discovered several that he considered obviously illegal—the result of inept record-keeping, poor administration, and political pressure. He concentrated on these permits and prepared a series of memos documenting their illegality and reasons for their cancellation. He saw national park land as sacred space, not cow pasture; removing the livestock would begin the process of healing.

As Shanks learned, a young local county commissioner, Clifford Hansen, earlier had joined two other cattle ranchers in moving their livestock to the monument lands. Legally they were trespassing, but Congress had cut off funds to manage or protect the national monument, and the Park Service had been powerless to enforce its laws. Meanwhile, Hansen rose in politics. He became a very popular governor, then a U.S. senator who sat on the Interior Committee governing public lands while his cattle grazed each summer on irrigated public land.

When he completed his research and documentation Shanks concluded that while several ranchers held permits, Senator Hansen held the largest, for 569 cattle—the largest permit in the park and in the entire park system.[10] Consistent with the law and with its own regulations, the Park Service would have to cancel Hansen's permit and others like it, returning the cow pasture in the park to wildlife.

After reading Shanks's memorandum, the chief ranger called Shanks to his office. He was concerned and sympathetic but ventured to be a political realist. "I don't care what you find in the records. As long as Cliff Hansen sits on the Senate Interior Committee, we're not going to touch his cows."[11]

Shanks quit, as have others who find the simple mission of protecting park lands complicated to the point of futility. He returned to college for graduate studies, ultimately earning a doctorate in natural resource development. He taught first at the University of Nevada and then at Utah State University as a specialist in resource policy. It was the time of the Sagebrush Rebellion, sparked by Secretary James G. Watt, which aimed at transferring federal lands and resources to states and private developers. The Sagebrush Rebellion was the West's own McCarthyism, gaining momentum with fear and distortion. Because Shanks saw it as an attack on public agencies and their personnel, he felt the leadership in the resource profession should defend its own kind. Shanks delivered important speeches in different parts of the West, hoping to influence policy by using factual accuracy and valid research data. His dean, however, expressed sympathy and support for the Sagebrush Rebellion, and Shanks was invited to leave. (His successor at Utah State, Rosemary Nichols, who obtained her doctorate with a study of politics in the administration of Great Smoky Mountains National Park, was destined to meet a similar fate.)

Shanks learned that many resource academics regard political science and politics as dirty words. They don't want to be tainted. They want to maintain "professional objectivity," with professionals being analysts who look at data and make some sort of rational, scientific decision. From his own experience in the Tetons and from reports of former students, he knew that decisions aren't made that way.

Shanks went on to hold positions as special assistant to the secretary of resources in California and to the governor of Arizona, and as director of the Institute of California Studies at California State University at Sacramento. The following story sums up his insights:

When I worked in California, I received a plain brown envelope from a friend in the Bureau of Land Management. That envelope contained a copy of the media plan Watt and his henchmen had developed in preparation for Reagan rescinding Nixon's tough executive order restricting the use of off-road vehicles on public lands. It was a detailed public relations campaign—mapping out day-by-day selling of the order after the fact. It was raw and reprehensible. We discussed it with a few environmental groups and agreed Huey Johnson, the secretary of resources, would go to Washington and release it there. Huey made about a hundred copies, went to Washington, and held a press conference. The *New York Times* played it on the first page and there were all sorts of editorials. Reagan never signed his order. It died before it was born.

Later I talked with the guy who gave it to me. He'd been in the BLM about twenty years. "The most important thing I ever did was get that document and give it to you," he said. "I can't talk about it, but I'm prouder of that than anything I've done in my life."[12]

Another outspoken scholar, Alfred Runte, a university professor and author of an excellent history (*National Parks: The American Experience*), worked for several years as a seasonal ranger-naturalist in Yosemite National Park. In his interpretive talks he detailed the changes in Yosemite: from 5000 visitors in 1900 to 2.5 million in 1980, with full-time jail and court, police cars, fire trucks, and rangers equipped with nightsticks, six-guns, and handcuffs. He especially criticized the relationship between park administration and concessionaires. He refused to overlook the park's unhappy side or deal with it in the accepted manner. His candor got him in trouble. In the summer of 1980 Runte was directed to a week of "rehabilitation training," during which the assistant superintendent and chief park interpreter listened to a tape of a talk he gave to park visitors, reviewed the transcript, and made corrections. Then, dressed like tourists, they accompanied him while he led groups of visitors and made further changes.

Following his rehabilitation, Runte reverted to delivering the message exactly as he chose.[13] He would begin by asking the audience to recognize that national parks are in jeopardy. "What would you be willing to do to see that national parks remain part of the fabric of

American society for generations to come? Would you be willing to
give up some lighting and other power so that geothermal development would not destroy Old Faithful? Would you be willing to use
less so that strip mines and coal-fired power plants would not be
needed in the Southwest?"

Runte believed that a program, any program—or any lecture,
whether in a university or a public setting—without a theme is
pointless; that dispensing information for information's sake is not
what the Park Service ought to be doing. He did not think visitors
should be spoken to as if they were children, but should be informed
about what it takes to protect the park. His attitude was much like
that of Harold Ickes: if a visitor goes home disappointed because he
couldn't drink beer or swim in a hot tub, or whatever it was he wasn't
allowed to do, that's just too bad. He insisted that national parks
don't need more visitors; they do need more solid friends to protect
the resource. And, like Ickes, Runte regarded the Park Service as too
timid to stand up and say, "Here are the rules and here's why they
exist."

I've known Runte as a brilliant teacher and a hero to university students. He was much the same in his work at Yosemite. Leonard W.
McKenzie, the chief interpreter at Yosemite and the very same rehabilitation officer mentioned above, wrote of Runte in a letter dated
December 30, 1985:

> He developed dynamic and provocative programs that offered a
> measure of depth and diversity, such as "Railroads and the National
> Parks" and both a slide program and conducted walk on the park's
> impending General Management Plan, which had a high public
> profile. His interpretive activities stimulated visitor involvement
> and motivated participants to probe and analyze their perceptions of
> park values. He served as a catalyst, helping them dissect the cogent
> issues and management dilemmas that have grown increasingly in
> the last 20 years. He piqued intellects and stirred emotions, often
> leading people to reassess their value systems and engendering the
> seeds of a park ethic. His style of presentation exemplified the traits
> that probably best describe him—passionate, sincere, enthusiastic,
> articulate, challenging, thought-provoking, purposeful and unswerv-
> ing in his commitment both to truth and the national park ideal. His
> programs had impact, conviction, character and integrity.

McKenzie's letter was sent to William P. Gerberding, president of the University of Washington, following action to deny Runte tenure. It was said that his scholarship "lacked quality." But friends and admirers wrote to Gerberding that that assessment must be a mistake. It didn't work. A form letter from the university thanked correspondents for their interest, explaining that "many factors are considered in these important decisions, which are often difficult."

Important decisions often *are* difficult, which explains why rangers look good in their uniforms and stay out of trouble. The same can be said of many university professors. But the heroes, in any field, dare to take risks. It's the only way to make a difference, and it brings its own reward. Runte, for one, had the last word. He came back strong in 1990 with *Yosemite: The Embattled Wilderness*, a book that historians praised for its high quality.

8

In chapter 7 I related a talk with Jack Hughes at Olympic National Park. Inevitably, the dialogue turned to the bitter episode involving William J. Briggle and Riley McClelland.

"I've never been with Briggle just one-on-one," Jack said, "but when he comes over it's always kind of congenial. Everyone mellows. My impression is that if we could ever get together, like you and I are doing now, we could laugh and talk a little. Riley is a wonderful person, a really super guy. He's straight as an arrow. But I don't think he's loose and able to laugh about issues. That's why he was able to do what he did. I'd probably have gone down in a hail of gunfire. I couldn't have stonewalled for seven or eight years as he did."

Riley McClelland, the straight arrow, was fired from his position at Glacier National Park while Briggle was park superintendent. Riley fought his dismissal through legal channels. After eight years on the outside, he won his case, complete with back pay and thirty-eight weeks of annual leave, and went back to work at Glacier National Park. That is no small feat.

"It is a strange and empty feeling to be fired from NPS after eighteen years," Riley wrote in a letter dated July 31, 1973, soon after his dismissal. "I've done nothing to deserve being fired except speaking out and refusing a contrived and vindictive transfer."[1]

The U.S. Court of Appeals for the District of Columbia ultimately concurred, capsulizing the case in a few lines: "In July 1969 William Briggle became the superintendent of Glacier National Park. There is evidence in the record indicating that Briggle's conduct in managing Glacier was erratic. At his request an unusual number of employees were transferred out of Glacier. Concerning the relationship between Briggle and appellant, there was a philosophical difference between the two. Briggle was concerned with overall management of the park whereas appellant was concerned with preservation of resources. Preservation was appellant's job and he did it well."[2]

The park announced Riley's return (long after Briggle's departure) with a news release dated August 26, 1980, headed: "McClelland New Wildlife Research Biologist at Glacier." The news release explained that he would enter duty September 1 with a study of the fall concentration of bald eagles along McDonald Creek. Along with his work in the park, he would continue his association with the University of Montana as a professor in the School of Forestry. His reinstatement followed a settlement agreement in accord with the findings of the Court of Appeals and "to rectify an unwarranted personnel action."[3]

Riley McClelland was a whistleblower, a federal employee who takes his grievance to the public; that was the cause of his trouble. Actually he is not the best known of the Glacier Park dissenters. That distinction goes to his friend Art Sedlack, who in early January 1975 shot a snowmobile. His action embarrassed park officials but attracted nationwide attention and made Sedlack a Montana folk hero. It happened after two Great Falls men had illegally taken their snowmobiles into the park. Sedlack gave chase, catching up with them near the Java underpass just inside the park boundary. As he tells it, he tried but failed to turn off the machines, and he couldn't disconnect the engines. Sedlack didn't want them to ride off, so pulled out his .38 revolver and fired a shot into one of the engines. He was suspended for a time, then reinstated. His deed has since been memorialized in the Art Sedlack Award, which is presented annually by the Montana Wilderness Association to a worthy defender of machineless nature.[4]

Glacier, with its glorious peaks, ridges, forests, and waterfalls, its abundant grizzly bears, bighorn sheep, mountain goats, eagles, and hawks, has long stirred its champions. I think of George Bird Grinnell, whose name has been given to a glacier, mountain, waterfall, point, and lake, and to the reddish rock that colors many formations in the national park. He came to the West from New York in the 1880s to hunt and to study Indians, but in time he lost interest in killing and concentrated on preservation. The establishment in 1910 of Glacier National Park—the "Crown of the Continent," as he called it—was his greatest victory.[5] In recent years, James R. Habeck, a botany professor at the University of Montana, has been a diligent student of park ecology and a watchdog of park administration; he was particularly critical of the boardwalk at Logan Pass. When I interviewed him at the university in Missoula in February 1985, Habeck said construction of the boardwalk brought a legacy of ruination to almost everybody associated with it; that the park was paranoid about doing *anything* because of the fear of adverse publicity; and that administrators were picked for their ability to avoid making waves.

Riley McClelland was the principal victim of the dispute over Logan Pass because he did make waves, though he certainly didn't start that way. In 1949, when he was sixteen, after spending two family holidays away from his Denver home camping in Yellowstone, Riley set his sights on becoming a ranger. Six years later he began his career as a seasonal ranger in Yellowstone. During that same summer he met Pat Truman, who was working for one of the park concessionaires while her father, a Kansas botany professor, worked as a seasonal naturalist. A year later, after completing college, they were married and returned to Yellowstone. As a full-time ranger, Riley's summers were involved in law enforcement and backcountry patrol, and winters were spent on ski patrols. In the late 1950s he assisted the Craighead twins, John and Frank, in their studies of grizzly bears in the wild and became very interested in science and ecology.

In time Riley became a district naturalist; he remained in Yellowstone until 1964, always sensitive to the tradition of the place. "I've never understood how we could get so far away from the Olmsted style of architecture," he once said to me, "from the Norris Museum, Fishing Bridge Museum, even Old Faithful Lodge, buildings that harmonize with the surroundings."[6]

I've never understood it either. Riley's statement reminded me of traveling in the park in 1981 with John Townsley, the superintendent. We came to the Old Faithful area, where the visitor center, an anachronistic modern design, was misplaced at the edge of the thermal area and mismatched with everything but the notorious nearby highway overpass. The building was erected for the 1972 Yellowstone Centennial and World Parks Conference. Townsley told me that five years later, Director William J. Whalen came to Old Faithful, shuddered at the visitor center, and ordered him to "take it out, get rid of it!" But that's not how things usually happen. Once a structure or road is in place, it begets a life of its own. And that's how it was with the Logan Pass visitor center and boardwalk in Glacier National Park.

Riley went to Glacier in 1964. Three years later, as a well-regarded young ranger and naturalist, he was chosen to study for a master's degree in ecology and wildland resources management at Colorado State University, preparing himself, as the official order declared, "for direct involvement in research, in resources management program development and execution, as a staff adviser to the superintendent."[7] Riley completed his thesis in June 1968. Most graduate theses are readily filed and forgotten, being designed to prove competency in statistics and research methods, not original or important ideas. Riley's thesis, "The Ecosystem—A Unifying Concept for the Management of Natural Areas in the National Park System," was different; it foresaw the oncoming calamity at Yellowstone and elsewhere. Note this brief excerpt:

> Evidence is put forth that less than five percent of Yellowstone is developed and it is therefore relatively unimpaired. This overlooks the fact that all of the geyser basins which contain active major geysers are vandalized nearly everywhere and also contain roads. It is not much consolation that there are hundreds of square miles of "undeveloped" lodgepole pine forest; it is fine that this is so, but it does not make up for the totally irreplaceable loss of non-renewable hot springs or geysers. . . .
>
> Currently drawn lines seldom bear logical relationships to natural ecosystem boundaries. Proximity to an existing road bears no intrinsic relationship to value, fragility, or desirable construction site potential of national park ecosystems. Land-use zones cannot possibly be determined on resource management priorities until the ecosystem and management units have been delineated.[8]

Riley's thesis cited the ecological studies conducted by Bettie Willard at Rocky Mountain National Park on the destruction caused by visitors walking over high-elevation tundra. Effects were observed in

1958, when the Park Service opened a new parking area but constructed no paths from it. Visitors wandered away from their cars, and
within two weeks distinct "freelance" paths were visible. Tiny plants
were matted, flower stalks were broken, and attrition on cushion
plants was beginning. By the end of August, two-thirds of the
cushion-plant surface was destroyed, so the Park Service installed a
blacktop trail routed to the principal attractive features. Visitors for
the most part stayed on the trail but shortcut across the tundra when
returning to their cars. So the following summer the shortcut area
was blacktopped—diminishing what the visitors had actually come
to observe. Elsewhere on the alpine ridge the effects of intense visitor
use for thirty-eight seasons had been total destruction. All plants
were gone except for the few protected by large boulders; five inches
of topsoil were eroded, leaving bare mineral surface. Willard estimated that a minimum of five hundred years would be needed to restore the tundra ecosystem.[9]

Riley wanted to apply the lesson of Rocky Mountain National Park
to Glacier. That might have saved a lot of grief and expense, to say
nothing of saving tundra. The same was true of Riley's point about
"constructive aspects of inaction." "Decisions not to build a road
through a wilderness, not to build a parking lot, not to expand the
campground, not to build a marina—all can be management decisions which are constructive when viewed within the context of the
goals of perpetuating naturalness."[10]

He might have been right, and he scored high in ecoconsciousness,
but the timing was wrong. The official emphasis was now on "people
serving." Nevertheless, once he returned to Glacier, Riley produced
a detailed 142-page Resources Management Plan. As luck would have
it, Superintendent Keith Neilson, who had strongly supported Riley's
studies at Colorado State, was transferred. He was well respected, but
Glacier had its problems—the aftermath of the deaths of two young
women campers killed by grizzly bears in 1967, extensive fires, the
reaction of private landowners against a proposed ban on water
skiing at Lake McDonald—and Neilson was sixty-four. He was
shifted to finish his time in a more benign setting, as superintendent
of Great Smoky Mountains National Park in the southern Appala-
chians, and was replaced by an up-and-coming powerhouse named
William J. Briggle, age forty-three.

When Briggle came to Glacier in June 1969 he already had twenty years of Park Service experience, in the field and in Washington, and he was a protégé of Director George B. Hartzog, Jr. In an interview published in the *Great Falls Tribune* of December 21, 1969, Briggle enunciated a laudable goal. "Development must be negligible and the area kept primitive," he said. "If people expect to pack in, they must do it on back country terms. They can't expect to take the city with them."

But James R. Habeck, the University of Montana botanist, watched closely and did not see him fulfilling the promise. In a letter published in the *Missoulian* on December 22, 1971, Habeck wrote:

> The pattern of Mr. Briggle's behavior in Glacier Park since 1969 can be better understood when it is revealed that he arrived in Glacier Park after a decade of training and experience in recreation areas and recreation planning. It also now makes sense why news releases from Glacier have been captioned, "Briggle Boosts Glacier for Winter Playground" and "Glacier Park Features Variety of Winter Fun." Mr. Briggle did not, of course, write the captions, but the information printed is accurately summarized in these titles.
>
> Most of us in western Montana are also familiar with what appears to be an inordinate preoccupation with visitor numbers, and we are told that Glacier has "enjoyed a good year" whenever a new visitor attendance record is set.

The management style of the park administration changed sharply. Within three years after Briggle became superintendent, thirty-three employees out of a staff of about fifty had been transferred, retired, or chose to resign.[11] It's difficult to believe that he acted wholly on his own initiative, without orders from Hartzog (or at least some understanding with him) to clean house, but Briggle went at it with gusto.

All of this might have been lost in the records had it not been for the Logan Pass boardwalk and the challenge of Riley McClelland. He learned about the proposed boardwalk for the first time at a meeting of the resource management committee attended by the park superintendent, district ranger, and representatives of the maintenance division and ranger division. Logan Pass, at 6664 feet on the Continental Divide, is a special place in Glacier, the key point of interest on Going-to-the-Sun Highway crossing the park between the east and west. For years it was a primitive stop, with a primitive toilet facility.

Then the visitor center was built in the Mission 66 period. A parking lot and water line went in, and a sewage line came out. More people came and toilets malfunctioned. People wandered off marked trails, feathering across the meadows, picking off lichen and chipping rock. Park personnel recommended improving trails with crushed native rock material, which would settle like a driveway.[12] This led to the idea of the boardwalk, which, it was believed, would cause less damage than a trail.

Riley did not initially object to the boardwalk; he was, however, inclined to question the method of selecting it as the best option, considering that his job was to evaluate the potential impact of proposed changes on park resources. He assumed that the purpose of the meeting was to get input from all those attending. The initial discussion, in fact, centered on whether an environmental impact statement, or EIS, should be prepared.

But Briggle shortly issued a memorandum with his decision that an EIS wasn't necessary. The first protest came not from McClelland but from the trail crew assigned to install the boardwalk; during the 1971 summer season fourteen members of the crew resisted their assignment. The men were mostly college trained, including several teachers, and all were enthusiasts of Glacier. In a bitter showdown with the superintendent they argued that the boardwalk was not consistent with the park's wilderness theme. They claimed it would not keep visitors off the fragile meadows, and that the $49,000 construction fund could be better spent on other trails in need of maintenance and repair.[13]

The trail crew members were dismissed from their jobs, stirring concern in western Montana. "I'm sorry that park management wasn't stable enough to respond with interest rather than be defensive about power and authority," lamented the Reverend Tom Best of Kalispell. "This reaction is just what creates so much unwarranted tension in our society. The power structure refuses to listen."[14] Park Superintendent Briggle did listen, to the extent of rescinding the dismissal, although some members complained of demotion and harassment.[15]

Riley didn't see any evidence at the time that a boardwalk wouldn't work. He favored a broad, open evaluation of options, though people like Habeck, in Missoula, strongly concurred with the trail crew. Habeck called the boardwalk an example of "undue artificiality." "Many alpine ecologists (including myself)," he declared, "believe that building the boardwalk is a terrible mistake, both esthetically and ecologically."[16]

Superintendent Briggle was supported in his decision to construct the boardwalk by Robert Linn, chief scientist of the National Park Service. In a statement quoted in the *Hungry Horse News* of October 15, 1971, Linn declared: "Boardwalks of one kind or another have been successfully used in similar circumstances. A boardwalk permits light to penetrate to the ground beneath, assuming that generous cracks are left, and boardwalks do not obstruct the flow of water and air, such as would be the case with other types of walk ways. Boardwalks are also more flexible in that they can be moved with little additional damage to the environment when and if they are no longer required."

A good case could be made for the boardwalk. It would open access to the summer wildflower display in alpine meadows and to vistas of classic alpine mountain panoramas extending for miles. It would comprise an "ecosystem model" to explain to visitors the wonders of holistic nature: the chill wind, almost constant, shaping plants, eroding earth, scattering seed and pollen; the snowbanks, protecting plants from wind, keeping the ground warm and temperature steady, while at the same time compressing plants, restricting their height, and limiting the growing season; and every living thing adapting to fill its niche, like the ptarmigan, mottled brown and white, blending into rocky terrain, a camouflage defense against predators, changing to white for winter.

Besides, the parking lot, visitor center, and comfort station (which had been erected in 1967) were the only visitor facilities for twenty-five miles. The boardwalk would be 3700 feet long and 8 feet wide, composed of Douglas fir timbers chemically treated to retard rot. Admittedly, construction activity would require some soil excavation to permit leveling the stringers supporting the boardwalk planks and elevating the planks 1 to 3 feet above the ground, but these were considered minimal disturbance.

Following the decision to build the boardwalk, the engineering staff chose to treat the boards with pentachlorophenol to prevent decay. But the chemical leached into the ground and killed vegetation, quite visibly.[17] So the boards had to be removed. Instead of being a solution, the boardwalk became a problem—a problem that might have shown up in an EIS.

Then there was the sewage. The Park Service was already dumping raw, untreated sewage onto alpine vegetation (mistakenly assuming that the plants would absorb the nutrients) and planned additional spray fields. Conservationists caught wind of it, and Habeck, for one, wrote letters to newspapers and to Congress.[18] The plan was scrapped, and the following summer the park sought a different approach. A number of options might have been considered, but the choice was made to have tank trucks haul the sewage down the mountain and dump it into an unsealed pit within a few hundred feet of an attractive stretch of McDonald Creek. This new spray field proved both unsightly and smelly, with the aroma extending a considerable distance. And it was located on the floodplain next to the area where bald eagles come in late fall to feed on kokanee salmon.[19]

Riley persisted in questioning the wisdom of these and other developments, but Briggle tolerated no opposition to his decisions; the superintendent was critical of research into the effects of the sewage dump on the bald eagles. Inside and outside the park it became known that McClelland's assigned role to bring ecological concerns to the superintendent was meaningless. "Riley McClelland is heroically trying to tell us that our revered Glacier National Park, together with other great national parks, are systematically being broken down," declared Loren Kreck of Columbia Falls, Montana, a prominent conservationist, during the heat of the issue. "Piece by piece, we lose a little of the naturalness and see it replaced by an unneeded visitor center or an unwanted chalet, a horse by a helicopter in the name of expediency, and a concerned ranger by a desk man isolated from the land. When somebody of Riley McClelland's ability breaks from the inside out we had better listen."[20]

In September 1971 McClelland's position was abolished. Riley was given the choice of transferring to another park or remaining at Glacier as a naturalist. Though he chose to remain, on February 25, 1972, he was ordered transferred to Bighorn Canyon National Recreation Area, which is centered on the Yellowtail Reservoir on the Montana-Wyoming border south of Billings.[21] He could not possibly have known that Robert Taylor, the man he was scheduled to replace, was going through the same paces. Before receiving *his* order of transfer (to Herbert Hoover National Historic Site in Iowa), Taylor had questioned impending construction of a road through the area. The road threatened ancient sites of the Crow Indians and the wild horse range in the Pryor Mountains, but it was promoted by commercial interests in nearby Lovell, Wyoming, and favored by Senator Clifford Hansen.[22] Taylor was not alone in his protest. The Montana Wildlife Federation and Montana Wilderness Association charged that the plan was ill-conceived, hasty, and environmentally degrading. "The National Park Service's apparent preoccupation with intensive development in the area," these conservation groups declared, "has spawned and nurtured commercial political pressure groups, while ignoring the necessity for objective analysis and meaningful public involvement in the decision-making process." Taylor was investigated by an operations evaluation team (a Big Brother unit dispatched from the regional office) and accused of activities, unspecified, "not to the benefit of the Service." He was warned to steer clear of Crow Indians, as though something in them might be sinfully seditious. Taylor ventured to protest, but a telephoned warning from the regional director, Leonard Volz, sped him on his way to Iowa.

Riley refused to go to Bighorn Canyon, asserting the transfer was intended as punishment for an unproved wrongful act. He was then ordered to move to the regional office at Omaha, accompanied by warnings of "adverse action" if he did not accept. On April 25, with guidance and counsel from the American Federation of Government Employees, he filed a formal grievance. The first step, in accord with civil service regulations, was a request to the director of the National Park Service to rescind the transfer and assign him to a field position at Glacier consistent with his career goals, education, and experience.[23]

The McClelland case became a matter of public interest; it was covered by the media and discussed widely within the agency. Riley received encouragement from the Professional Rangers Organization, founded the year before to protect the ranger role. Jack Hughes and the PRO established the Glacier Defense Fund to raise money for Riley's legal expenses. A letter to park people, dated March 30, 1972, read as follows:

> Glacier National Park administration has come under attack
> nationally for violation of environmental practices in park manage-

ment. Rather than counter the charges, the administration has withheld information and dismissed or transferred concerned employees. A case involving fourteen trail crew men is still being fought by friends of the national parks.

As resource management ranger, Riley was in position to know of this, and the cases of disregard of the park environment by the park administration. While he spoke against several items practiced in Glacier in official memos—bear feeding at Granite Park Chalet, use of herbicides in the wilderness, building a boardwalk across alpine tundra, discharge of sewage in alpine streams, to name a few—he always did so through channels. This official stand, and "knowing too much," appears to be the reason for the present purge of Glacier's resource management ranger.

If this can happen to a ranger for doing his job in Glacier, it can happen in your park! Please help us to stand up for park values.

Many contributed, but the challenge to authority was not universally cheered. Richard Boyer, superintendent of Lassen Volcanic National Park, wrote Director Hartzog on April 11: "I do not feel that the action to gather funds for 'the defense' of the former Glacier ranger smacks of anything other than a misguided attempt of the flamboyant 'free Father Berrigan' or 'free Angela' or 'free anybody else' types. We can do without this sort of action, which is certainly not in the best interest of the fair (although sometimes harsh, when necessary) administrative image which has developed over the years of the Service."

Hartzog's response to Boyer took a more benign view: "While I deplore the fact that 'the Park Ranger in Olympic' ignores the channels of communication, based on the knowledge I have of his actions, I propose, at this time, to treat them simply as an irregular method of exercising his right to protest."[24]

Riley was summoned to three conferences with agency officials. In the first, Lemuel (Lon) Garrison, a nonconformist himself, once a ranger and superintendent and now supervisor of the Albright Training Center at the Grand Canyon, said he would recommend canceling the Omaha transfer and reinstatement at Glacier. The second session was with Director Hartzog at Ozark National Riverways, the director's old stomping ground and hideaway in Missouri. "I hear you are capable and intelligent but you are an opinionated, self-centered individual," Hartzog said for openers. Riley responded that since he had subjected himself and his family to ostracism and harassment at Glacier, his objective could hardly be self-serving. They talked for ninety minutes. Hartzog counseled Riley to become a research biologist, a position less subject to transfer. "You will hear from me shortly concerning the grievance settlement. I'll be in touch with you concerning the biologist matter in a month or so." It didn't quite work that way. On his return to Glacier, Riley received a message to meet with Robert Linn, the chief scientist of the Park Service (who had endorsed the boardwalk), in Santa Fe the first week in June. Linn brought three others, all working the theme "Who do you think you are to challenge the Park Service's motives?" The discussion ultimately turned to the possibility of Riley undertaking a doctoral study on wilderness ecology and human use. Linn said he would recommend that Riley be assigned to complete this graduate program, either funded by the service or on leave without pay.[25] But on June 16 Riley heard from Hartzog: since he had rejected all reasonable offers, a formal grievance hearing would be conducted by an administrative law judge.

Conservationists were concerned. On June 7 George Alderson, legislative director of Friends of the Earth, wrote Secretary of the Interior Rogers C. B. Morton warning of deterioration of the national parks. Though his main purpose was to urge the dismissal of Hartzog as director, he referred to the McClelland case: "The use of transfers as a reprisal technique discourages park employees from trying to save the parks. If a park naturalist, like the one at Glacier earlier this spring, warns against practices and developments that will hurt the park, he can be transferred to Omaha the next day. The reprisal technique is hurting the parks, and it is also breaking down the esprit de corps that has always made the National Park Service a great agency."

The secretary's response of July 27 supported the agency (and possibly was drafted for him by agency personnel, as was often the case). The situation, Morton wrote Alderson, was blown out of perspective by inaccurate and inflammatory articles. A superintendent must count on the support of his fellow employees. Loyalty does not mean accepting abuses, but there is no excuse for willfully disregarding accepted standards of conduct.

The formal grievance hearing was held at West Glacier on August 14 and 15, with Riley represented by a field officer of the American Federation of Government Employees. The public was not allowed to attend. It took the administrative law judge, Robert Snashall, six months—until January 22, 1973—to announce his findings and recommendations. He acknowledged evidence that the superintendent ran roughshod over personnel, but not enough to determine whether there were "intended acts of recrimination or merely manifestations of frustration created by the necessity of a somewhat massive servicewide reorganization."

Riley's attorney, Donald Marble, filed an appeal with the secretary of the interior; it was denied on May 21, without discussing its merits. On June 6 Riley received a notice from Briggle evicting his family from park housing. The McClellands left on July 27. Riley's last official memorandum insisted that the action against him was cruel, unethical, and an illegal abuse of managerial power.

The hearing officer, Snashall, while failing to grant Riley's plea for reinstatement, had recommended further inquiry into Briggle's management. A study was conducted in February 1973 by two deputy associate directors of the Park Service, Charles Mangers and Joseph Rumberg, who were dispatched directly from Hartzog's office. All the public would learn of their findings was a recommendation that Briggle be counseled about his management practices; the supporting details were withheld. Another investigation, this one on behalf of Congress, was conducted by Jerry Verkler, staff director of the Senate Committee on Interior and Insular Affairs. It produced as much as the study by Mangers and Rumberg. In a letter to McClelland dated June 7, 1973, Verkler noted that the outcome was inevitable. "It is my hope, however, that the atmosphere at Glacier Park will improve for the benefit of the workers as well as the visitors. I think your efforts toward this end will be a major contribution."

The deck was stacked, but Riley and Pat stuck to the long, tough road, even while she was ill with pneumonia and pleurisy. Things looked up when a Civil Service Commission field examiner ruled in his favor on July 29, 1974, declaring the Park Service regional director had been "unreasonable, unfair, arbitrary and capricious in his decision to remove."[26] But the Interior Department appealed to the commission's appeals review board, which overruled the examiner, asserting that any transfer must be considered mandatory as long as the agency presents some reason for it—not necessarily a good reason, but *any* reason.[27]

The McClelland case ultimately was settled following the decision by the U.S. Court of Appeals mentioned earlier in this chapter. The court ordered the Interior Department to deliver the Mangers-Rumberg report, hitherto suppressed, to the Civil Service Commission, giving the appellant access to it except for portions considered validly withheld. The court directed the commission, in turn, to apply a different standard than its previous recognition of reassignment "supportable on any rational basis." The alleged need for Riley's services in Omaha, the decision noted, was a sham—a way of achieving a predetermined result; there must be "a nexus between the action taken and the good of the service."[28]

The Park Service chose to accept its fate, offering to settle rather than press the case further. It assigned two principal negotiators: Nancy Garrett, an associate director hired by Director William J. Whalen despite her lack of background in conservation work, and James Thompson, a "team player" presently working in the Washington office and later to be rewarded with the superintendency of Rocky Mountain National Park. They made the negotiation painful, consistent with the Park Service response every step of the way. Throughout the entire process of appeal and litigation the Park Service took its allotted time and more, exceeding deadlines to produce information or to answer legal motions, plainly a lesson for anyone else with a mind to challenge the service.[29]

The only kind of position Garrett and Thompson would offer Riley was in research. They refused to consider management. Thompson in particular resisted the idea of Riley returning to Glacier, arguing that all the research needed in Glacier had been completed (a strange assertion since the "Threats to the Parks" study that came out soon afterward identified Glacier as the park in greatest jeopardy of all U.S. national parks, with abundant threats not fully understood).

Riley did return to Glacier, not in management but in research. Still, it *was* Glacier. Riley wrote in a letter dated August 15: "Most importantly the Circuit Court's decision establishes standards which should help prevent transfers being used so blatantly as tools of intimidation. Hopefully the outcome will benefit many agency employees and particularly those willing to speak openly and honestly on management issues."

And on August 26, 1980, Russell E. Dickenson, who had succeeded Whalen as director, extended a hand of welcome, writing as follows: "It is neither necessary nor appropriate for me to comment on the disagreement of the past eight years. However, I want you to know that I respect your integrity and appreciate your strong commitment to national park principles. There is a tremendous amount of work to be done. We need every bit of talent and energy to meet the issues of the day. I will be counting on the input of your considerable skills and talent."

Following his dismissal, Riley had enrolled as a doctoral student at the University of Montana, concentrating on the relationship between hole-nesting birds and decay in standing trees of western larch and Douglas fir.[30] The Forest Service provided funding for three years of fieldwork, portions of which were conducted in Glacier National Park. Thus, in a sense, he never left home.

After completing his Ph.D., McClelland was appointed to the University of Montana faculty, and he advanced through the ranks to full professor in almost record time. Even after his return to the park, he continued to teach two courses—park management and bird conservation and management—in one quarter. In park management he stressed at the outset that he was preparing people not for work in the Park Service, but to understand the parks and make better input as citizens. In bird conservation he emphasized the qualitative aesthetic aspects. Despite his success at the university, he felt the real meaning of higher education had been lost, that academic curricula for the most part were now reduced to job training. By comparison, when he attended Colorado State, every student entering the School of Forestry took a first course called "Principles of Conservation." To be sure, lots of courses are required at land-grant universities like Montana and Colorado State, but they are specialized and technical, with scant attention to conservation principles and ethics. And outspoken rebels are as rare in higher education as they are in public agencies.

While I was in Glacier during the summers of 1984 and 1985 I visited the home Riley and Pat occupied in the park employees' complex. Riley, over six feet tall, well built, and square jawed, wore a brown beard—trimmed, but not too trimmed. Most of his time was spent researching the McDonald Creek bald eagles, attempting to identify their yearly ecology: where they go, what they do, what they need. More than a thousand birds pass through, spending part of the year in Canada, three months in Glacier, then another part of the year farther south. Pat McClelland, an attractive, pert fifty-year-old who had raised a family, was back in college working on a graduate degree in biology. They lived in a rambling old frame-and-stone house, appealing on the outside but basically just old and plain. It was one house away from the one they had occupied when Riley was the resource management specialist, while directly behind them, about a hundred yards away across an open lawn, was the superintendent's house where Briggle had lived.

Riley recalled that a lot of people regarded the issue as a personality conflict between Briggle and himself, but he saw it as a difference in views on how the internal park system should operate—whether on openness or on hierarchical authority alone, and whether a transfer could be used to suppress openness.

"I've never been able to understand why superintendents, or any managers, didn't want to be open," said Riley. "It would be a rare case when they wouldn't generate support for their decisions as long as they could be openly discussed and options weighed carefully. No one expects his or her point of view to be adopted every time, but you do expect to be heard if that's what you're being paid for."

For Riley and Pat the Park Service was never just a job. They confessed to feeling extremely emotional about national parks and what parks stand for. But Riley saw the emotionalism that once was widespread throughout the service slowly and steadily drain away. Now, for most personnel it's great fun to work in Glacier, but that gutsy something—it isn't there. It isn't only Glacier, alas; the old Park Service magic, the *mystique*, is tough to find.

The boardwalk, as I last saw it, extends two miles to the Hidden Lake Overlook, with faults and failures every foot of the way. Little wonder that in 1985 the park conceded, via an environmental assessment, its mistakes: the existing comfort station at the Logan Pass Visitor Center did not meet public needs in several ways. There were not enough stalls, and there was an excessive amount of down time due to plumbing malfunctions. Large tour groups arriving in buses operated by the hotel concession created surges of users throughout the day when the facilities were in almost constant use. Even worse were shutdowns in which the entire men's or women's side had to be closed because one stall malfunctioned. The sewer line from the comfort station to the underground vault in the parking lot had an inadequate slope, stopping up periodically and causing the shutdown of the entire comfort station.

The comfort station was closed to visitor use and replaced by a

temporary mobile toilet in 1983. The mobile facility greatly increased visitor capacity, but it was a temporary structure requiring
much setup and takedown time; it was located away from the visitor
center at a corner of the parking lot and was inconsistent with the
permanent architecture of the Logan Pass visitor center.

The proposed solution was to build and expand. The visitor center
would be enlarged to more than twice its size. The number of toilet
fixtures would be increased, and the plumbing redesigned to allow
shutting one stall when it becomes plugged. The sewer line would be
rebuilt with a trenching method to minimize vegetation disturbance.
The walking approach from the parking lot would be rebuilt, too,
with a 225-foot curving ramp, plus stairs, to replace the existing 120-
foot ramp. Undisturbed vegetation broken during construction
would be salvaged and set aside in a nursery area for reuse the following year.[31]

Following the period for review and comment, the park announced
on April 24, 1985, that the two-year reconstruction project at Logan
Pass would soon begin: "The environmental assessment adequately
considered the environmental consequences and the fact that environmental aspects will be rendered insignificant by implementing
mitigating measures. The proposal is justified as an improvement
which will meet demonstrated needs of sanitation and accessibility
in a manner in keeping with National Park Service standards."[32] In
other words, National Park Service standards were being refitted to
allow the disappearance of another defenseless fragment of wild nature.

The unhappy history at Glacier illustrates the value of openness at
all levels within an institution and the importance of considering
criticism from without. Must the internal dissenter be sidetracked
as a "renegade"? Must the external critic be treated as the "enemy"?
Superintendent Briggle in autumn 1972 might have benefited by
heeding the warnings of James Habeck, the University of Montana
botany professor, instead of complaining about Habeck to his superiors. In this case, the university president, Robert T. Pantzer, replied
as follows: "I can assure you that the park and not the administrators
of the park are the main subject of Professor Habeck's study. You are
not the subject of a formal program at the University; but the park,
specifically the plant ecology, treated according to tried methodolo-
gies in the biological sciences, I am confident you will agree, is an

appropriate study for a university scientist. Professor Habeck's inquiries, then, are those made by a professor and ecologist whose field of specialization includes the vegetation of the park. In that capacity, he conducts public research open to refutation or acceptance according to its quality and merits."[33]

Briggle's responses, as I see them, represent those bred into any authority-dominated system. In time I observed that he had broadened his outlook. I wish he could have been present when I drove Going-to-the-Sun Highway with Riley and Pat from West Glacier to Logan Pass. The day was clear and bright, emboldening the high cliffs. The fifty-mile road between St. Mary on the east side and West Glacier opens the heart of the northern Rockies wilderness to those who might never know it except from pictures. But what's the value of a vista from a car window? If the value is inspirational, then it must be greater still without the road.

Ultimately we reached Logan Pass on one of its busiest days. The parking lot overflowed. Queues were lined up before the portable johns. Clusters of bicyclists lounged in the shade while awaiting the hour when traffic would diminish so they could resume riding. We walked the boardwalk that rambles over the tundra to the hanging gardens and Hidden Lake overlook. Many visitors carried Park Service descriptive leaflets along with their cameras and binoculars, reflecting a genuine interest and desire to know. But there were so many of us. At their first encounter with snow, young people would jump off the boardwalk for a snowball fight. On spotting a marmot or ground squirrel, or anything living, taking refuge under the boardwalk, somebody would stoop down and try to shag it out or entice it with candy or salted peanuts.

My most vivid recollection is of the young mountain goat that wandered down from the ledges and suddenly was surrounded, I mean totally engulfed and hemmed in by curious humans eager for a close look, perhaps a touch, to connect them with this strange critter, as though it had come from outer space instead of from out of the wild. For the good of the goat, the meadows, and the public, there must be some better way than the boardwalk at Logan Pass.

9

The Nature of Naturalness

In 1970 a lone male gypsy moth was trapped in Shenandoah National Park in the highlands of Virginia. No egg masses were found, and no female, nor any other evidence of infestation. Nevertheless, Superintendent Taylor Hoskins and the park staff felt the need of strong measures to prevent gypsy moths from chewing up the mountain forests. After due deliberation, heavy doses of Sevin-4, or Carbaryl, a Union Carbide product, were sprayed extensively. Although gypsy moths bring an influx of cuckoos, nuthatches, orioles, tanagers, red-winged blackbirds, woodpeckers, parasitic wasps, flies, and white-footed mice—all of which prey on insect larvae, pupae, and adults—this consideration was set aside. It was known that Sevin-4 might stay lethal for seven days and seven nights, wiping out bees and butterflies; that it might eliminate or contaminate the food supply of fledgling birds during the nesting season and leave long-term adverse effects on the ecosystem. But this knowledge also was set aside.[1]

It was then seven years after the publication of Rachel Carson's *Silent Spring*, with its warnings of chemical damage to the environment. A park scientist might have taken the view that gypsy moths don't kill trees, that most of those defoliated in June grow new leaves by August, and that patience, allowing nature to take its course, would prove the best remedy. But this was not to be.

The gypsy moth episode is not an isolated case, not even with the passage of time. A 1977 report, *Pest Control in the National Park System*, revealed that one national park after another was dosed with poisons bearing names like Inject-a-cide, I-so-sect, Kill-Ko, Formula 40, Esteron 99, Silvex 4L, Mirex, Tordon 22K, Chlordane, Carbaryl, and Malathion 5, 8, 50, 51, and 55. All these were designed to sanitize the parks of aphids, ticks, chiggers, caterpillars, beetles, mosquitoes, moths, mice, nematodes, pocket gophers, snails, slugs, wasps, and webworms.

The late-1970s "management plan" for the black-tailed prairie dog in Badlands National Park of South Dakota aimed to eradicate thirteen prairie dog colonies along the inner boundaries of the park by applying zinc phosphide, a highly toxic chemical.[2] The plan was a response to ranchers and stockmen outside the park boundaries who complained their lands were heavily affected and degraded—that the burrowing of prairie dogs destroyed grasses and induced erosion.[3] Park administrators were prepared to comply with the demand of private landowners, though the national park constitutes one of the last significant sanctuaries of prairie dogs. Their colonies have been part of life in the Badlands for thousands of years, furnishing shelter, food, nest sites, and courtship grounds for snakes, salamanders, burrowing owls, and sharp-tailed grouse. Prairie dogs themselves are the food staple of the black-footed ferret, now endangered because the dogs have dwindled in number as a consequence of poisoning programs. A park spokesperson defended zinc phosphide, the proposed chemical, as "fairly specific," though it is recorded as an intense, extremely dangerous, long-lasting poison, toxic to all forms of life, with a record of poisoning humans as well as domestic and wild animals.[4] Because the very areas designated for prairie dog eradication appeared to offer potential ferret habitat, conservationists protested, leading William J. Whalen, then director of the Park Service, to defer the management plan. I'm not sure of the ultimate outcome at Badlands, but in 1986 Ernest W. Ortega, superintendent of Wind Cave National Park, also in South Dakota, outlined to me his prairie dog reduction program then under way, based on the use of zinc phosphide.

The National Park Service has its corps of scientists and resource management specialists, but little has changed. The experts gather baseline data. They discuss ecosystem values. Sometimes they are heeded by park administrators. Rarely do they complain when they are not.

Adolph Murie, however, in 1966 felt that his responsibility as a scientist transcended his long employment by the National Park Service. He openly protested pesticide spraying in Grand Teton National Park designed to eradicate bark beetles preying on lodgepole pines. Park foresters for years had promoted beetle control, but Murie disagreed, citing the so-called epidemic as the high point in beetle population in the historic beetle-lodgepole cycle. He reasoned that the beetle serves as a thinning agent to make room for more lodgepoles or for firs and spruce, and when beetles run out of old, susceptible lodgepoles the cycle subsides naturally. In the meantime, dead and dying trees provide favored perches for hawks and owls and habitat for woodpeckers, nuthatches, and brown creepers. Moreover, with opening of the woods, vegetation takes on more variety to become a genuine rather than a phony landscape.

Park officials couldn't see it that way. One explained that spraying was meant to save the natural scenery. "Will it," Adolph asked, "be natural after spraying?" "Well, the brown needles of dead trees might cause visitors to think the Park Service negligent in its custodianship."[5] That viewpoint, and the extensive use of pesticides, is still widespread. Park officials feel compelled to provide a sanitized environment that *looks* natural but is nonetheless free of poisonous plants, pesky bugs, and dangerous animals.

Murie's life and work suggest him as a model for scientists and science in the national parks, but his superiors gave him little support or encouragement. On November 8, 1956, for example, Murie sent a fourteen-page memorandum to the superintendent of Mount McKinley (later renamed Denali) National Park commenting on the plans for Mission 66, the ten-year national park system development plan. He urged open discussion, with guidance and assistance from conservationists and others outside the Park Service. Murie was concerned about the future of the wilderness. The construction of lodgings and the intrusion of a road across the park with everything on both sides of it labeled like a museum were grave threats to the area.

For his troubles he was brushed off by the park superintendent of the time, Duane D. Jacobs, with this response: "I think it is quite reasonable for anyone of your many years of intimate knowledge of McKinley as purely a wilderness area to be somewhat alarmed as Mt.

McKinley finally emerges across the threshold of a new era, that of a great national park set aside for the use and enjoyment of the people, which is soon to receive this intended use and enjoyment."[6]

Other scientists have received the same response. In 1973 John Craighead reported that he and his brother Frank had recorded ninety-one grizzly bear deaths within the Yellowstone ecosystem during the two preceding years, more than double the birth rate, leading to the conclusion that the population was in very serious trouble.[7] If respected authorities like the Craighead team raise some significant doubt or challenge, then the administrator is well advised to follow a cautious, conservative approach. But in Yellowstone in 1975 the park superintendent, Jack Anderson, declared: "We're finding grizzly. My concern would be that because of a low sub-adult mortality the numbers might get too high." Numbers of grizzly too high? One can only conclude that he had the same idea as Superintendent Jacobs: that naturalness must have its bounds, as defined by public use and enjoyment.[8]

Adolph Murie and his older half brother, Olaus, were outspoken field naturalists, both widely known for their research and writing. They were born in Minnesota, where they camped, fished, swam, and canoed as a prelude to academic study. In 1920, at the age of thirty-one, Olaus made the first of many trips to Alaska for the U.S. Biological Survey (later renamed the Fish and Wildlife Service); from then on he traveled hundreds of miles by dogsled each winter and by boat or on foot each summer conducting a biological survey of the Alaska wilderness, with emphasis on the life history of caribou.

In 1927 Olaus came to Jackson, Wyoming, with his wife, Margaret, who had spent her childhood in Fairbanks and shared his love of wild country. He began his study of elk, which later resulted in the definitive work *The Elk of North America*, and over the years led pioneering scientific expeditions to the Aleutians, the Brooks Range (influencing establishment of the Arctic National Wildlife Refuge), and New Zealand. He was a self-taught artist who tended to details in field sketches—head, ears, mouth, nostrils, legs, the true colors—and left behind a legacy of wildlife art. In 1946 he resigned from the government to become director, and later president, of the Wilderness Society. Olaus took a few words that he and his wife found on an old tombstone in Cumberland, England, and reproduced them on a plaque that hung on the mantle in their log home at Jackson Hole:

"The wonder of the world, the beauty and the power, the shape of things, their colours, lights and shades—these I saw. Look ye also while life lasts." The words are a guide to the living; for the Muries they reinforced a perception of nature stronger and richer than scientific analysis, yet invaluable to it. Olaus died in 1963. Margaret, or "Mardy," Murie carried on, with considerable influence derived from heartfelt human caring free of self-righteousness. Twenty-five years later she told me that she missed Olaus every day, but that he would want her to persevere. Even into her late eighties, though less active, she still spoke strongly on environmental issues.

Adolph Murie worked for the National Park Service for thirty-two years. Starting in 1922 he spent twenty-five summers conducting field research in Denali. In 1939 he walked 1700 miles from April to October in his field study of the relationship between wolves and Dall sheep.[9] He returned the following year for fifteen months in the field, traveling on skis and snowshoes in winter. He knew the birds, wolves, coyotes, lynx, foxes, caribou, moose, sheep, and other species from intimate experience with them in the days before research was conducted by harnessing the animals with electronic devices. Adolph learned by living among the animals, on their own ground. Once he wanted to test the temperament of wolves. He approached a den, reached in, and succeeded in picking up and withdrawing a pup—for the wolves were friendly and trusting. After the mid-1950s he concentrated on grizzly bears, often following a family for days so that he knew and understood each member. He wrote monographs in the National Park Service Fauna Series, long since discontinued, and park handbooks and natural history articles for both popular and scientific journals. He heeded the advice of his brother: "It seems to me we should get away from the strictly scientific method of today, so much like the laboratory technique. We have to speak the truth but we can use human language in doing so." Adolph concurred: "I have, I think, avoided the ecologist's jargon, the scientific phrases so frequently created by ecologists and animal behaviorists to make simple facts sound profound and impressive."[10]

In 1932 Adolph married Louise, Mardy's younger half sister. Louise, or "Weezy," was born and raised in Fairbanks and easily took to the wilderness. In 1945 the younger Muries settled in Jackson Hole, adjacent to Olaus and Mardy, where they lived until Ade died in 1974.

The Murie brothers thought much alike. They believed in naturalness in their lives and work. Olaus wrote: "Poisoning and trapping of so-called predators and killing rodents, and the related insecticide and herbicide programs, are evidences of human immaturity. The use of the term 'vermin' as applied to so many wild creatures is a thoughtless criticism of nature's arrangement of producing varied life on this planet."

And Adolph, in the foreword to *The Mammals of Mount McKinley*: "No species of plant or animal is favored above the rest, and they grow together, quietly competing, or living in adjusted composure. Our task is to perpetuate this freedom and purity of nature, this ebb and flow of life—first by ensuring ample park boundaries so that the region is large enough to maintain the natural relationships, and secondly to hold man's intrusions to the minimum."[11]

Providing sanctuary for wild creatures surely must be the single most important role of the parks at a time when diversity on the planet is so thoroughly endangered. The National Park Service should be the apostle of wildlife preservation and the advocate of a pesticide-free landscape. But this has not been the case. Until the mid-1930s most of the so-called predators in Yellowstone—principally coyotes but also mountain lions, wolves, and wolverines— were trapped, poisoned, or shot on sight. Ultimately coyote control was stopped, over the objections of the park staff, who insisted that those villainous critters disrupted the naturalness of the good animals—deer, elk, antelope, and bighorn sheep—on which they preyed.

The view of park administrators reflected outmoded federal programs that emerged from the bounty system and were biologically unsound, costly, and corruptible. Theodore Roosevelt, the big-game hunter, described a cougar treed at the rim of the Grand Canyon as "a big horse-killing cat, the destroyer of the deer, the lord of stealthy murder, facing his doom with a heart both craven and cruel."[12] Predator control as a federal function began during World War I as a means of eradicating wolves in order to save beef for our troops and allies. Then sheepmen enlisted the government in a program to kill coyotes on their behalf. Trapping, shooting, and poisoning reduced rare species to near extinction—wolf, cougar, grizzly, bobcat, ferret, fox, hawk, owl, badger, golden eagle, bald eagle, lynx, and wolverine. States demanded jurisdiction over game species but welcomed the federal government's attempts to exterminate the so-called nongame species.

The same costly mistake was made all over the West. In Yellowstone, cougars and wolves were eliminated, and coyotes reduced, while ancient winter migration routes were cut off by human settlements. Elk numbers consequently exploded, then they starved. Few biologists stood up to declare that predators take only small numbers of the animals they prey upon and probably are beneficial to a healthy population. Scarcely any of the experts asserted predation as part of the harmonics of life, like the pitcher plant feeding on insects, the lark devouring grasshoppers, the bass swallowing minnows.[13] Wildlife management professionals have largely concentrated their interest and efforts on "producing" desirable game species for "harvest" by recreational shooters.

Predator control was long provided by the Fish and Wildlife Service, a companion agency of the Park Service at the Department of the Interior (until shifted to the Department of Agriculture). For years Fish and Wildlife officials despaired over national parks as "reservoirs of predation" that required extra control measures around their borders, if not within them, instead of seeing them as sanctuaries and laboratories of predator-prey relationships deserving buffer zones where predators are not subject to systematic "control."

In 1964 Secretary of the Interior Stewart L. Udall responded to complaints by appointing an advisory committee, headed by A. Starker Leopold, to review the predator control program. The committee in due course reported that "control has developed into a semi-autonomous bureaucracy whose function in many localities bears scant relationship to real need and still less to scientific management."[14] Unfortunately, the Leopold Committee concluded that "when properly applied" Compound 1080 (the favorite and deadliest poison then in use) does an effective and humane job of controlling coyotes with little damaging effect on other wildlife, when, in fact, all evidence shows there is no application—no matter how "proper"—that does not directly affect or threaten other wildlife.[15] On receiving the report one year later, the secretary renamed the old Branch of Predator and Rodent Control the Division of Wildlife Services, but only the name was changed. In the same vein, on February 4, 1981, Russell E. Dickenson, then director of the National Park Service, announced a tightening of the process of chemical review. "A decision to use chemicals in parks must be made with care, mindful of employees and visitor health and safety. Where there are alternative means to accomplish control, we will not use chemicals." But the legendary pattern of poisoning goes on, an activity inimical to naturalness.

Adolph Murie pleaded for purity in the parks because he believed them to be imbued with special spirits deserving human acknowledgment and protection. In an article in *National Parks Magazine* (July 1965) he decried improvement of the ninety-mile road through the heart of Mount McKinley National Park. He saw the old road as being in harmony with the enjoyment of flowers, lichens, wandering tattlers, and grizzlies, charming all visitors seeking the sublime, while the new road clearly was designed to dominate, creating a conspicuous scar over many miles of landscape and showing an obsessive regard for superhighway standards and a lack of appreciation for the spirit of wilderness.

Murie received scant encouragement. His strongest support came from Charlie Ott, who worked for years as a maintenance man in Denali until his retirement in 1970, all the while taking magnificent pictures of wildlife that have illustrated books, won awards, and ranked him among the world's finest photographers of animals in the wild. When we were together in Denali in 1986, Ott recalled that in his early years wildlife was easy to see in large numbers and diverse species. He estimated that less than a quarter of the wildlife remain in the park as compared with 1950s numbers; as visitor numbers rose, and development with them, both inside and outside the park, wildlife declined.

Ultimately the Park Service instituted restrictions on the park road and installed a system of shuttle bus transportation that allows people to get on and off along the way. This has helped to some degree, but questions remain regarding the influences of human activity on wildlife. For instance, what are the behavioral effects when solitary species like bear and wolverine intrude into the territories of their neighbors? Tourism the world over has affected the habitat of wild animals and modified their behavior. The road, the bus, the fumes, the sight, smell, and sounds of humans, harassment by amateur (and professional) photographers—these unnatural influences are not understood, yet little if any attention has been directed toward comprehending their effects.

Denali in 1980 was enlarged from 1.9 million acres to 6 million acres, as Adolph Murie had long urged. However, pressures have increased many times over and have led to drastic changes. First came the modern ninety-mile road through the park, then the main-stem highway linking Denali with Anchorage and Fairbanks, Alaska's major population centers. Within thirty years the yearly number of visitors rose from less than 1000 to more than 400,000. Many arrive by train or bus on package tours, overnighting at standardized tourist hotels at the park border and spending a few hours sightseeing in the park by bus as their brief experience of wild Alaska before continuing on their itinerary. But then, much the same is true at the Tetons in Wyoming. The lake that appears so natural is an artificial, fluctuating reservoir with artificially stocked fish. The visitor to the Tetons finds a river, the Snake, whose flow is artificially controlled, plus livestock grazing, luxury hotels, dude ranches, airport, high-speed highway, big-game hunting in fall, and mechanized snowmobiling in winter, all in the national park.

For most visitors the disturbances are acceptable because they generally add to convenience; besides, their negative effects on wild nature are scarcely understood. Nevertheless, as early as 1933, personnel in the National Park Service pointed to the need of broader considerations. In *Fauna of the National Parks of the United States*, George M. Wright, Ben H. Thompson, and Joseph S. Dixon asserted that the greatest natural heritage comprised more than scenic features. Nature itself—"the intimate details of living things, the plants, the animals that live on them, and the animals that live on those animals"—is our birthright.[16]

That view has never taken hold. Although grizzly bears, as a case in point, depend for survival on national parks (and designated wilderness in national forests), park people think their job is to protect visitors from grizzly bears. In 1975 the Fish and Wildlife Service classified the grizzly as "a threatened species." But it also called *Ursus arctos horribilis* "an aggressive animal that is highly intolerant of man." That kind of prima facie assumption—prevalent in Park Service publications and warnings to visitors—overlooks *Homo sapiens* as the most *horribilis* of them all, an aggressive critter intolerant of anything that gets in its way. From all I've read and heard, a bear rarely attacks unless wounded, provoked, or startled, or unless it thinks its home, food supply, or family is in danger. When bears aren't bothered, they are less dangerous than most animals; they pre-fer to avoid contact with humans. Of course, bears are never to be fully trusted because they are wild, but they certainly ought to be respected on their own terrain. I'm against conditioning bears to be more fearful of humans. I like bears natural—condition the humans, I'd say, to be respectful of bears. Stated another way, it's not really an issue of the future of the grizzly at stake, or not that alone. The pres-ence of the grizzly means that natural law remains in force, at least in the national parks, and that fragments of the planet have not been fouled by the disorder of human-dominated contemporary society.

The least management of wild nature is the best management. "Wildlife managers want to manage everything," Adolph Murie wrote in *The Grizzlies of Mount McKinley*, "just as a forester wants to practice forestry in parks, and engineers want to build more and wider roads."[17] Wolf control, coyote control, insect control, mosquito control, wildlife salting, exposed garbage dumps in bear country—these and other manipulative techniques show that preservation of nature itself is not the principal focus.

In 1962 Secretary Udall appointed a committee headed by A. Star-ker Leopold to review wildlife management in national parks (much the same committee referred to above that reviewed predator con-trol). In its 1963 report the committee cited indiscriminate logging, burning, grazing, hunting, suppression of fires, suppression of insect outbreaks, predator control, and introduction of exotic species and diseases as having reduced the parks to "artifacts, pure and simple." Thus it recommended against public hunting to reduce overpopula-tion of herbivores and against the use of chemical poisons to eradi-cate forest insects in the parks. But the second Leopold Committee had its own management emphasis, proposing that "a reasonable il-lusion of primitive America could be re-created, using the utmost in skill, judgment and ecological sensitivity." It wanted each park to maintain, or re-create, as nearly as possible, biotic associations that prevailed when the area was first visited by Europeans so that it would represent "a vignette of original America." That in itself, de-spite the ring of idealism, focused on freezing the environment at a certain stage by management, with human experts, of course, doing the managing. If nature encroached on a meadow that was present when man first arrived, that area would be managed to forestall na-ture and keep it in meadow. If a pond is, under natural ecological process, becoming a marsh or swamp, it would be managed so as to pre-serve the pond. The Leopold definition on the face of it gives license for such controls.[18]

In 1966 Adolph Murie wrote a paper titled "A Plea for Idealism in National Parks," a critique of the Leopold report. He cited the ex-ample of an old river bar in Denali covered with thin sod and used by caribou for grazing and by grizzly bears for root digging. But shifting channels kept eroding and cutting away the thin sod, leaving bare gravel, thus modifying the entire scene. "Shall we manage in order to preserve the primitive, as it was when white man first arrived, by calling on bulldozers to build protective gravel embankments? Or are we more interested in natural processes, a wild river that is forever doing these things, destroying old bars and permitting the formation of new ones, with man left out of the picture except to marvel and to wonder?"

Alston Chase, in *Playing God in Yellowstone* (1986), documents the decline of wildlife in the nation's oldest national park. He makes a compelling case that political expediency has governed wildlife de-cisions, reflecting the historic weakness and inadequacy of science in the parks. In this connection, I recall a study in 1969 by Edward E. C. Clebsch, professor of botany at the University of Tennessee, "concerning the values to science of wilderness." Clebsch prepared his paper for presentation to Secretary of the Interior Walter J. Hickel as part of the effort of citizens to prevent construction of a highway across the Great Smoky Mountains as proposed by the National Park Service.

Nary a national park scientist nor resource specialist was heard from when the highway plan was announced. It remained for Profes-sor Clebsch to come forward and declare: "I regard it my responsi-bility to show you the ecological consequences of poor stewardship of one small fragment of our already small wilderness parkscape. . . . The benefits of the proposed transmountain highway to the com-munity of scientists is virtually non-existent. I believe the liabilities of such a road outweigh the benefits—not just to the scientists, but to the population at large as well."[19]

Clebsch gave reasons why the road should not be built. It would: split a wilderness into two parts; alter the chemical constituents of several very fine streams; cause physical changes in the streams by siltation, with only gross consequences predictable; alter groundwater patterns for an unpredictable distance from the cuts and fills necessary to build the road; require that cuts and fills be stabilized by plants, most likely species exotic to the region (as are many plants commonly used for such purposes); create a barrier to the movement of animal species; provide avenues for the introduction of new pests and pathogens into the adjacent wilderness; and serve as a point source for contamination and disturbance of the adjacent wilderness by people and their refuse.

Perhaps the strongest point Clebsch made was that eminent world scientists, already then, in 1969, were alarmed at the rate of destruction of plant cover and foresaw serious problems and global consequences. Thus, while the amount of green cover to be destroyed by the transmountain highway might be very small, when added to the destruction in other places, its significance would grow.

No such data or warning was provided to the public by National Park Service scientists. They might speak of an ecosystems approach in lofty, general terms, but certainly not in specifics, not when their director in Washington was aggressively promoting the Smoky Mountains road,[20] and when, as Alston Chase charged, political convenience and expediency often govern decisions. The scientist who insists on speaking independently from his conscience pays a price. In 1958 Adolph Murie was directed by his superiors to move to Medford, Oregon, to spend his winters. He didn't want to relocate from Jackson, Wyoming, where he had all his books and papers, but he was warned that he would not be able to continue his Alaska studies unless he accepted the transfer.[21] As independent research biologists, John and Frank Craighead between 1959 and 1971 studied the movement of bears in Yellowstone through the use of radio-tracking collars, a system they pioneered. When their findings differed from official policy, they were subjected to harsh criticism and denied their permit for research in the park.

The Yellowstone fires of 1988 illustrate a more recent side of park politics and science. One morning late that summer, as it happened, I was hiking the trail from Jenny Lake up Cascade Canyon in Grand Teton National Park. The monumental wildfires burning in Yellowstone not far to the north clouded the skies and covered the lake like a shroud of gloom. My two companions and I talked of smelling the smoke, of feeling it penetrate our clothes.

That was the morning scene. As we headed back down the trail in the afternoon, a fair wind blew off the smoke. The peaks of the Tetons shone against a clear blue sky, while Jenny Lake became its old self, reflecting the glory of the earth around and above it. I felt a lesson in the experience: a reassurance that all would be well if only we were patient, allowing nature and time the chance to heal.

The fires were unquestionably extensive, but the damage was more commercial than ecological. The park was not "destroyed." Parks are destroyed by human impacts and influences, not by inevitable natural events. Those fires resulted from extremely high temperatures, dry conditions, and high winds, but fire has long been natural to the northern plains. It sweeps through periodically and recycles nutrients for new growth. Indian tribes considered fire a friend, just as primitive peoples in various parts of the world even now set fire to "green up the grass" and stimulate new growth. But wildfires of a century ago that were devastating to commercial timber forests led to a public policy to suppress all fires. It was considered good forestry to protect the timber crop, and then it was considered a good resource practice even without the timber crop. Fire became a particular specialty in professional management; it made jobs for smoke-jumpers, the shock troops, and for temporaries of all kinds to supplement professional firefighters, and it stimulated business in nearby communities. The forestry policy prevailed in the parks until 1972, when "natural regulation," or "let burn," became the policy, allowing natural fires—those caused by lightning—to run their course except when human life and property were threatened.

Then came June 1988, when lightning danced in the sky and sparked in the trees. Severe drought had turned trees into tinder. Dead litter on the forest floor, untouched during the years of fire suppression, made it worse. A carelessly tossed cigarette butt set off a massive new blaze in July. Park concessionaires and commercial interests in nearby communities complained that fire was bad for business. Politicians demanded more aggressive suppression and charged that national parks were being run as "quasi-religious sanctuaries." They ridiculed Yellowstone superintendent Bob Barbee as "Bob Barbecue" and urged the dismissal of William Penn Mott, director of the Park Service. The media descended on Yellowstone, though most of the fires burned on national forests outside the park. Television reporters showed America the billowing flames and smoke, firefighters in yellow clothing, and assorted local critics complaining about mismanagement, scarcely touching on the story of fire as a powerful historic force. The real values of Ycllowstone were ignored.

Again, while attending a conference in May 1989 at Bozeman, Montana, on wilderness, parks, and fire, I felt that the real values of Yellowstone were ignored. The participants were mostly from the Forest Service, Park Service, and land-grant universities—technical people communicating with each other in technical jargon, as though the earth had no soul, natural forces were meant to be catalogued and controlled, and these experts were privy to knowledge beyond the ken of ordinary people. One reported that the fire at Old Faithful would have been sheer disaster had it not been for the firefighting force; such an assessment was in keeping with the tremendous outlay of manpower and money—more than twenty-five thousand firefighters and $145 million during the summer of 1988.[22] Yet the "disaster" at Old Faithful would have been disastrous for human-made structures rather than the geysers that were born of vulcanism and have endured through the upheavals of natural history. The big issue was how to "manage" fire—whether, for instance, fire managers should continue to have more to say than wilderness managers in defining the appropriate level of protection in wilderness, and how extensively fire should be deliberately set to compensate for all those years it was suppressed.

Nature, alas, is perceived as requiring guidance, correction, and control, without recognizing that forces like blizzard, cold, drought, earthquake, fire, flood, heat, hurricane, storm, and volcano are both beneficial and inevitable, and all predate human existence. Like architects, these forces shape and reshape land into landscape and recast the form and function of plants and animals. They are nature's art and poetry and dance and music. A wildfire is like a wildflower or wild trout or wild wind, sisters and brothers of wild places called national parks.

In this age of fallout there are no places on earth free of human disturbance. Roads, development, and deforestation around national parks have reduced them from the spacious havens that they once were. Still, any place, of any size, where human sounds, chemicals, and other by-products of civilized life are not dominant—any area where nature prevails, or might prevail, given time—merits attention and respect. That is wilderness to me; that is what a national park should be.

John Ruskin once wrote: "Great art accepts Nature as she is, but directs the eyes and thoughts to what is most perfect in her; false art saves itself the trouble of direction by removing or altering whatever it thinks objectionable." A dead tree or blackened snag or ghost forest, when natural, has its own beauty and significance. For beauty in its deepest sense requires truth to achieve significance.

10 Concessionaire Profits and Public Access

During his truncated tenure as director of the National Park Service from July 1977 to May 1980, William J. Whalen tried to clamp down on concessionaires, the commercial entrepreneurs licensed to provide lodgings, food, and other visitor services in the parks. He charged that in many cases they allowed facilities to deteriorate, failed to provide adequate services, and made excessive profits. Whalen initiated an annual evaluation of concessionaire performance, introduced a new standard contract, and increased the franchise fees. He wanted to end the "possessory interest" through which a concessionaire cannot be removed without a government buyout. The one to be removed, however, was Whalen.

Other factors were involved (as related in chapter 5), but the concessions conflict was critical to Whalen's career, especially after Representative Morris Udall, chairman of the House Interior Committee, demanded his dismissal. Udall's intercession was sparked by an indelicate remark made by Whalen at a meeting of concessionaires, but Don Hummel, chairman of the Conference of National Park Concessioners, played a special role in getting rid of Whalen. Hummel at one time or other operated concessions in Glacier, Lassen, Yosemite, and Mount McKinley; in addition, he was a former mayor of Tucson, Arizona, and a political supporter of Representative Udall in their common hometown.

Hummel, an attorney and public official (assistant secretary of housing under Lyndon B. Johnson) as well as a concessionaire, was an articulate, combative chairman of the trade association for fourteen years. His viewpoint was always clear. "We've ignored the people. We've protected the animals. We protect the ecosystems, but we haven't put the money where the people can use it," he declared at the 1981 Concessions Conference.[1] "The Park Service is cutting back the concessioners methodically so that we have less and less security."

Hummel pursued the cause even after he was succeeded as chairman and sold his last concession contract. He wrote *Stealing the National Parks: The Destruction of Concessions and Park Access*, a rambling personal memoir which he paid to publish in 1987, a year before he died at the age of eighty-one. He wanted to show that parks are not overrun, as charged by environmentalists and their bureaucratic allies in government. According to Hummel, the Park Service reported 346 million total visits for the year 1985, but only 50 million of that total was recorded at the forty-eight national parks. Most of the visits were to urban day-use sites like Golden Gate National Recreation Area in San Francisco and Gateway National Recreation Area in New York; moreover, only 9.2 million visitors stayed overnight in the national parks.[2] Hummel had a valid point, insofar as numbers go. He also insisted that "the private national park concessioners are the true champions of public access and reliable front-line fighters for the right of the people to use and enjoy their parks."[3]

Nevertheless, L. E. "Buddy" Surles, the Park Service chief of concessions management during the late 1970s and early 1980s, was critical of what he considered substandard and unsafe operations by Hummel's concession at Glacier National Park. He felt much the same about the concession at Big Bend National Park operated by National Park Concessions, Inc. Surles moved against them both, but after Whalen's dismissal he got little support. He later told me (in December 1985) that Russell Dickenson, Whalen's successor, deliberately went easy on the concessionaires: "It took me two years to get Don Hummel and Garner Hanson [president of National Park Concessions, Inc.] to a point to actually start performing under terms of the contract. I had meeting after meeting with the concessionaires where I went in with a preapproved plan from Russ and he'd come in and pour water over the coals and kick my knees right out from me.

His philosophy was to give the concessionaires what they wanted to keep his job."[4]

Not all the rules are in the books. Surles was a new man who had joined the Park Service after serving as director of state parks in Arkansas, while Dickenson was an old hand who understood the unwritten rule of survival: avoid making powerful enemies; they'll complain and get you. "Hummel and Hanson first complained to Russ," Surles continued. "Then they went to Secretary Watt."

Thus, at the 1981 conference Watt assured the concessionaires he was with them, that they would be invited to play a larger role in the administration of national parks: "If a personality is giving you a problem, we're going to get rid of the problem or the personality, whichever is faster."[5] Surles left soon after, to be replaced by David Gackenbach, Hanson's future son-in-law.

Watt was introduced at the conference with admiration and praise by Rex Maughan, who succeeded Hummel as chairman of the association. Maughan, a self-made magnate, came into the concessions scene through his association with the Del Webb Corporation, which held concessions in Arizona and southern Utah. In due course he became involved with the concession at Glacier National Park (when Hummel sold out and retired) and with Signal Mountain Lodge in Grand Teton National Park. These were sidelines, however; Maughan's principal business was Forever Living Products, a door-to-door network selling shampoo, diet pills, suntan lotion, and skin moisturizers, all based on the aloe vera plant.

Hummel and Maughan shared the viewpoint that parks become meaningful when visited by people, that people must be accommodated and served, and that private, profit-making enterprise is the best way to furnish necessary and appropriate services. In *Stealing the National Parks* Hummel quoted Stephen T. Mather, first director of the National Park Service: "Scenery is a hollow enjoyment to a tourist who sets out in the morning after an indigestible breakfast and a fitful sleep on an impossible bed."[6] Maughan, for his part, stressed the tradition and importance of the "partnership" between concessionaires and the National Park Service.

At a meeting of park superintendents following the 1981 Concessions Conference Maughan explained what this meant. He wanted the superintendents to "cut out anything that represents an ivory tower concept." He told them too many decisions were influenced by extraneous, outside-the-park elements, notably environmentalists. "They've tried to convert major areas to wilderness areas, which we feel takes away the majority of the park for most people in favor of providing pristine areas for a minority of park users. Parks are for all the people, not just the environmentalists." Thus, continued Maughan:

> if you haven't been to Yellowstone in the winter on a snowmobile, you haven't really seen Yellowstone, and more people should have that opportunity. You can travel into other areas of the park; perhaps we might develop different areas. Yellowstone hasn't opened up any new thermal areas since 1905, as I recall. If Yellowstone is overtaxed, as we're always hearing, possibly we need to open up a new area or two and take some traffic to these new areas. . . .
>
> If you don't have a profitable concessioner, you're not going to have a very happy concessioner. If you don't have a happy concessioner, he's not going to provide very good services to the public.

Many concessionaires feel constantly put-upon; they see themselves as targets of elitist ecologist types working in collusion with park administrators who know little about the particular parks they run for two or three years before moving on, and know even less about business. They, the concessionaires, live in chronic fear that the Park Service will eliminate them and, maybe even worse, purchase their facilities without respect for the "possessory interest" in whatever they have built or remodeled on government land. Consequently they strike back, individually and collectively, locally and in Washington, for what they believe is theirs by right—and right, as they see it, in the public interest.

Representative Udall, in his criticism of Whalen, insisted that a concessionaire, like any citizen, is entitled to state his case to Congress.[7] That makes sense. On the other hand, although commerce is a main pillar of American society, in the national parks commerce colors and clouds any meaningful discussion of appropriate human activity and the pressures of increasing visitor use. Private enterprise by its nature promotes business to maximize profit. Entrepreneurs in (and around) the parks generally advocate recreational tourism, from which they benefit, rather than spiritual sanctuary and ecosystem preservation with fitting restrictions and restraints. Wherever visitor service is commercialized, it tends to feature and promote convenience and crowd pleasing. It leads to advertising to keep accommodations full during the "shoulder seasons," to stay open during winter, to lengthen the "season." It rationalizes selling tawdry souvenirs and package liquor as a way to lower prices for backpacking supplies and peanut butter. The bar trade encourages barroom behavior, brawls, and enforcement problems. Such enterprises and activities influence the entire tenor of a park: it doesn't look like a parcel of primitive America and doesn't feel like one. The park becomes a popcorn playground to which visitors adjust their expectations and behavior. Even when National Park Service employees try to maintain a high level of visitor information and other service responsibilities, that standard sometimes is lost in concessionaire-operated portions of visitor services—inadequately trained staff, poor maintenance, institutional food, substandard employee housing, below-minimum wages.

The Park Service is presumed to control concessionaires in terms of service, prices, wages, housing, and maintenance standards; in practice, it doesn't always work that way, and hasn't for years. In Sequoia–Kings Canyon National Park during 1985, for example, I interviewed Marvin Jensen of the park staff regarding the planned relocation of concession facilities out of Giant Forest. Jensen (later superintendent of Glacier Bay National Park) was directly involved in negotiations with the concessionaire, Guest Services, Inc., or GSI, represented principally by its general counsel, George B. Hartzog, Jr., a former director of the National Park Service. Jensen told me: "We have tried to move the concession out of Giant Forest because of the human impact on sequoia trees. This has been proposed since 1924. We felt we had a stronger position because in 1979 we'd gone through the development concept planning process, including public involvement and a full environmental impact statement. What's been happening is procrastination, continual slippage of dates for removal as a result of political maneuvering by the concessionaire."

Howard Chapman provided further evidence in an opinion article in the *Marin Independent Journal*, published at San Rafael, California, on January 22, 1990:

As a National Park Service regional director for seventeen years, I had responsibility for Yosemite during the events that led to the

1980 [general management] plan as well as the years that followed. I have sat in the board rooms of the Music Corporation of America (MCA)—the corporate parent of the Yosemite Park and Curry Company—in the early seventies when we found ourselves outgunned by the financial, political and downright economic aggressiveness of their executives who measured success by the bottom line of each day's profit and loss statement. A national park was to them a place to make money! . . .

The National Park Service makes lofty statements about national parks being special places. But special places—national parks—demand special attention. That doesn't have to mean removing every convenience, but it does mean choices about location, numbers and timing with respect to what affects the park scene—whether it is a car, a cabin, a restaurant, or park offices and shops.

Chapman waited to speak until after he retired. Park employees recognize that if a concessionaire wants to implement some new revenue-producing program and meets resistance from the park administration, the concessionaire can appeal to levels way above the park. They know where and how to push the right buttons until approval is given and handed down the line. Because park administrators fear concession power and pressure, they tread lightly, acquiesce, and rationalize.

Concessions are as old as the national parks, and lodgings are even older. Yosemite Valley, as a case in point, was opened after the Mariposa Battalion, a posse dispatched in 1851 by the governor of California, drove out Indians blocking the path of the gold rush. Accounts directly thereafter attracted tourists to marvel at massive El Capitan and Half Dome, Bridal Veil Falls and Yosemite Falls, and the Mariposa Grove of giant sequoias. Because entrepreneurs preempted choice sites and built hotels, Congress in 1864 turned over the valley and the Mariposa big trees, then still part of the public domain, to the state of California "to be held inalienable for all time." Even so, by the time Yosemite became a national park in 1890, hotels had been in the valley more than thirty years, with still more abuilding. At the turn of the century the largest of them was operated by David Curry and his wife. Starting with six cabins under Glacier Point, within a few years they had six hundred. Curry promoted the famous firefall, pushing burning embers over the cliff to cascade slowly to a

ledge far below—artificial, but destined to become as much a Yosemite attraction as waterfalls and granite domes.[8]

Yellowstone likewise was subject to early development.[9] The Yellowstone Act of 1872 authorized the secretary of the interior to grant
leases of small parcels of land for the erection of visitor accommodations, and entrepreneurs opened for business. By the 1880s the
Mammoth Hot Springs vicinity was the principal center of action,
with livery stables, stores, tent camps, and a "house of doubtful character." Visitors came, many evidently with vandalism in their hearts.
They threw sticks, stones, stumps, garbage, and clothing into geysers
and hot springs. Fish by the thousands were left to rot on riverbanks
and lakeshores. In 1875, only three years after the park was established, an army captain reported that nearly all the craters showed
signs of unrestrained barbarity by the visitors, who were shattering
and destroying nature's handiwork with axes.[10] Nonetheless, two
years later, in 1877, Superintendent Philatus W. Norris established
bear-feeding stations near the hotels, using garbage from hotel kitch-
ens to attract bears to entertain visitors. In 1881 F. Jay Haynes opened
the first of the photographic shops that would continue in his family
until 1968. Silas S. Huntley, with his brother-in-law, Harry Child, in
1891 obtained transportation rights in the park, laying the basis of
the Yellowstone Park Company that would continue in their family
for three quarters of a century. Canvas towns presently gave way to
great cavernous wooden structures such as the Lake Hotel, completed in 1899, and Old Faithful Inn, completed in time for the 1904
season.[11]

Railroads were early concessionaires and park boosters. Jay Cooke,
financier of the Northern Pacific, retained Nathaniel P. Langford, the
first superintendent of Yellowstone, to lecture throughout the East
about the park. The Northern Pacific identified itself as the "Yellowstone Park Line." The Southern Pacific, in California, lobbied for establishment in 1890 of Sequoia, Yosemite, and General Grant national parks; eight years later the railroad founded *Sunset* magazine
to bring these parks to the attention of tourists and settlers. The
Santa Fe in 1905 built the elegant El Tovar at the south rim of the
Grand Canyon and urged the proclamation by President Theodore
Roosevelt in 1908 of Grand Canyon National Monument (which subsequently led to designation as a national park). Great Northern built

grand hotels and Swiss-style alpine chalets at Glacier National Park. Union Pacific operated hotels at the north rim of the Grand Canyon, as well as at Zion and Bryce. They were self-serving, of course; before World War I, railroads accounted for 85 to 90 percent of all park visitors. The hotels they built are still environmental intrusions, yet railroads helped the parks gain status and security. "We do not want to see the Falls of the Yellowstone driving the looms of a cotton factory," wrote Charles S. Fee, general passenger agent of the Northern Pacific, in the first of a series of Western guidebooks he and his line commissioned, "or the great geysers boiling pork for some gigantic packing-house, but in all the native majesty and grandeur in which they appear today, without, as yet, a single trace of that adornment which is desecration, that improvement which is equivalent to ruin, or that utilization which means utter destruction."

When Stephen T. Mather came along, he decided that competition was destroying the parks and determined to institute a new system. Facilities in Yellowstone, as Mather found them, included a chain of five hotels and lunch stations run by the Yellowstone Park Hotel Company, three stagecoach lines, three systems of permanent camps offering overnight lodgings, and assorted lunch stations along the main loop through the park. Mather thought it was all too much and insisted on merging companies and their facilities. He also changed the park orientation from stagecoach to motorcar, thus cleaning out camps, corrals, fences, and four thousand horses; that was considered progress. At Yosemite Mather forced the merger of the Yosemite Park Company and Curry Camping Company, the two major operators. Convinced that visitors would better enjoy the parks free of competitive, hustling entrepreneurs, Mather and his associate, Horace Albright, launched the concessions system of "regulated monopoly" through which lodging, transportation, food, and other services are contracted to chosen companies; the company is granted a monopoly and guaranteed a profit in return for furnishing desired services, whether profitable or unprofitable. That is the foundation of the present system.

Mather felt he could work with his allies, the railroads. The Yosemite Park and Curry Company was also good to deal with. It was a family concession of considerable status, fitting Mather's notion of noblesse oblige adapted to outdoor America. At his initiative the company in 1927 built the elegant Ahwahnee Hotel (in keeping with his concept of three levels of park accommodation: tent cabin, room with bath, and quality hostelry).

In those early years some concessionaires did as much to protect the parks as to promote them. William Gladstone Steel first saw Crater Lake in Oregon in 1885 and devoted the rest of his life to it. He campaigned to make it a national park, and once that came to pass in 1902, he operated a concession so he could stay close to the lake. "All the money I have is in the park, and if I had more it would go there too. This is my life's work," Steel said at the 1911 National Parks Conference. Ansel Hall, pioneer park naturalist, established the concession at Mesa Verde in southwest Colorado, and was succeeded by his son-in-law, William Winkler, a former park ranger who concerned himself with park interpretation until he sold the franchise to ARA, a large lodging and food service company. Horace Albright once said of Jack Ellis Haynes, who in 1916 succeeded his father, F. Jay Haynes, in operating the Yellowstone photographic studios, and who lived seventy-five of his seventy-seven years in Yellowstone: "Jack Haynes placed public service—and service to the public—above personal interests, profit, and prestige," Horace told me. "He was always as ready to aid the park as he was to safeguard his family and his business. No man in business in a national park was ever more cooperative, more generous, and more unselfish."

Concessionaire-conservationists were not only found in the West. George Freeman Pollock began his resort, Skyland, in the Blue Ridge Mountains of Virginia in the 1890s, first with a tent camp, then with log cabins. He was a naturalist who knew the mountains and mountain people, a colorful character who would lead guests on overnight trips, though there were no trails. He held snake shows in the dining hall, picking up rattlers in his mouth in the style of the Hopi Indians in their famous snake dances. Pollock was the prime mover in the establishment of Shenandoah National Park, by influencing Governor Harry F. Byrd to support the land acquisition with state funds. In 1937 he sold Skyland to the Virginia Sky-Line Company, which largely followed his tradition until it too, like Winkler in Mesa Verde, sold controlling interest to ARA. Pollock died in 1949, a few weeks before his eightieth birthday. Funeral services were conducted in Washington by Swami Premananda, a close friend, who recalled that Pollock was not a religious man and had not been to a church in years, but had built a cathedral where anthems are sung by bird choirs and which would last as long as America lasted. Two years later, in October 1951, when Pollock Knob was dedicated in the mountains, the Washington, D.C., *Evening Star* editorialized:

> Mr. Pollock loved the Appalachians and it was his vision of their permanent value to successive generations that finally led to Shenandoah Park's being set aside as a permanent recreational property of the whole Federal commonwealth. He was a Washingtonian who "discovered" the Blue Ridge in boyhood and never ceased to be devoted to its attractions. His campaign for the preservation of the Skyline ridge was a one-man endeavor for decades, but it gradually enlisted hundreds of supporters, many of whom attended the dedication assembly October 14. Senator Harry F. Byrd, principal speaker of the occasion, declared that naming Pollock Knob for "the Father of Shenandoah National Park" was an act of "simple justice to a great American character."[12]

There were others like them, and there are others even now who, given the choice between preservation and profit, would choose the former. But they are not the major players, and not too many of the minor players, either. In *Yellowstone: A Wilderness Besieged*, historian Richard A. Bartlett details the concessions saga in the nation's oldest national park. With reference to the longtime principals of the Yellowstone Park Company, Bartlett says: "There is very little evidence that the Child-Nichols interests ever manifested much concern over the park proper."[13] They may be proud of their hotels, buses, boats, and souvenir shops, but to many concessionaires a national park is primarily a place to do business, albeit a pleasant place, and concern is directed to restraints on business or the introduction of a competitor in business, and scarcely ever to environmental threats to the park.

During the 1940s the Interior Department campaigned to take over the facilities in the parks and operate them publicly. The concessionaires retaliated by refusing to invest in modernization or improvement. They fought Interior over issues of building ownership, term of contract, rate of franchise fee, and method of valuating concession buildings. Consequently, postwar visitors were subjected to antiquated facilities, poor service, and poor food. Ultimately the concessionaires got what they wanted. In 1958 the maximum term of concession contracts was extended from twenty to thirty years.

The Concessions Policy Act of 1965 assured the "preferential right" of renewal, and more besides: if a concessionaire chooses to sell, the buyer must purchase his "possessory interest" at current market rate. The Park Service generously accepted the possessory interest concept, believing it would give concessionaires security to invest their own money or to use for collateral in applying for business loans.[14] In this way, private corporations were given a vested interest in public land—somewhat akin to stockmen holding grazing permits on rangelands administered by the Forest Service and Bureau of Land Management. The improvements they make enhance proprietary rights and add value to franchises (in the parks) and permits (on the range).

In 1978, when Don Hummel was in the process of selling out at Glacier, I was interested in determining the fitness of the potential new concessionaire and made inquiries of the Interior Department. After all, a national park is public land, so the public might assume the right to understand how and by whom the land is run. The response, however, from Assistant Secretary Robert L. Herbst declared: "I must admit that the public voice is not heard before such transfer takes place. This was one of the most adamant of the demands of the Conference of National Park Concessioners. It is their position that this would place an abnormal restraint on the property rights of stockholders, would restrain trade, and would preclude normal open market transactions of publicly owned stock, thus infringing on property rights."[15]

In other words, the critical lands involved may be public in name, but those lands are recognized as private in fact, the protected provinces of concessionaires. I recall also the early history of Everglades National Park, established in 1947 at the southern tip of the Florida peninsula, free of resort facilities. In the 1950s Devereux Butcher, executive director of the National Parks Association, fought to keep it that way. So did Conrad L. Wirth, director of the Park Service. But local tourist interests prevailed through political means, and a concession facility was installed at Flamingo, at the very tip of the peninsula. The first concessionaire failed, then another took over, and it failed too. On a visit I made to the park in the early 1970s, I found the concession in shambles. Jack E. Stark, then superintendent (later a regional director and superintendent of Grand Teton National Park), shared with me data on poor conditions of lodging and food facilities and the drug-related and alcohol-related difficulties of concession employees. Successive superintendents recommended removing overnight accommodations, considering the abundance of facilities in nearby communities and the desirability of restoring part of a sensitive area. But no, when the contract expired, the superintendents' recommendations were ignored and, without public notice or involvement, another concessionaire was introduced.

In *Yellowstone: A Wilderness Besieged*, Bartlett deals with the political influence of concessionaires and the acquiescence of government officials. "Again and again," writes Bartlett, "incidents appear indicating Park Service cooperation with the concessionaires that seem to place consideration for these businesses above the public welfare."[16] He cites the case history of the Childs, the Huntleys, their children, and their children's children, who continued to run Yellowstone's transportation system, the great hotels, and the tent camps, and shared in the profits until 1967, three quarters of a century in all, in a national park where concessions supposedly are reviewed periodically and granted in a democratic way.[17]

Harry Child, the pioneer of the family, apparently made a point to be on good terms with whoever was in the White House, regardless of party. Harry's sister married a Yellowstone park superintendent, and a daughter married a national park concessionaire in California, so the power of their common link was felt in Washington. When the government was reluctant to allow Child to run the stores in Yellowstone, he subsidized one of his employees, Charles Hamilton, thus starting another concessions powerhouse.

Hamilton Stores was established in 1915, a year before the National Park Service, and continues to thrive to this day, with the third generation in charge. Hamilton service stations, snack bars, grocery and general merchandise stores, and camera shops are scattered throughout the park. They sell something of almost everything: groceries, liquor, wine, auto supplies, camera equipment, clothing, fishing and camping gear, jewelry, Black Hills gold, curios, gifts, souvenirs, handicrafts, books, proprietary drugs, cosmetics and sundries, hardware and furniture, smokers' supplies, and, through the former Haynes photo studios, which Hamilton acquired, cameras, film, picture frames, decals, paintings, and assorted photographic services. Food and beverage services at the stores offer soft drinks, ice, light lunches, beer, and other refreshments. "Ham Stores" also provides twelve dormitories for eight hundred summer employees.

The Yellowstone Park Company has not fared nearly as well. Heirs of the Huntleys and Childs were still around in the 1950s, the beginning of Mission 66. Then the Park Service encouraged the construction of Canyon Village, a massive tourist development in the heart of the wild country, which proved a disaster, financial as well as otherwise, and finished off the old families.

The history of the principal Yellowstone concession turned into a comic tragedy. The National Park Service shopped for a new concessionaire and in 1966 proudly presented the Goldfield Corporation, which agreed to spend $10 million on capital improvements in Yellowstone. It was not exactly a parks outfit; in fact, the principal in Goldfield, Richard Pistell, was a securities dealer whose prior firm had been suspended by the Securities and Exchange Commission for selling securities without being registered.[18]

But Pistell didn't last. Goldfield evolved into the General Host Corporation, an entity distant and uncaring, with profits from a captive audience going out and nothing coming in. Lodgings were poorly maintained and run-down: roofs, windows, screens, draperies, shades, blinds—all were unclean or unsafe. Employees received low wages and worked long hours. They were housed inadequately, poorly trained and supervised, unhappy in their jobs, and rude or indifferent to guests. Complaints forced the National Park Service to face its own fiasco. A Yellowstone Concessions Study Team in October 1976 conceded: "Visitors are not getting the same quality of service that would be expected or received in most other national parks or in the free enterprise system outside of a park environment."[19]

The government paid off General Hosts with $19.9 million, then spent $34.7 million to renovate many of the buildings it purchased and looked for a new outfit to take over. Edward C. Hardy, president of the Yosemite Park and Curry Company, was invited to consider the possibility. He came to Yellowstone to study the scene. Later (in 1985) Hardy told me: "That concession got milked. It got milked beyond where I could figure how a prudent businessman could justify the investment for his stockholders, without making it a giveaway. I don't think the government did right when it bought out the concession. They paid too much; they should have gotten it for half, or a third, of what they paid."[20]

TW Services became the next concessionaire. It was a unit of the Trans World Corporation, the holding company of TWA, the airline, but after corporate shuffling the airline flew off and the Canteen Corporation became the parent. Under the new arrangement at Yellowstone, Canteen agreed to invest $12 million in upgrading facilities, to operate with a management contract, including a cap on profits, and to allocate a significant percentage to repair and maintenance. Conditions have improved considerably.

But the improvement in fortune for one Yellowstone concessionaire, TW Services, has not sat well with the other concessionaire, Hamilton Stores, which in 1985 sued the government, accusing the Park Service of "callous disregard of its statutory and contractual obligations."[21] Hamilton Stores charged that because the Park Service breached its contract, TWS was systematically encroaching on Hamilton Stores's operations in Yellowstone National Park "to the extent that it has greatly impaired HSI's ability to realize a profit on its operations as a whole commensurate with the capital invested and the obligations assumed."[22]

This particular hassle had its origin in an arrangement over the Yellowstone Park service stations, formerly jointly controlled by Hamilton Stores and the old Yellowstone Park Company. However, General Host, when it came on the scene, was given a 55 percent share in the service stations, plus the right to develop and fully own a service station at the new Grant Village tourist complex. The Park Service wanted to be good to General Host and help it establish a sound economic base, since it had largest capital investment and highest operating risk; if the company made more profits, it could afford to give better service. However, after Hamilton Stores complained bitterly, General Host agreed to return to the fifty-fifty split and to sell Hamilton 50 percent of the Grant Village service station. But it gained and held onto the right to sell "limited gift and photo items"[23] in its own facilities. This became the bone of legal contention, since Hamilton Stores insisted that souvenirs are solely its domain, guaranteed with preferential right. Hamilton didn't win its case in court, but TWS doesn't sell souvenirs in its hotels. It may operate gift shops, but they sell gifts, definitely not souvenirs, which are defined as "items that are localized, whether they are screened, imprinted or otherwise have the locality of the park applied."[24] If a visitor wants a T-shirt, sweatshirt, glassware, or item of cedar emblazoned with the word "Yellowstone," he or she must get it at a Hamilton Store, because it's a souvenir. To a concessionaire such things really count.

Grant Village was designed to replace an older development at Fishing Bridge, a key point on the park loop (where the Hamilton Store does the greatest volume of all its stores in the park). Recommendations to phase out 300 campsites and 350 recreational vehicle sites and other facilities at Fishing Bridge to restore the area to wildlife, notably grizzly bears, were made in the 1973 Yellowstone master plan. Nine years later, in June 1984, the park announced it would close the facilities, but commercial tourist interests in Cody, Wyoming, the gateway to Yellowstone from the east, objected; so did the Wyoming congressional delegation, and new studies were begun.[25] Meanwhile, construction proceeded at Grant Village, the replacement area. In the winter of 1985 I went to see the new development, a massive tourist enclave bordering Yellowstone Lake—buildings to accommodate three hundred units already constructed, with an additional four hundred units still to come, plus the Hamilton Store, of course—located on spawning streams used by grizzly bears. And Fishing Bridge is still in place.

Visitors tend to get wrapped up in Yellowstone as an entertainment center. The same is true of all the parks, but Yellowstone is largely the model, and that's the way it was laid out. Visitors drive the loop from point A to point B, stopping at another tourist site and convenient concession facility, with scant understanding of ecological cost and consequence.

I mentioned how an early superintendent introduced the bear-feeding shows. When he was superintendent, Horace Albright built "Greek theaters" of logs at the dumps, patrolled by a mounted ranger armed with a rifle. The shows lasted until 1948; the garbage dumps finally closed in the 1960s. In place of dumps the park introduced "bear-proof" waste containers, increased efforts to educate visitors on sanitation and dangers posed by bears, and removed "nuisance bears." Today, during the summer season, no garbage is held in the park more than twelve hours; approximately one hundred employees twice daily empty more than two thousand bear-proof cans from 2400 campsites, picnic sites, roadside pullouts, and park residences. They empty the garbage into eight trucks, which compact and transfer it to large trailers, which move 1800 tons eighty-five miles to a disposal station at Livingston and 700 hundred tons to a landfill near Ennis.

To be sure, nobody wants to know where garbage goes. Maybe that has something to do with what people toss, shove, or roll into the Yellowstone hot springs and geysers. On a visit to the park in the mid-1980s I took a close look in company with Roderick A. Hutchinson, the park specialist in thermal geology (the "geyser-gazer," as he calls himself). He told me that rocks, coins, frying pans, whiskey bottles, engagement rings, sticks, stumps, marbles, shell cases, dentures, bath towels, and clothing at one time or other have all been tossed in and cleaned out. Curiosity apparently is the principal motivation. Some people think of hot springs as wishing wells. Others want to get rid of their Black Hills or Grand Teton souvenir token because they can't use it anywhere else. Or they have a grudge against the government and this is one way of striking back. Hutchinson mentioned that at least there are no sacrifices to the gods. "I mean they don't toss in their infants, but now and then somebody jumps in on a dare or because he's intoxicated. They don't realize they're damaging something important or that could be important. There are all kinds of little secrets in Yellowstone's thermal basins. As long as we help to preserve them, and allow these small plants and animals to live, something may come along to make our lives better."[26]

Only a few concessionaires concern themselves with the condition of small plants and animals or the little secrets in thermal basins. Others would agree with Rex Maughan in his derogation of elitist ivory-tower extraneities and the need to protect their position as regulated monopolies with preferential rights and assured profit. Toward that end they work diligently to sustain proper friends and contacts—and Park Service people are ever mindful.

A 1976 joint study conducted by two subcommittees of the House of Representatives concluded that:

1. National Park Service administration of concessions has been inadequate and ineffective.
2. Concessionaires have, in effect, been allowed to do business with little overall control or supervision by the NPS.
3. The concessionaires have undue influence over NPS concession management and policies.

4. Concession contracts are vague, ambiguous, and generally do not adequately protect the government's interest.[27]

These were not the subcommittees that count, however. Power over the parks belongs to the Interior Committee in the House, Energy and Natural Resources in the Senate, and appropriations committees in both Senate and House. Others may meddle and blow smoke, but considering the way Congress divides power, they have a tough time making things happen. It was a different story when Senator Mark Hatfield of Oregon, ranking Republican on the Committee on Energy and Natural Resources, received a memo on June 17, 1980, from Tony Bevinetto, of the committee staff, that began: "The forthcoming GAO report will identify the national park system as a dangerous place to visit. The NPS has numerous report documents which substantiate the GAO report."

Those NPS documents included a study directed the year before by Philip Iverson, superintendent of Glacier National Park, who had decided that he must challenge Don Hummel, the park concessionaire. Iverson commissioned outside fire and safety experts to inspect the old wood-frame Lake McDonald and Many Glacier hotels. They reported the facilities in need of emergency measures such as alarms, smoke detectors, and lighting to ensure public and employee safety from fire and smoke.[28]

The General Accounting Office (GAO) went much further. It reviewed drinking water systems, sewage, bridges, tunnels, hotels, and employee dormitories in Glacier, Crater Lake, Denali, Everglades, Grand Canyon, Isle Royale, Mount Rainier, Rocky Mountain, Voyageurs, Yellowstone, and Yosemite national parks, the Blue Ridge Parkway, and ten national forests. Health and safety inspectors identified health and safety deficiencies so hazardous that they recommended immediate closure pending repair.[29]

Senator Hatfield had requested the GAO study following a series of unhappy incidents in Western parks. At Crater Lake, in his home state, about sixteen hundred visitors and employees in June 1975 were stricken with gastroenteritis after drinking from the park's water system. At Glacier National Park two years later, in September 1977, fifty-five visitors and concession employees became ill with giardiasis after drinking from the Many Glacier water system (supplying water to the Many Glacier Hotel, Swiftcurrent Creek Motel, and Many Glacier Campground). Consequently, the GAO reported that drinking-water systems in these and other national parks did not meet state or federal standards.[30]

Old wood-frame, combustible lodges and dormitories likewise were reported as substandard: they were deficient in smoke alarms, fire alarms, sprinkler systems, fire-retardant materials in hallways and stairwells, emergency lighting, and emergency exits, and failed to comply with building and fire codes. The Lake Hotel and Old Faithful Inn in Yellowstone, El Tovar in Grand Canyon, Paradise Inn in Mount Rainier, Many Glacier in Glacier (built by railroad magnate Louis Hill in 1914 as the "showplace of the Rockies"), Crater Lake Lodge in Crater Lake, the Ahwahnee in Yosemite—all were celebrated relics of early periods but now worn with time. The Kettle Falls Inn built in the Minnesota north woods in 1913, many years before Voyageurs National Park was established, was picturesque in its decline, with its sloping lobby floor, but structurally defective. Facilities at Flamingo in the Everglades, however, were not nearly as old. Nevertheless, in November 1978 the assistant safety manager for the Southeast Region stated in an inspection report that "the Smith Hall complex [five buildings elevated on pilings and providing living units for concession employees] represents a serious threat to the lives of its occupants. This situation has existed for many years under concession and now under U.S. Government ownership. We can no longer rely on 'good luck' to protect the operation."

Park officials in charge were interviewed. They were aware, they conceded to GAO inspectors, that facilities were substandard, and they took action in some cases. In others, however, they deliberately failed to act because: they didn't consider public health a high priority; closing a facility would deny park visitors and employees overnight accommodations within the park and cause a hardship on employees; it would diminish visitor enjoyment; closing the park would be politically unacceptable; concessionaires were responsible for hotels and dormitories; the facilities in question were no more hazardous than other frame buildings.

Some significant measures have been taken in the years following the GAO report. In 1979 the Park Service negotiated a fifteen-year contract requiring the concessionaire at Everglades to spend $1.6 million to improve and rehabilitate facilities. That same year the contract with TW Services at Yellowstone required spending 13 percent of gross receipts for repairs and improvements. The Park Repair and Improvement Program undertaken during James G. Watt's time as secretary of the interior (see chapter 3) was aimed specifically at correcting abundant health and safety hazards. One might ask, however, why such a program should be necessary, why it takes outbreaks of gastrointestinal sickness caused by feces in water and substandard systems to protect public health. With the National Park Service and its concessionaires on duty, which partner is minding the store?

"The National Park Service is 'in charge.' It sets policies and guidelines for both concessions operations and public use. The concessionaires provide the services deemed appropriate by the NPS,"[31] stated Edward C. Hardy, president of Yosemite Park and Curry Company, in 1987. He should know; he directs the largest and most extensive individual concession in the park system: lodgings at twelve locations, thirty places to eat, twenty-four stores, tennis courts, swimming pools, nine-hole golf course, bike rental, river raft rental, garage, service stations, and stables with nearly four hundred horses, ponies, and mules.

The Yosemite concession is a lucrative year-round operation (unlike those in the Rockies, which must make their profits during the short summer season). This helps explain its appeal to the Music Corporation of America, or MCA, the Hollywood entertainment conglomerate that acquired the concession in 1973. At the very outset MCA came on strong with money-making ideas of its own: to attract convention business, build an aerial tramway from the valley floor to the Glacier Point overlook, and replace traditional low-cost accommodations with higher-priced units—at the very time the Park Service was working on a master plan to *reduce* services and facilities in the valley.[32] MCA hired the law firm headed by William Ruckelshaus to represent it in Washington, which gave the appearance of insider wheeling and dealing within the Nixon administration.

Then came the ill-fated television series "Sierra." Universal Studios, an MCA subsidiary, moved a large crew into the park. Ron Walker, director of the National Park Service, raved over the show's potential. Jack Morehead, the chief ranger, who coordinated the park's role with the film people, was also enthusiastic, explaining in the Park Service house organ, the *Courier*, that while "Sierra" wasn't truly factual or authentic, it would bring desirable recognition to the agency. Rangers and other personnel were assigned as technical assistants. Then problems arose. During months of filming, the Universal crew slowed or stopped traffic on the valley floor, angering park visitors; for one sequence rocks were painted—and that set off a furor.

"Ron Walker wanted to show the rangers with white hats, like emergency crews and fire departments," Hardy recalled later. "Writers in Hollywood came up with scripts that were very hokey. It didn't work and it shouldn't have. I didn't see any resistance; the park superintendent, regional director, all of them, were supportive. After the thing flopped it was another story. We were accused of painting the rocks, when actually it was the Park Service that gathered the dust and water to make a paste and paint it on about nine square yards of granite."[33]

The "Sierra" fiasco became part of the dialogue of dissent over the management plan. The first draft had been presented for public comment in 1971, but many objections were raised to the proposed increases in visitor accommodations in Yosemite Valley and Tuolumne Meadows. A revised study in 1974 also generated strong complaints. Environmentalist Democrats in Congress tuned in. They saw visitor facilities in the national parks controlled by a handful of money-minded outfits; besides MCA, TW Services were at Yellowstone, Everglades, Zion, Bryce, North Rim of the Grand Canyon, and Death Valley; AMFAC controlled the old Fred Harvey concession at the South Rim of the Grand Canyon and in Death Valley; ARA was at Mesa Verde and Shenandoah (and later in Denali); GSI, a corporation without stockholders, was at Mount Rainier, Sequoia–Kings Canyon, and the National Capital Region; and National Park Concessions, Inc., controlled Big Bend, the Blue Ridge Parkway, and Mammoth Cave. House hearings in December 1974 conducted by Representatives John Dingell and Henry Reuss fired salvos at the Nixon administration, Director Walker, MCA, and conglomerate concessionaires. The Park Service looked like a weak sister, an outfit easy to manipulate, especially at Yosemite.

Yosemite has been a continual hot spot and the scene of a sequence of fumbling and stumbling without solution to its problems. In 1968 the Park Service eliminated the traditional firefall, begun early in the century by David Curry, but not the attendant traffic jam, nor the chronic congestion problems of Yosemite Valley, barely seven miles long and a mile and a half wide. The wild counterculture July Fourth celebration in 1971 at Stoneman Meadow turned rangers into cops and was subdued only by violence. Perhaps worst of all, many of the rangers liked the idea of being cops, and so did their leaders. As Director Gary Everhardt declared in testimony on March 3, 1975, before a House appropriations subcommittee: "Protection of the visitor can be accomplished only through an aggressive professional law enforcement program." But crowds and congestion still brought problems to Yosemite. An investigation of people working in Yosemite Valley, including personnel of the Yosemite Park and Curry Company, begun in 1981 led to guilty pleas, indictments, and convictions for cocaine dealing.[34]

The fiascos continued. In 1986 the park superintendent, Robert O. Binnewies, was removed after an investigation showed he had secretly tape-recorded a meeting with Charles Cushman, a longtime opponent of Park Service policies on private landholdings within park boundaries. "This action on my part," he confessed, "was a lapse in judgment."[35] Binnewies was replaced by Jack Morehead, the former chief ranger who had advanced through the ranks as superintendent of Isle Royale and Everglades national parks. I was curious to get his retrospective view on "Sierra." Morehead told me that he and other field personnel had wanted to please Park Service director Ron Walker, but the Hollywood hacks had shown little appreciation of the park and needed continual restraint. They wanted female rangers to unbutton their blouses and rangers in uniform beering up at parties. "It failed miserably. I would not do it now."[36] It was another of those "lapses in judgment" which themselves often go unjudged.

Meanwhile, following the 1974 congressional hearings, the planning process began anew as an extensive and serious venture. More than sixty thousand planning kits were distributed for workshops in California and in cities as distant as New York, Washington, and Atlanta. The new Yosemite General Master Plan, completed in October 1980, called for reduction of overnight accommodations by 10 percent and for eventual elimination of automobiles from Yosemite Valley.

Some sections of the master plan have been implemented. The concessionaire moved part of its operation to a new million-dollar supply depot in Fresno, thus reducing its work force and its impact on Yosemite. A concession-operated free shuttle system, bike paths, and a reservation system for accommodations in the valley also help. On the other hand, in late 1987 Superintendent Morehead dismissed other sections of the plan as impractical and unfeasible, justifying construction of new housing units for almost five hundred concession employees, complete with water, sewage, electrical hookups, and parking—contrary to the park plan but wholly compatible with the concessionaire's plan.

"We have basically eighteen hundred employees," Hardy told me in 1985. "If you put them all in cars and commute them back and forth, and tried to have customers do the same, you'd have quite a traffic jam. The staff should be efficient, well trained, and not become commuters." My contacts with Hardy have shown that he is not insensitive to natural values and the responsibility of concessionaires to protect them. As he put it:

> I don't think you can limit the numbers of people, or need to. Where bodies do the most damage is to trample a meadow or misuse their automobiles. The automobile is the toughest management problem. If we manage the automobile, we've dealt with the largest part of the problem. It's difficult to divorce the Californian from his car, but ideally you have him bring it here and then park it. He's given a card on his windshield and he doesn't move that car until he leaves. If he goes to the store, he walks, rides his bike, or rides the shuttle bus. I can foresee alternative fuels for the transit system. Ideally it ought to be electric.
>
> We think MCA's ownership is the best thing that could have happened. I'm looking at funding to preserve and restore historical structures. That takes somebody with large capital. Yosemite has to lead with the most environmentally astute type of structures, with minimum visual impact and a minimum of pollution and consumption. The number of employees is the tail wagging the dog. You've got to start by determining the appropriate services. What do you really need, or want, in Yosemite?[37]

Late in 1990, however, Matsushita, a Japanese electronics giant, announced its plans to acquire MCA, and proceeded to do so (for $6.6 billion). Though the Yosemite Park and Curry Company was only a small part of the MCA package, it attracted the most public attention. Interior Secretary Manuel Lujan led a superpatriotic chorus of opposition to the idea of Japanese interests taking over the national parks, conveniently ignoring both his own responsibility as the administrator who sets the rules and the fundamental issue of whether parks are meant for profit or preservation. MCA/Matsushita saved face for itself and trouble for Lujan by agreeing to sell its possessory interest in Yosemite to the National Park Foundation (which Congress established to funnel private contributions for land acquisition, but essentially an obscure player in the parks scene) for $49.5 million. It also relinquished its preferential right to renew its contract, which runs out in 1993.

What happens then? In 1993 the National Park Foundation will transfer title to the National Park Service, which will choose an operator to lease the concession, somewhat along the lines of TW Services in Yellowstone. One contender will be the nonprofit Yosemite Restoration Trust, which promises to curtail commercial activity in the park. Before the contract is offered, however, the government must attend to the basic question posed by Ed Hardy: "What do you really need, or want, in Yosemite?"

One problem is that, of thirty thousand visitors moving through the park daily, many are part of package-tour groups brought in and shuffled through lodges, restaurants, and shops, lightening purses and billfolds along the way, then shuffled out, having seen little and sensed less of the true grandeur. Moreover, as Alfred Runte, historian and irreverent onetime park interpreter, asks: "How can a national park justify the expansion of barroom facilities precisely at a time when outside the park Mothers Against Drunk Driving, Students Against Drunk Driving, and other groups are campaigning against the disease of alcohol? The Yosemite Park and Curry Company was having 'happy hours,' actually encouraging drinking, with two-for-one drinks between 4:30 and 7:30, describing the drinks as 'cool as the mist of Yosemite Falls.' "[38]

Early one June I heard Hardy speak at a training program for seasonal interpreters preparing for the oncoming summer. I felt that he was forthright with them. Several complained about amplified music disrupting the experience on the Upper Falls Trail. He conceded that they had a valid point, that he shouldn't (as he said) allow amplified music to blare out through Yosemite. But if amplified music is inappropriate on the Upper Falls Trail, is happy hour in the cocktail lounge, with television blaring, any more appropriate?

In the spring of 1987 I stayed at the Yosemite Lodge, a contemporary motel with bar, pool, gift shop, and considerable personnel to run it. It was a pleasant tourist facility, but Yosemite Valley would be better off without it. If that valley was relieved of one-half of its buildings, automobiles, and people, it would become twice the national park it is today. Yet, where the 1980 master plan sought a 17 percent reduction in overnight accommodations, the Curry Company proposed to maintain the total number and replace six hundred simple tent cabins with higher-priced motel units.

In 1990 an enterprising California journalist discovered that the company pays the government a fee of three quarters of 1 percent of its annual gross sales.[39] In 1988 that amounted to $570,774 on gross sales of $76.1 million—a puny pittance for doing business in a national park.[40]

But perhaps profit in itself is not the key issue in assessing concessionaires and their operations; neither, necessarily, are the advent and influence of conglomerates. Some of the big ones, like ARA and TWS, have tried to exercise corporate responsibility and respect for park values. Robert Giersdorf, the principal concessionaire at Glacier Bay in Alaska, has cooperated with local environmental groups and consciously improved his own environmental awareness and involvement. A reasonable profit fairly earned for serving the public is not improper. Hardy pointed to something more fundamental when he said that you've got to start by determining the appropriate services you really need and want.

That's a basic question. And I found a basic answer in the *San Francisco Examiner* of January 21, 1990. "Uproar over Another Look at Yosemite" headlined an article on the new battle over the old master plan. The Park Service had received three thousand letters of comment in a month, the paper reported, including this one from Julie Miller of the Yosemite Institute, a nonprofit environmental education group: "John Muir said, 'Come to the mountains, for here there is rest.' He didn't say it would be in a lodging facility with bath, bar, restaurant, entertainment, bike rentals, ice skating and room service."

Julie Miller, as it happens, is a former student of mine, who studied her lessons and got an A for the course. And she earned it.

11

Crashing through the Snow

I picked up a copy of the lush color brochure provided by TW Services, Inc., the concessionaire, proclaiming Yellowstone as "the world's winter park." The intent, I noted, was not to promote snow camping the old fashioned way, but snowmobiling. Adventurers on snowmobiles were assured they would find Old Faithful a warm home base from which to explore the park's miles of groomed roads, with convenient stops at warming huts along the way. Winter would be hospitable indeed, turning the geyser basins into an otherworldly landscape wreathed with the steam of the bubbling hot pools, hot springs, and spouting geysers. Elk, bison, and other wildlife would be much in evidence, and friendly, often wandering right into the Old Faithful visitor complex for their winter forage. And then, "after a brisk and busy day in the clear winter air, there's a warm fire, a hot drink and a good meal to return to while reliving days that make for years of memories!" And so off I went, from West Yellowstone, "the snowmobile capital of the world," crashing through the snow on my trusty snow machine.

I could proceed with the assurance that national park administrators heartily approved and encouraged me and many others to pursue this form of touring. They used it themselves in their work. In 1973 Superintendent Jack Anderson of Yellowstone National Park received the First International Award of Merit from the International

Snowmobile Industry Association for showing "enlightened leadership and sincere dedication to the improvement and advancement of snowmobiling in the United States."[1]

Three years later, in October 1976, the same industry association issued a report titled *Snowmobiling and Our Environment—Facts and Fancies*, which advised that despite high use levels in some sections of Yellowstone, no significant adverse reactions to snowmobiling had been detected. It quoted Anderson, then recently retired:

> We found that elk, bison, moose, even the fawns, wouldn't move away unless a machine was stopped and a person started walking. As long as you stayed on the machine and the machine was running, they never paid any attention. If you stopped the machine, got off and started moving, that was a different story. The thing that seemed disturbing to them was a man walking on foot.
>
> Now in reference to snowmobile operation infringing upon the intrinsic majesty of the area or threatening the wilderness characteristic of the park, I'd have to say this simply is not the case. I think one of the things the snowmobile did was finally let the people see what a great experience it is to get out in the wintertime and really see the park.[2]

The National Park Service hierarchy in Washington felt much the same. The January 1977 issue of the *Courier* carried the headline "Crashing through the Snow" on its first page, followed by an extensive feature on the endowments of snow machinery. It quoted Yellowstone's chief ranger, Harold Estey: "Snowmobiles are kind of a natural for this part of the country." He was proud that Yellowstone was a leader "to get into the oversnow business." The article also quoted Mac Forsell, chief ranger of Acadia National Park in Maine, who was sure that snowmobiles do not affect wildlife, since (as he said) the wildlife just stays away from the noisy areas.

The "oversnow business" at parks like Yellowstone and Acadia, building alliances with the local tourist industry, has inspired administrators of Voyageurs National Park to follow suit. That particular area along the Canadian border in northern Minnesota comprises the western portion of the wonderful watery wilderness ecosystem that includes the Boundary Waters Canoe Area Wilderness. When the park was established in 1975, the Park Service pledged that its principal objective would be to restore and preserve the wild woodland scene that had greeted the early French voyageurs. Commercial local interests, however, thought they could establish a different kind of area, to be called Voyageurs but administered as Snowmobile National Park. Congress did indeed consider a proposal directing the secretary of the interior to include provisions for winter sports, snowmobiling among them. But conservationists insisted that national parks must not be vulgarized. Sigurd Olson, master outdoorsman and inspirational writer about the north woods, testifying on behalf of the Wilderness Society, declared: "In our opinion, the entire section is at best confusing, at worst inimical to park stewardship. We believe it is neither necessary, desirable nor appropriate and therefore urge its complete removal."[3] Consequently the legislative language was changed: the Park Service could provide for snowmobiling, but it had no mandate to do so.

Nevertheless, Voyageurs today is the most heavily motorized of all national parks, with motorboats on the large lakes in summer and snowmobiles anywhere and everywhere in winter. In 1989 the national park issued a draft trail plan and environmental assessment (as required by the National Environmental Policy Act) proposing construction of snowmobile trails down the length of the Kabetogama Peninsula, the core of the area's remaining wilderness. Environmental groups objected. All the large lakes, they said, already were open to snowmobile use, and snowmobilers can find many trails available to them within easy range outside the park. Besides, the Kabetogama was designed by nature for wolves, which still survive there in one of their last sanctuaries. A new snowmobile trail would only increase poacher access; besides, studies everywhere show that wild animals of all kinds are best left alone and protected during winter.

The park superintendent, Russell Berry, campaigned diligently for snowmobiling. He was supported by his superiors right up the line. Director William Penn Mott, in rejecting an appeal from the Voyageurs Regional National Park Association, cited a congressional reference, in an early report on Voyageurs, to the use of over-the-snow vehicles in other national parks—as though that justified more of same. Mott expressed his personal support on the ground that Congress had allowed snowmobile use "where appropriate."[4] Or, as Berry put it, such mechanized recreation provides "balance." Soon thereafter he was rewarded with promotion to the position of superintendent of Denali, the great wilderness park of the north, while the assistant superintendent of Yellowstone, Ben Clary, another believer in snowmobiling, succeeded Berry at Voyageurs.

Support for snowmobiling is certainly not universal in the agency. In the late 1970s Philip Iverson, superintendent of Glacier National Park, denied snowmobiles access, despite congressional pressure. In the early 1980s Assistant Secretary of the Interior G. Ray Arnett tried to open California parks to snowmobiling, but park officials resisted, and prevailed. Grand Teton National Park has long been a battleground, and it is still the only park in the system where snowmobiles are allowed off established roads, despite efforts by many people inside and outside the Park Service to eliminate them.

In August 1979 the Park Service announced that the contested twenty-thousand-acre Potholes area in the Tetons would be closed to snowmobiles, which would henceforth be confined to unplowed roads, frozen lake surfaces, and other routes used by motorized vehicles in summer. The local chamber of commerce and tourist interests complained, and an ad hoc committee in opposition to the park decision was formed, including former U.S. senator Clifford Hansen and State Senator John F. Turner, a concessionaire in the park (and later appointed director of the U.S. Fish and Wildlife Service during the Bush administration). The protest made its mark in Washington politics: William J. Whalen, then director of the Park Service, after meeting with the Wyoming congressional delegation, reversed the position of his field personnel.[5] The park's chief ranger, chief naturalist, resource management specialist, north district ranger, south district ranger, research biologist, and aquatic biologist vented their distress in a seven-page memorandum to the superintendent dated June 27, 1980, about the sanction of off-road snowmobiling. Research biologist William J. Barmore, Jr., and aquatic biologist Peter S. Hayden wrote further, on July 15, 1980, to the director in Washington, through channels: "We believe the issues raised in our memorandum are not inconsequential in that they involve basic park management philosophy, national park values, and the credibility of the Service."

There is no such problem in Yellowstone. Administrators can say that snow machines are restricted to unplowed roads and other routes used by motor vehicles in summer, and therefore anything and everything must be okay. Nevertheless, in presnowmobile days Yellowstone during winter reverted to its own, affording respite for wildlife. It doesn't require special expertise to recognize winter as the toughest season for animals in the wild. Winter can last from October to June. On a clear, calm night, the temperature may drop to forty or fifty degrees below zero. Elk and bison may be able to forage through snow four feet deep, but in time their reserves must run thin. As snow deepens and crusts with an icy layer, animals turn to thermal areas for the shallow snow, easy walking, and warm ground; they crowd into the valleys to feed on plants preserved beneath the snow and insulated by it. Coyotes and ravens pick the remains of elk, deer, buffalo, and moose, sometimes feeding at the same carcass.

Early in 1985 I took off from West Yellowstone, mounted astride a powerful machine and wearing a big snuggly snowsuit. I had snowmobiled once before, in Utah, and recalled how easy it can be. The snowmobile came complete with hand warmers in the handles, so it was quite cozy. I rode in company with Tom Hobbs, then chief ranger at Yellowstone, starting slowly and gradually increasing speed to fifty miles per hour. Zipping over the snow was fun in itself, I readily concede, but it was impossible to focus on the tiny crystals of ice catching the sun's light, the feathery frost clinging to stalks of grass, the geese, swans, and ducks on unfrozen ponds and streams.

Heading for the center of winter activity at Old Faithful, we passed an enclosed buslike snow coach carrying ten or a dozen passengers, Japanese travel agents on a "fam trip" surveying Yellowstone as a winter market. What, I wondered, could they possibly see of the park? What could they feel of it? What could they tell their clients about it? Moving from one hotel cocktail party to another, as travel agents and writers do on such trips, their exposure can be only superficial; yet they do indeed dispatch cash customers to fill the rooms and "extend the season." We stopped en route at Madison Junction to visit the maintenance shop that houses equipment essential to keeping the park open during winter. These included large tractorlike vehicles that groom snowmobile routes, rolling new snow and smoothing rough spots, dips, and bumps—a generous public service provided by the government.

We stopped again along the road, and Tom endeavored to show that buffalo and people mix without problem. Maybe so, but buffalo trying to cross the road seemed confused by the machines. Here and there a buffalo wanted to rest or sleep in the road, sending a message that contradicted Tom's. I felt like an uninvited guest, arriving at the very time when wildlife is weakest. At the Firehole Bridge a crowd of parked snowmobilers had stopped to observe a bull elk with an impressive six-point rack. But close at hand a yearling bison lay on the ground, its bones bulging through the skin, without enough energy to get up and move. That little buffalo, I thought, deserves to die in peace, without this audience. In short, the animals may appear to accept the intrusion, complete with noises and smells alien to them, but I don't believe it. Appearances alone don't mean that they remain unaffected or unchanged.

I stayed a few days at the Snow Lodge, the concession facility open during the winter in the Old Faithful area, and skied around and above the thermal features. One midday in front of the Snow Lodge I saw a hundred or more snowmobiles arrayed like a military battalion on the move into enemy territory. Their drivers—men, women, and children—paraded in helmets and colorful, bulky winter clothing, as though they had arrived from some "other-worldly" place to annex this wild new land. The "intrinsic majesty" to which Superintendent Anderson referred was effectively transferred from Yellowstone to the machine and machine-people.

The last time I asked, in 1990, snowmobilers totaled more than sixty-five thousand, and numbers were rising annually. It was great for business. "Where else," as they like to ask, "can you snowmobile in three states in one day?"

12   The Silly Souvenirs They Sell

In late 1967 Secretary of the Interior Stewart L. Udall appointed an advisory committee of six citizens, "prominent in their respective fields of endeavor," to review the souvenirs sold by concessionaires in national parks. The secretary asked the committee to recommend a comprehensive program aimed at meeting the reasonable needs of visitors with souvenirs appropriate to the national park environment. The idea of the review had been conceived by George B. Hartzog, Jr., director of the National Park Service, possibly as one way of reining in the concessionaires, but doubtless also in response to criticism of assorted curios and contrivances on sale in the parks.

The agency already had a policy of noble intent, as evidenced in a statement published in the July 1960 issue of *National Parks Magazine*: "The National Park Service recognizes its responsibilities in having the concessioners maintain appropriate standards in the selection of souvenirs and is constantly working with them to eliminate objectionable items from the sales counter displays." A subsequent Souvenir Policy Statement spelled it out: concessionaires were expected to offer items of good taste and high intrinsic value, particularly Indian and other authentic handicrafts associated with and interpretive of the areas where sold. They were allowed to sell machine-made pseudo-Indian merchandise, but it must be displayed separately from the real thing. They were *not* allowed to display or sell animal skins, nor unusual quantities of low-cost novelty souvenirs. Park superintendents were delegated "to determine, evaluate, and insure the suitability, quality, and appropriateness of all such merchandise."

Those pronouncements read well, but only on paper. The concession shops were like novelty stores specializing in trinkets, pulp magazines, and comic books. The gift shop at Canyon Village in Yellowstone carried eight thousand separate items, principally cheap importations from the Far East, including imitation English Wedgewood, Spanish toreador figurines in several colors, bells of Sarna, pine-scented pottery, and bongo drums. At Mount Rushmore National Memorial the mammoth souvenir shop displayed a meager assortment of native handicrafts made by Sioux Indians, but the emphasis was on such items as nylon flags of all nations, Japanese-made plates of President and Mrs. John F. Kennedy, and figurines of Jesus Christ. The shop at Glacier National Park featured animal skins, an ironic memento of a great wildlife sanctuary where hunting is prohibited. The shop was lavishly inelegant, offering sweatshirts imprinted with slogans like "School Drop Out, Flunk NOW, Avoid the Rush," and "I'm an alcoholic. In case of emergency, buy me a beer."

Many superintendents felt (and still feel) the gift shops were beyond their domain. They tolerated the tawdriest trinkets, asserting that souvenir profiteering enabled concessionaires to furnish low-cost lodgings and other less profitable services.

The secretary's Souvenir Committee was expected to provide some positive, palatable compromise for the Park Service and the concessionaires that they had been unable to find on their own. I was appointed as a member; largely, I suppose, because of critical articles I had written. I had also from time to time brought to Washington for exhibit before Director Hartzog and Secretary Udall a collection of souvenirs—"the little chamber of horrors collected at America's shrines"—that made them shudder.

I felt there must be a better way. The superintendent of the Blue Ridge Parkway, Sam P. Weems, had initiated a successful program at Cone Memorial Park, in North Carolina, introducing craftsmen at work with native materials producing native products in an appropriate environment. The program gives visitors an enhanced understanding of the people of the region as well as something worthwhile to take away with them. I could point to the same sort of thing at the craft shops of Colonial Williamsburg in Virginia, which produce and sell attractive items of intrinsic value at moderate prices. I wanted the shops in national parks to be worthy of their settings, like museum shops, and the Park Service and concessionaires to work with crafts groups like the Southern Highland Handicrafts Guild and Indian Arts and Crafts Board (a unit of the Interior Department but detached, luckily, from the inept Bureau of Indian Affairs).

The other members of the Souvenir Committee were Charles Eames, industrial designer, best known for the stylish Eames chair; Stanley J. Goodman, president of the May Company department stores in St. Louis, who chose not to serve; Lloyd Kiva New, a Native American textile designer and director of the Institute of American Indian Arts at Santa Fe; Hilmer Oehlmann, chairman of the Yosemite Park and Curry Company, a well-reasoned concessionaire who served as chairman of the committee; and Paul Phillips, president of the United Papermakers and Paperworkers. The committee convened first in Washington, then made two field trips: to Grand Teton, Yellowstone, Glacier, and Mount Rushmore; and to Yosemite. I was struck by the caution of the park superintendents in any open discussion with concessionaires, and by the congenial hospitality provided by the concessionaires up to the point of discussing their products and profits. For example, Trevor Povah, president of Hamilton Stores in Yellowstone, wined and dined the committee at his ranch home in West Yellowstone, then delivered a stern warning against communistic meddling with the right of free enterprise—which seemed strange considering the socialistic protection he received to do business in a public preserve.

Charles Eames and Lloyd New reached much the same conclusions that I had started with. "Why do you sell this trash to the public that you wouldn't have in your own home?" Eames demanded of John Amerman, president of the Yellowstone Park Company. Amerman tried to brush off the question with a laugh. "Oh well, sometimes you have to sell things or do things you don't believe in." But Eames wouldn't have it. He snorted, "I can't imagine Ansel Adams taking a picture *he* doesn't believe in."

Udall sought to help by waiving concession sales fees on Indian handmade craft items, but that stimulated concessionaires to merchandise carloads of trinkets labeled "Indian," "handmade," and "craft items," which increased their profit and degraded Indian culture. Concessionaires and most of the park people repeatedly gave the same rationale: they could not find local crafts . . . Indian crafts were expensive . . . they needed something inexpensive for children . . . it wasn't fair to dictate public taste. But it all seemed transparent; the bottom line was to maximize profit by cultivating and catering to the lowest common denominator of taste.

The committee chair, Oehlmann, reported to the secretary in a detailed letter dated October 25, 1968. The committee, he wrote, had inspected shops and museums inside the national parks and outside them as well. Conferences with park officials and concessionaires were candid and lively exchanges covering standards of quality, need for guidance, scarcity of appropriate merchandise, massive displays, profitability of souvenir shops, questionable "handcrafted" Indian articles, and crowded sales areas. The committee, wrote Oehlmann, was soberly conscious of the difficulties confronting the Park Service in achieving meaningful improvement. Thus it made various uplifting recommendations about the purpose of souvenirs—what should and should not be sold. Individual members sent supplementary views of their own. Oehlmann felt that some of the judgments against concessionaires were unduly harsh, and he cited substantial progress in cleaning up their act, notwithstanding "the manifest indifference of the principal wholesalers of souvenirs."

Lloyd New commented that some concessionaires offered the cheapest kind of souvenir merchandise in mass displays not in keeping with the general overall standards of a national public institution; some manufactured-by-Indian products were among the worst. Other concessionaires showed quality merchandise in attractive settings, but it was often of foreign origin and unrelated to the visitor's park experience. "The banal aspects of the problem," continued New, "could best be overcome by park superintendents if they would exercise proper supervision of existing policies having to do with the general mission of conservation and interpretation of nature havens. In my opinion no superintendent should have to have it spelled out to him whether a concession is of an acceptable standard or not; this responsibility is no different than others superintendents seem to meet very well."[1]

Eames offered three recommendations: 1 / keep selection and sale of souvenirs entirely separate from the financial problems of running a food and lodging operation in the national parks; 2 / select souvenirs that serve as a reasonable extension of what the national park experience is intended to be; and 3 / see that the park superintendents have a conviction about what the park experience should be to a visitor—and the imagination to recognize how that experience can be extended into the selection of a souvenir. See that certain superintendents have the authority and sense of involvement to enforce their convictions.[2]

My view then (as now) was that a souvenir must have relevance to the mission of the particular park and the National Park Service. No concessionaire needs to duplicate machine-made souvenirs and curios that are available immediately outside a park area. I felt the concessionaires and the National Park Service had let down the children who came into the parks in great numbers with eyes and minds wide open, ready for their first lesson in environmental conservation. As I wrote:

> It's not the volume and variety of merchandise that should count, but the selective quality and what it does to motivate a child to ask and answer questions on his own, such as: What is soil? What is water? What is light? What is a bird? What is a forest? What is a boy in relation to a bird or a wild animal?
>
> Instead, children are offered tawdry playtoys of the lowest order. They are diverted from their true aspiration to listen and learn by drums, tomahawks and assorted other pseudo-Indian fakements produced under the label of various tribes. The names of the tribes have been expropriated by non-Indian entrepreneurs who exploit Indian labor. The native culture and capability deserve better treatment and interpretation in our national parks. . . .
>
> It seems ludicrous to hear a superintendent declare that he hasn't thought much about souvenirs, as though millions of visitors are shopping for them under some other jurisdiction. Every superintendent should be encouraged to develop a usefulness out of souvenirs as part of the interpretive mission of the agency.[3]

The secretary acknowledged the Souvenir Committee report with appreciation; he pledged it would become official policy. Following the election that year, however, Udall departed and it was all filed and forgotten. The following year, when I returned to the parks, little, if anything, was different.

Some improvements have been made over the years. Shops in the parks as a whole sell merchandise of somewhat better quality, but there is still plenty of the old schlock that concessionaires would not have in their own homes. The most significant improvement has come through the growing presence and influence of natural history associations designed to promote historical, scientific, and educational activities in the parks, and to provide funding support for research, interpretation, and conservation programs. These nonprofit associations operate bookstores in the parks; I've never seen a single item on their shelves not in keeping with park philosophy and purpose. For three years during the late 1970s I served as a member of the board of directors of the Great Smoky Mountains Natural History Association, observing (and approving) the allocation of money spent by visitors to enhance the very park where they spent it. For a time the concessionaires complained about the natural history associations poaching on their exclusive preserve. The late 1980s brought peaceful accommodation, but to a preservationist the question still remains: Why assign a parcel of valuable public parkland to the sale of comic books, girlie magazines, and tawdry trinkets for private profit?

13
Conservationists and Compromise

Horace Albright, pioneer and then patriarch of the national park system, appreciated the activity of conservationists and conservation groups, even when he did not agree with them. I can attest that he encouraged me in my work, providing invaluable historic data but always allowing me room to reach an independent conclusion. He never showed resentment when I felt the need to write critically of one aspect or another of his tenure as director or when I disagreed with him on any score.

Horace expressed his viewpoint on the role of conservationists in an essay published in 1957 as the epilogue to *A Contribution to the Heritage of Every American*, by Nancy Newhall. It was a limited-edition book underwritten by the Rockefeller organization to recount the conservation activities of John D. Rockefeller, Jr., whom Horace had long served as an adviser. He recalled in the essay his time with Mather and in Yellowstone, and "the improvising and the stubborn persistence that were necessary to get things done in those days"; things, he said, that could not have been done at all if many Americans had not shared a basic human compulsion to save the country's treasures. He continued: "This mission takes many forms of expression in different individuals. We have had eloquent spokesmen, who have talked and written with great effectiveness of some of the challenges of conservation. We have had men of organizational genius, who have rallied the people of the country in great voluntary associations to answer specific needs. We have had conscientious, perceptive men who have quietly stepped in at critical times and turned the tide when everything seemed to be going against us."[1]

Others in leadership of the National Park Service have felt differently, resenting and rebuffing what they consider meddling in internal professional affairs by unprofessional outsiders. The historic record essentially supports Horace's view, although conservationists are mortal, too, and have not always been the purest of the pure or the wisest of the wise.

Human frailty notwithstanding, citizen concern more than any other force has made and saved the national parks. From the very beginning, and continuing to this day, parks have been established through the efforts and energy of particular individuals and public groups. John Muir not only crusaded to establish Yosemite and Sequoia national parks in 1890 but also sparked a citizen movement leading to the creation of the National Park Service in 1916. George Bird Grinnell is considered the father of Glacier National Park, William Gladstone Steel the father of Crater Lake National Park, and down the line, including mothers of national parks as well—Mrs. Anne M. Davis, associated with the Great Smoky Mountains; Marjory Stoneman Douglas, whose book *River of Grass* gave voice to the Everglades; Peggy Wayburn, Lucille Vinyard, and other wonderful women who fought for the Redwoods. More recently established parks—Great Basin, North Cascades, Redwoods, and lesser-known Obed River and Big South Fork, both wonderful areas in Tennessee—came into being because people outside government campaigned for them. The Alaska Coalition of conservation groups fought for the vast parks in Alaska. Moreover, when officials fail, for whatever reason, to speak in defense of their parks, the citizen advocates are heard from. Muir fought and lost to save Hetch Hetchy Valley in Yosemite from being dammed. Howard Zahniser, David Brower, and others fought and won to protect Dinosaur National Monument from dams. Brower inspired the nationwide effort to block dams at the Grand Canyon. Irving Brant for years tirelessly tracked issues in Olympic National Park to save its rain forests from logging. Harvey Broome and many others living near the Great Smoky Mountains and far from the region stopped the transmountain road which the National Park

Service itself had proposed. These few names represent a citizen movement closely connected with national parks.

Stephen T. Mather, first director of the National Park Service, saw the value of a constituent organization. In 1919, with his own money, he established the National Parks Association "to defend the National Parks and the National Monuments fearlessly against the assaults of private interests and aggressive commercialism" and dispatched Robert Sterling Yard, the publicist of the Park Service and his old crony at the *New York Sun*, as executive director. Trouble developed, however, when Yard became too fearless; he chose an independent course critical of the Park Service over what he considered lowering standards and insufficient emphasis on preservation. Mather was upset and withdrew his support.

Thus conservationists are not automatically or universally appreciated. Conrad L. Wirth welcomed those he considered Constructive Thinkers, Professionals, and Consultants, while shunning the Pests. In his book *Parks, Politics, and the People*, Wirth categorized and described six different kinds of conservationists:

1. *Pests.* Constantly after the government about something of no importance, except to them. Never consistent in their demands. Lack experience, but stick cotton-picking fingers into everything. Hardest to avoid. Last to contribute constructive ideas.

2. *Endrunners.* Always on the job, running to congressman, Interior secretary, governor—anybody in authority—to complain, to ask for overruling an administrator, to request almost anything they think the bureaucrat would not approve.

3. *Followers.* Will sign any petition. Pests and Endrunners circulate petitions for and against projects, and some names will be found on both. Signers just don't think, perhaps don't even read petitions, but simply sign when asked.

4. *Constructive Thinkers.* Usually competent, will study a problem carefully, then offer constructive, helpful suggestions. Invariably kind and courteous, can be reasoned with, understand when told why something cannot be done.

5. *Professionals.* Good to have around. When highly specialized, however, may not understand necessity of blending principles of all professional fields to satisfy requirements and habits of park users while also protecting park features. With a little broader vision, most professionals would fit into next classification.

6. *Consultants.* Based on experience, study and observation can analyze a problem from many angles, thus willing to help work out plans for solving it. While consultant's analysis may differ from the administrator's, he introduces new thoughts worth considering, with positive effect on final solution.[2]

The most pestiferous conservationist during Wirth's time as director was Devereux Butcher, executive secretary of the National Parks Association and editor of *National Parks Magazine.* Much like his predecessor, Robert Sterling Yard, Butcher conceived the parks as preserves where natural systems prevail. He at first supported Mission 66, Wirth's ten-year park improvement program, as an opportunity to remove hotels and lodges without building new ones. Instead, Mission 66 *expanded* the carrying capacity of the parks while doing little for plants and animals. (Between 1955 and 1974 park visitation more than tripled.)[3] Butcher became extremely critical and left the association in 1959. For several years he published *National Wildland News,* "an independent newspaper dedicated to the preservation of national parks, monuments and wildlife refuges as sanctuaries."

In the first issue Butcher lamented construction of the resort at Flamingo in the Everglades, asserting it would have been better to locate sleeping and eating accommodations at the park's entrance, a site better protected from hurricanes, and to limit development at Flamingo to a modest interpretive building, snack bar, small dock, and launches for guided naturalist cruises. Less than a year later, in September 1960, Hurricane Donna left Flamingo almost a total wreck. The *New York Times* (September 18) reported: "The storm gutted almost all the buildings, leaving only the walls standing. Both the marina and the motel must be rebuilt." The *Miami Herald* said the marina was destroyed beyond recognition, leading the November *National Wildland News* of that year to headline "Another Opportunity in Everglades" and urge elimination of "a big yachting-fishing resort of the kind that are a dime a dozen in Florida"; but the Park Service rebuilt the whole thing. Butcher wrote a book, *Exploring Our National Parks and Monuments,* in the eighth edition of which (1985), he included a chapter, "Threat After Threat," with sections on "dam building," "road building," "increasing misuse of the parks," "national parks in name only," "architecture gone wild," and "menace of inholdings."[4]

In 1987 I received a letter from Butcher detailing "infringements on national park integrity." Though no longer organizationally involved, he remained personally concerned; his deep, desperate caring for the parks remained undiminished. Among issues of concern Butcher listed the misuse of the Grand Canyon by sightseeing planes and helicopters; the entry into Glacier Bay each summer of large cruise ships and countless smaller craft, affecting humpback whales and other aquatic wildlife; hang gliding in Yosemite; downhill skiing in various parks; snowmobiling, "whose incessant noise shatters the peace and quiet visitors come to enjoy"; and hunting. With reference to the last issue, Butcher cited the precedent of opening Grand Teton to elk shooting on the grounds that it would help reduce the size of the southern Yellowstone elk herd: "When the park was opened for this purpose, it was said the practice would be terminated when the herd had been sufficiently reduced, but after more than thirty years there is not the least sign of any intention of putting an end to the shooting. What is worse, it has served as a precedent not only to open more Park Service areas to shooting, but to devise an entirely new land category to be called 'national preserves,' areas often adjoining national parks which are to be open to sport shooting—and these in care of the National Park Service!" He had it all down, with feeling, in words scarcely heard from officials of the agency. Butcher was like a precursor of that irreverent, free-lance conservationist Edward Abbey, who years later wrote in *Desert Solitaire* his ode to raw, undiluted natural beauty: "No more cars in the national parks. Let the people walk. Or ride horses, bicycles, mules, wild pigs—anything—but keep the automobiles and motorcycles and all their motorized relatives out."

As a confirmed individualist, Abbey was free to speak his piece. David Brower, as executive director of the Sierra Club, didn't have that freedom, but he preempted it anyway to make major contributions to the cause of national parks. On Wirth's list Brower might not be a Pest; he might be an Endrunner (always on the job, running to anybody in authority—and more besides), but he definitely was not a Constructive Thinker (invariably kind and courteous, can be reasoned with). Curiously, the first time I met Brower I was with Wirth.

It was in the mid-1950s in Washington, D.C. I had invited the parks director to lunch at the National Press Club to hear his boss, Secretary of the Interior Douglas McKay. Wirth asked if he could bring along a guest from California. It was Brower: tall, handsome, reserved, aloof, on guard, as though distrusting the whole scene. In retrospect, I can understand his behavior then—I still worked for the American Automobile Association, a highway lobby—but in the thirty-five years since then, after speaking on the same program at least half a dozen times, sitting next to him at dinners, next to him on an airplane at least once, and hosting him overnight in my home, I find him to be much the same, a man of singular achievement based on principle, but without personal warmth. Once I shared this view with Brock Evans, who worked as northwest regional representative of the Sierra Club and then as vice president of the National Audubon Society. "I understand," he said. "Dave hired me. I worked with him closely for years, but never knew him."[5]

Another friend, Martin Litton, saw Brower as so consumed with the next crusade that he didn't have time for small talk with mere mortals. Brower became executive director of the Sierra Club in 1952, when it was still essentially oriented toward outdoor recreation. In those days you didn't apply to join the Sierra Club, you were properly invited. Brower changed the club into the militant environmental vanguard of the postwar period. Martin Litton, then on the editorial staff of *Sunset* magazine, became a board member in 1964 and was irreverent as well as militant. "The knowledge of the board members was so fuzzy and thin they didn't even know where the Grand Canyon was," Martin would say later in reflecting on the approval by some of his colleagues of proposed dams in the canyon.[6]

The idea was to build two dams, neither actually in the national park but both too close for comfort. The upstream dam would have been 60 miles below Glen Canyon Dam, but inside Marble Canyon National Monument; the other was to be 200 miles downstream at Bridge Canyon, near the point where the Colorado River flows into Lake Mead—both together flooding 146 miles of the Colorado River and the bottom six hundred feet of much of the Grand Canyon. It was an engineer's delight designed by the Bureau of Reclamation, an agency of the Interior Department commanding bigger bucks and therefore more political punch than the National Park Service.

The bureau had lately, in 1963, closed the floodgates on Glen Canyon Dam, submerging a wild desert of sandstone cliffs and beautiful side canyons beneath a flat-water reservoir called Lake Powell. The threat to violate the Grand Canyon as well was too much to take. On June 9, 1966, the Sierra Club published a full-page advertisement in the *New York Times* and *Washington Post*, written in commanding and eloquent language, urging public opposition. One day later the Internal Revenue Service warned the Sierra Club that its tax-exempt status was in jeopardy for lobbying. The club defiantly placed another advertisement headlined "Should We Also Flood the Sistine Chapel So Tourists Can Get Nearer the Ceiling?"

"The weakness of the arguments in favor of the dams," wrote Morris K. Udall in his book *Too Funny to Be President*, "was borne home to me the day I had to debate David Brower—as clever, tough, and tenacious an opponent as you could want—in front of a gaggle of national press at the worst possible venue: *the rim of the Grand Canyon*." Udall was then a young Arizona congressman doing what was necessary to stay in office. I was there and observed that Brower, with a strong cadre of vocal supporters, controlled the show. Udall had a hard time speaking. "This was a tough assignment," his narrative continues, "comparable to debating the merits of chastity in Hugh Hefner's hot tub in front of an audience of centerfold models, and me being on the side of abstinence."[7]

In Udall's view, the conservationists' victory in stopping the Grand Canyon dams marked a turning point in American history: from then on, those big-bucks projects would not be taken for granted. It was Brower's doing; not his alone, but he sparked the public outcry that turned the tide. In the process, however, he upset Sierra Club directors. They disliked his uncompromising challenge of government officials, agencies, and scientists. Boards of directors, even of conservation groups, often are composed of reasonable, wholly respectable people. Some directors, like Litton, are crusaders steeped in their subjects. Others, however, don't go around looking for fights; they gravitate to the lesser of evils. In 1949, while considering the issue at Dinosaur National Monument, Sierra Club directors were willing to accept one dam rather than two; at one point they were willing to accept dams in the Grand Canyon if the Bureau of Reclamation first built other, smaller dams to retain silt and then built recreation facilities on the reservoirs. In these and other cases Brower insisted on holding tight, building support, and letting someone else propose the compromise.

The directors felt he was emotional, irresponsible, and insubordinate. Brower took the limelight; they were left out. He published classic books on one endangered place after another, but the books didn't make money, and the directors didn't like that either. In 1969 Brower resigned and established Friends of the Earth, where ultimately similar problems arose, leading to a second departure.

The Sierra Club has grown steadily in membership, though not in militancy. It has lost the cutting edge. The old *Sierra Club Bulletin* is now the glitzy, slick *Sierra*, lush with color and loaded with ads merchandising high-tech products for upscale yuppies.

The National Parks Association went through its own metamorphosis. Devereux Butcher was succeeded by Fred Packard, who toned things down and sought to help rather than harass the Park Service leadership. When he left in 1958, Anthony Wayne Smith, a tough labor lawyer, took over. He was strong on park issues but ran a one-man show, refusing to tolerate dissenting views from his staff or directors. Despite an effort to broaden the organization's base by changing its name to National Parks and Conservation Association, membership declined. After considerable internal acrimony, Smith left in 1980. His successor, Paul C. Pritchard, who had worked in government during the Carter administration, picked up the pieces and put them together, rebuilding the association in membership and influence.

Many conservation leaders tend to think in the realm of the possible, the attainable. They would rather build bridges than barricades. During the Carter presidency, for example, they were more than tolerant, more than hopeful; they were generous to a fault on the president's behalf. "It looks amazingly good," wrote Michael McCloskey, of the Sierra Club, in reviewing Carter's first year. "There are a few disappointments, but the overall record is good enough to cause environmentalists to regard the future with relish, instead of the gloom of previous years."[8] Carter's completion of his second year in office in early 1979 became the occasion for renewed adulation. At a Washington press conference, spokesmen for environmental organizations pronounced the president's performance "outstanding." A joint statement declared: "His efforts, supported by environmental leaders in Congress, have renewed our commitment as a nation to cleaning up our air and water and to protecting our natural land heritage."[9]

The groups sounded the same when speaking on their own. "The aspirations toward greatness which President Carter voiced after his election may find their fulfillment first of all in the environmental field," wrote Anthony Wayne Smith in *National Parks Magazine*.[10] The halo glowed over others as well. "The first two years of your administration," David Brower and Chuck Williams of Friends of the Earth wrote to Interior Secretary Cecil D. Andrus in January 1979, "have been one of the brightest spots in the history of the National Park System."

That is not the way I saw it. In two years under Carter and Andrus, the department, without public notice, opened the parks to mineral exploration by the Department of Energy, though parks are expressly protected by law; approved expansion of the airport terminal at Grand Teton National Park, when the whole airport should be closed; elected to build roads "to provide easy access to outstanding viewing areas" in Canyonlands National Park, rather than safeguarding wilderness; and gave its blessing to snowmobiling, the mechanized intrusion against defenseless nature.

True, Carter and Andrus did their bit on behalf of resources in Alaska; but as Aldo Leopold said, "There seems to be a tacit assumption that if grizzlies survive in Canada and Alaska, that is good enough. It is not good enough for me. Relegating grizzlies to Alaska is about like relegating happiness to heaven; one may never get there." Under Carter and Andrus, wildlife programs bogged down in politics and bureaucratic inertia. Programs for whales, elephants, grizzly bears, and endangered species were lost in the shuffle to look good.

In 1985 the National Audubon Society, Sierra Club, and Wilderness Society all were shopping for new executive directors. Those organizations were at mid-life, facing a marked transformation from volunteer effort to multi-million-dollar business enterprise. They hired professional search companies to find new executives. They were looking for leaders strong in finance and budgets, management specialists—and willing to pay high prices, in the $90,000-plus level. They had grown away from the grass roots to mirror the foxes they'd been chasing.

The Wilderness Society, as a case in point, was conceived in Tennessee during a meeting of like-minded people, including Robert Marshall, Benton MacKaye, and Harvey Broome, who shared a concern over New Deal programs to build highways in the Great Smokies and other Eastern mountains. Aldo Leopold, who had seen national forest wilderness disturbed and destroyed, joined the group soon after, and then so did Olaus J. Murie, the respected field biologist. Robert Sterling Yard in 1935 became the part-time executive secretary (and later president) of the Wilderness Society while continuing his association with the National Parks Association. Following Yard's death in 1945 (at the age of eighty-four), Olaus Murie became director, based in Wyoming, and Howard Zahniser, formerly a government editor, became executive secretary, based in Washington. Zahniser, or "Zahnie," was the principal author of the Wilderness Act of 1964. He was studious, soft-spoken, patient, always willing to listen, always resisting the seduction of compromise. But both Murie and Zahniser died within a year before the act was passed.

Stewart Brandborg, Zahniser's deputy and protégé, succeeded him. "Brandy" had grown up with the great Idaho-Montana wilderness as his backyard and studied wildlife management before coming East. He was a go-getter, at the center of conservation activism, who cultivated the political power of the grass roots to influence decision making in Washington. His door was open to little people from frontier towns coming to the big city with an issue that seemed obscure to everybody but them. He patiently cultivated and enlightened media people. Brandborg was fundamentally earthy, and never snobbish. At a congressional hearing I heard him say, "We have had plenty of documentation—and too many symposia—in which the intellectually elite gather together, bathe in their own erudition, and generously document the case of the environmental degradation to show that the world is going to hell. We are now ready to get down to the grassroots with meaningful programs to show people how to become responsibly involved."[11]

But like Brower, Brandborg learned, painfully, the difficulties in dealing with a board, budget, members, other organizations, bureaucrats, and politicians. Following internal hassles he was dismissed in January 1976. Two years later, following interim leadership, a whole new era began with the arrival of William Turnage, who presently was named president, cleaned house of the old staff, and made clear that earthiness was out and urbanity was in. Turnage had studied at

Yale and Oxford, worked for the State Department, then became business manager for Ansel Adams, the celebrated photographer. Everything about the society went upscale. People who worked for Turnage have told me about the fancy sterling silver tea set he had in his office. He would ring a little silver bell and his executive assistant would come in and prepare the imported tea—the water exactly the right temperature, a certain number of sugar cubes; if it was done at all wrong, he rejected it. It was a system that worked, in its own way, for Turnage brought in large grants and gifts, and attracted Gaylord Nelson, a former senator from Wisconsin, to come aboard as spokesman for the society.

When the Wilderness Society marked its fiftieth anniversary in 1984, Stephen Fox, a conservation historian, contributed a lengthy essay on its history to *Wilderness*, the society's quarterly publication. Brandborg received short shrift. His critics, wrote Fox, felt he operated at too feverish an emotional pitch, turning even routine matters into crises; he emphasized Alaska, while some of the society's Western field staff wanted to pay more attention to de facto wilderness areas in their own part of the country; he ran large annual deficits.

Turnage, on the other hand, was depicted as an intrepid outdoorsman and fearless leader. "When I'm in the mountains the feelings are, I think, strongly religious—with a small *r*. I am almost overwhelmed—indeed, I feel as though I'm in the proverbial throne room of the mountain gods," Fox quoted Turnage as saying, then added, "He has no tolerance for fools and an absolute passion for excellence."[12]

In June 1979 Turnage assembled eight or ten of the regional field representatives of the society to a rendezvous in California. This revealing little episode has not been recorded in *Wilderness*. The "reps" were holdovers imbued with a wilderness mission who worked without complaint for low pay. They were woodsy, rough-and-ready, and not Turnage's type. One or two had already quit or been fired, and the ax clearly was ready to fall on others. They insisted on a backpack of at least one night in the Sierra Nevada. Jim Eaton, the California representative, who lived in his pickup with his celebrated dog Stikeen, wanted them to see the proposed Granite Chief Lakes Wilderness (a national forest area), and they headed up the trail for the site, a little more than three miles away. The ground was still covered with snow and Turnage expressed a desire to sleep indoors. He and Chuck Clusen, of the Washington office, observed a Sierra Club cross-country ski cabin along the way and announced they would go there after supper.

Presently the group arrived at the lake, pitched tents, and started cooking. Turnage had brought a six-pack of Perrier water with him to avoid drinking water out of a stream or lake. He set up his stove and pulled out his tea bag. It was imported tea in a cheesecloth bag. "Cheesecloth tea bags!" exclaimed Dave Foreman, the New Mexico field rep. "My God!" echoed Dick Carter, of Utah. "Leave it alone. Cool it," pleaded Eaton. But it was too late.

Foreman, irreverent and independent, had had enough. He felt the national conservation groups, including the Wilderness Society, had turned tame, corporate, and compromising. They were professionalized by Ivy Leaguers who were career oriented and concerned with perks, benefits, and status, had never been hungry and never slept outdoors (not, at least, without high-tech gear); they were raging moderates, replacing activism and ethics with pragmatic politics, willing to settle for paper victories. Foreman erupted.

From his backpack he brought out a large steak he had planned to cook, sat down next to Jim Eaton's big black Labrador retriever, and ridiculed Turnage. Despite the cold weather, he ripped off his coat, then his shirt. He shouted about the challenge of being rugged in wilderness and the wimpiness of bringing Perrier, imported tea, and staying in a hut. Turnage stood his ground and argued. "I've had it," shouted Foreman. "We're going to be men around here." He rubbed the greasy steak over his chest, across his face, in his hair. He ripped off a piece of the raw meat and chewed it. He took another piece and gave it to Stikeen. He and Stikeen shared bite after bite.

Turnage watched in dismay. He stood up, looked around the camp in disbelief, packed his pack, and he and Clusen went off down the trail. They hiked back up the next morning. It was the last time the old reps were together; that was the end of it.[13]

Foreman resigned early in 1980. He rejected a vision defined by the modern corporate state, complete with throwaway culture, nuclear dependency, and wilderness in compartmentalized parcels. The defiant stand was in keeping with his past.[14] He had started as a high school Republican campaigning for Barry Goldwater as president because he rejected government paternalism, and bigness in general. As a student at the University of New Mexico he campaigned for no grades, no compulsory class attendance, no dorm hours. After graduation he joined the Marines but rejected the discipline. He returned for graduate work in biology but objected to killing and pickling snakes and lizards and turned to saving wilderness instead. After placing the Wilderness Society behind him, he and like-minded spirits organized Earth First!, not an organization but a movement based on "no compromise in the defense of Mother Earth." With inspiration from the words and person of Edward Abbey, Earth Firsters adopted monkey-wrenching: spiking trees and roads, burning bulldozers, dismantling billboards, disabling helicopters. At Fishing Bridge in Yellowstone they paraded dressed as grizzly bears, then entered a restaurant and demanded trout because their habitat had been destroyed. They held a funeral procession on the twentieth anniversary of Glen Canyon Dam. In Idaho, where conservation groups asked for protection of three to four million acres of unclassified national forest wilderness, Earth First! demanded all nine million acres and restoration of more besides. The Earth First! movement put important issues on the front pages and nightly news shows. It made some people mad at the mischievous radicals, but it made others wonder what it was all about.

What is it about? I think it's about laws that don't work, that lull the public into complacency; laws like the National Environmental Policy Act, Clean Air Act, Endangered Species Act, and Surface Mining Act; laws of illusions that regulate, manage, control, and legitimize with "health standards" and "acceptable risks" and "legislative guidelines" and "timetables" and "variances." It's about the jargon of the bureaucracy and allied professionals, keeping the experts paid and busy with "risk assessment" and "citizen involvement" that scarcely genuinely involves citizens. It's about trade-offs and compromises when there is less and less of the earth to trade and give away.

I see the same in other social issues. Under Nixon, arms "control" in the form of SALT I produced multiple warheads and MIRV; under Ford and Carter it was SALT II, with cruise missile technology. "Realists" focused on "bilateral" agreements with the Soviet Union. "Freeze" in the 1980s compensated for approval of the latest nuclear weapons, while disarmament and challenges to U.S. military intervention overseas were obscured. In civil rights, most mainstream civil rights organizations concentrated on working inside the courts and Congress, cautioning against militant nonviolent action. Yet it was just such action, in Alabama, that enabled the civil rights movement to achieve historic breakthroughs.

On January 18, 1975, I was at a conference in Washington, D.C., initiated by the Coalition against Strip Mining and the Environmental Policy Center. Even while the meeting was under way, a staff person working for Ken Hechler, a congressman from West Virginia, walked around the hall distributing copies of a handwritten note and mimeographed statement. Hechler was a rare breed of congressman—literate, high-minded, and independent. His message included the following:

> RED ALERT: It is URGENT that the opposition to strip mining be *forcefully* communicated not only to Congress, but also to your own people in EPC and the Sierra Club who have been waffling in their opposition to strip mining.
>
> My people in West Virginia, and people throughout the nation, are getting more cynical about compromising politicians, Washington environmental groups that settle for the lowest common denominator, and those who enjoy the transient glory of winning a few commas or semi-colons while the people and the land continue to be exploited and destroyed. . . .
>
> You are now being asked to work for a regulatory bill which is actually weaker than the state laws of Ohio, Pennsylvania and Montana. Time after time, the leadership of the environmental groups here in Washington has succumbed to the temptation to move farther and farther away from abolition, to compromise and weaken their position before it was strategically necessary, and to enable the coal exploiters to move the whole forum of debate progressively and inexorably toward greater freedom to exploit. . . .
>
> I can understand the victory light which attracts the moths who demonstrate their lobbying sure-sightedness by flying toward the sweet and bright majority. I can appreciate the desperate desire to register the undeniable fact that something is assuredly superior to nothing. But in your actions and decisions, measure carefully how much you are really protecting your people, rather than how much may be temporarily expedient.
>
> In politics, one cannot court defeat. A little over ten years ago, I cast the worst vote in my life in support of the Gulf of Tonkin Resolution, which carried by 414-0 in the House of Representatives.

They said it was useless to oppose it. How silly would a few scattered votes have looked then, yet events have proven they would have been tremendously effective. . . .

Let's show the people we represent that we *demand* the right solution. Don't let anybody sell you any more lowest common denominators.

With reference to national parks, David Brower would feel that way, and so would Stewart Brandborg, and, to be sure, so would Devereux Butcher, Edward Abbey, David Foreman, John Muir, and Robert Sterling Yard—that demanding the right solution is better than buying into any more lowest common denominators. Abraham Lincoln had a word or two for it. "The probability that we may fail in the struggle," he wrote, "ought not to deter us from the support of a cause we believe to be just."

Horace Albright would see things differently, preferring dialogue, persuasion, and goodwill. Nevertheless, he recognized the material support to conservation projects given by many citizens through voluntary association. He urged wider involvement of "citizens who will take the trouble to inform themselves of new needs and weak spots in our conservation program."[15] The national parks and National Park Service would be lost without demands that they rise above the lowest common denominator.

14   Regreening the National Parks

I PROPOSE to close Yellowstone National Park for five years to automobile traffic.

Let visitors enter on foot or shuttle bus, maybe not even shuttle bus. Use that period to develop a whole new system of circulation, and to decide how the park should really be used, based on respect and veneration for Yellowstone as a sacred place. But that's only the first step in regreening the national parks.

I PROPOSE to eliminate half the overnight facilities in Yosemite Valley, and all the automobiles.

That's for John Muir, who lamented allowing those "blunt-nosed mechanical beetles" to puff their way into the valley and mingle their gas breath with the breath of pines and waterfalls.

I PROPOSE to close the transmountain road across the Great Smoky Mountains and by so doing make the wonderful wilderness of southern Appalachia whole again.

In the regreening process the administration of every park will focus on the mountains, canyons, glaciers, forests, prairies, songful rivers, and the natural life systems they support. Their welfare will come first, before commerce and crowds. The same principle will apply to the national historic and prehistoric sites; Americans will learn at last to walk lightly over the dead and to treat the ancient battlefields and structures of mud, brick, and stone as documents in trust.

Regreening won't be easy. The most devastating disruptions of park values, whether from within or externally, are commercial in nature. They manifest themselves in politics, but politicians generally are limited to short-term vision, extending to the next election rather than the next century. They ask: How many visitors did the park attract last year? How much money did they spend with the businesses in my communities? Why does the superintendent consider wilderness instead of facilities and access?

Years ago the National Park Service built a reputation as a bureau powered by professional ethics, free of political pressures. This is no longer the case. Democratic and Republican administrations alike and congressional power brokers have politicized the agency, influencing personnel selection and treating the parks like political pork. The National Park Service has caved in and lost its sense of mission, its commitment to protect national parks in perpetuity.

Compromise of principle with expediency is no way to run national parks. Regreening will bring a catharsis to the bureau, transforming it from a part of the problem to a leader in effecting the solution. It will refocus the entire organization, top to bottom, in a way that reestablishes professionalism, justifies public trust, and ensures the highest level of stewardship.

Regreening is demanding and unending, for one challenge leads to another. The future of the national parks will never be established, the parks will never be secure, until the country recognizes and corrects the wrongness of its old national agenda. Experts may argue the need of a better park science program or a better fire policy or better elk management or emphasis on interpretation or more funding for more parks, but those are surface concerns. America needs to dig deeper to reexamine goals and institutions. America needs to reclaim its wholeness in order to save its best parts.

Eddie Sue Judy, a prize student in my History 404 class at the University of Idaho, made that point clear to me. I tried to interest her in national parks history, but she had her mind set on Native Americans. We agreed, at least, that for her term paper Eddie Sue would discuss the question Why don't Indians go to national parks? But that wasn't the focus of her paper at all. It was only the title and opening line, a starting point to consider a larger issue about America and Americans that she insisted we both face.

Yellowstone in 1877, wrote Eddie Sue, was five years old as a national park, but already well traversed by tourists. They were not the only ones in the park. Their pleasures in the "pleasuring ground" were disrupted by hundreds of Nez Percé Indians, followers of Chief Joseph, on the prowl. The Indians had been dispossessed from their ancient homeland along the Idaho-Oregon border. They had come from the fierce two-day battle in Big Hole Valley in southwestern Montana, where many of their women and children were slain, and they were in Yellowstone on their epic attempt to reach freedom in Canada.

In the first flush of white settlement, the Nez Percé, like other native people, living as God made them, had wished for peaceful coexistence. But they stood in the way of the Brave New World, in which everything, even the earth, became a commodity. The government's solution to the "Indian problem" was the reservation system, which provided places where aborigines could be Christianized, civilized, and eventually merged into the American melting pot. The Nez Percé in the process were denied much of their homeland. Although President Grant in 1873 had designated a portion of the Wallowa Valley as a reservation, Governor L. F. Grover of Oregon forced a reversal with a tough letter of protest: "If the [white] families should be removed to make roaming ground for nomadic savages, a very serious check will be given to the growth of our frontier settlements, and to the spirit of our frontier people in their efforts to redeem the wilderness and make it fruitful for civilized life."[1]

Those who lived on reservations found themselves impoverished and their lifeways drastically changed, yet reservations became islands in the white tide where Indians could remember they were Indians. In that way, wrote Eddie Sue, they were similar to the parks, refuges where wild things could still live wild. And then to her main point regarding the 1870s: "It signified a juncture of two important themes: removal of Indians to reservations and withdrawal of parcels from the public domain for 'pleasuring grounds' and protection of natural wonders. Dispossessing native peoples and preserving native splendors might seem contradictory, but both policies had roots in a common national agenda and produced a common effect. They isolated tiny islands in a country created whole, and rendered the vast majority of remaining land fair game for pell-mell exploitation."

I remember also, when I was a columnist for *Field & Stream*, a reader writing to me in anguish, "Have we so much of earth that we can afford to sacrifice any part of it?" Those words make me continually aware of oil spills, nuclear disasters, release of toxic wastes, destructive dams and roads—plus the assorted external and internal threats to national parks—as symptoms of the larger issue. A national park is part of the world around it, and the futures of both are tied together.

Early in these pages I wrote that our supercivilization is troubled by pollution, overpopulation, corruption, and violence, to such a degree that a woman cannot hike alone safely in a national park and that the rangers must be police as well. Let me add now that it isn't even safe to be a ranger.

"Rangers Boost Firepower as Violence Rises" read a headline in the *Denver Post* of July 3, 1989. The article beneath it reported that rangers were ordered to replace their .38-caliber revolvers with .357 revolvers, providing them with nearly twice the stopping power. The change came after three separate incidents in four months, in which rangers shot and killed assailants who had tried to kill them. Assaults on rangers, the newspaper reported, rose sharply from thirty-one in 1986 to eighty-six in 1988. Some rangers, in fact, wanted Congress to give them a twenty-year retirement option similar to those already granted to agents of the FBI, Secret Service, and Border Patrol (instead of waiting thirty years or reaching the age of sixty-five). That is how it goes with the "new ranger," better oriented to law enforcement than to resource protection.

The answer is regreening the parks as the start to regreening America. Senator Harry Flood Byrd of Virginia understood and loved national parks. He was a conservative in all things, yet a political green. "I know that in them is to be found some of the most beautiful scenery in the world," Byrd declared on the Senate floor in 1963. "Through these areas the government is engaging in the highly constructive service of preserving and interpreting great scenic, scientific, and historic assets of our people." These noble thoughts are not much expressed in our time. Congress and the whole federal government have gone stale on the treasures of America that they are charged with protecting. Little wonder that everything down the line has changed and slipped, reaching to field personnel carrying guns instead of the dreams of John Muir.

Regreening will kindle new recognition of public parklands as precious places. Whether administered by city, county, state, or federal government, whether covering half a block in the heart of an urban community or ten million acres above the Arctic Circle in Alaska, public parkland provides an outlet for physical, emotional, artistic, spiritual, aesthetic, and intellectual senses. There is really no way to place a dollar value on a "park experience." I visualize a park as an art form in itself, with the land base as the canvas and each person free to express himself or herself as long as he or she does not damage the resource or disturb or harm others. Disneyland and other "theme parks" serve different purposes; they make their profits as entertaining popcorn playgounds. But public parks, like art galleries, theaters, museums, and libraries, enlighten and elevate individuals who come to them—they enrich society in immeasurable ways.

Each little bit of preserved nature serves its purpose. Nature belongs where people live, as part of life. The more of it in city, county, and state parks, the better the quality of community life. Nonetheless, a national park is a different kind of park. National parks approach the last representation of primeval life—to the degree possible within the artificial boundaries by which most park units were established. In a setting free of human intervention, the visitor absorbs the "feel" of nature—of plants, animals, and natural features—and the "weathering of the land" by winds, rivers, and other geological forces. Intangible values should prevail, and regreening will restore them. Beauty, timelessness, solitude, silence, harmony, awareness, simplicity, freedom, balance, and order are the essences of humanity. The national park will stimulate questions deeper than When does Old Faithful erupt? Where is the best fishing? Where is the nearest beer? Rather than seek the excitement of snowmobiling in Yellowstone, rock climbing in Yosemite, rafting the Colorado River in the Grand Canyon, or helicoptering over the Na Pali coast in Hawaii Volcanoes National Park, the green visitor will search for undisturbed beauty and the serenity of wild places, in the spirit of John Muir.

From Mission 66 to the present, visitor comfort, facilities, and enjoyment have received a higher priority than protection and perpetuation of the natural systems. There are too many people in the parks at a given time, spending only hours where they should spend days learning to appreciate and understand the natural systems, and themselves in the process of doing so. Too much space is given to large luxury vehicles complete with water systems, electrical hookups, and their own TV sets. That must change. Considering that we need a revolution of ideas and ideals for all of society, the regreened national parks are marvelous places to begin. Every park is full of lessons to help in the transformation from the Age of Greed and Corruption to the Age of Caring and Integrity. For example, in 1893, when Gifford Pinchot, the youngest member of the National Forest Commission, went to the Grand Canyon, John Muir became his companion. And when Pinchot prepared to kill a tarantula, Muir stopped him with soft, strong words. "It has as much right here as you have."

Let us appreciate anew the rights of the tarantula, the rights of all wild creatures, and the rights of trees and plants—all of them, including those derided in the controlled human environment as weeds. In the primeval landscape, all life is free and purposeful. Often I'm reminded by experts of imperfections in what I see to be wild, as a consequence of human intervention and influence ("the Indians deliberately set fires, you know"), but that's all the more reason to leave it be. Where better than a national park for the earth to restore itself?

The National Park Service, as we know it now, cannot provide the necessary leadership. The influence of the director has steadily declined; he follows orders from assorted political supernumeraries in the Interior Department. Consequently, the Park Service fails to speak on issues that degrade the parks; it pussyfoots around the issues and answers in cautious, politically acceptable terms. The bureau has lost professional stature and its respect in resource management, historic preservation, and park management. It postures and plans, but the plans go on the shelf, to be updated with more posturing a few years later. It dreads opening the planning process to full public participation and the accountability attendant to the process.

The bureau hierarchy dreads the input of its own people. When I interviewed Gary Everhardt, the former director, at Waynesboro, Virginia, in 1985, he volunteered his views on whistleblowing: "I just don't believe in it. My approach is, 'If you've got a problem, come talk to me about it. We'll resolve it.' Whistleblowing generates a way of saying, 'Well, I'm going to squeal on you but I don't have to be confronted with it.' I think the accuser ought to stand up and confront the person he's talking about. These people don't seem to be responsible for their actions."

But the concerned employee has the legal right to "go public" when he or she feels that internal channels are inadequate. As the Civil Service Reform Act of 1978 stipulates, employees are free to make public without reprisal, or fear of reprisal, information concerning acts or failures to act by their employer which they believe harmful to the public interest. And the Code of Ethics for Government Service opens with a declaration that "any person in government service should put loyalty to the highest moral principles and to country above loyalty to persons, party or government department."

Regreening the national parks begins with regreening the National Park Service. That is where I list it in the ten-point program that follows.

1. Encourage all employees of the National Park Service to contribute consciously and conscientiously to making parks into genuine demonstration models of ecological harmony. Open channels to better internal communication, free of intimidation and risk. All organizations, once they become large and self-perpetuating, repress independent expression, but diversity of opinion and even dissent should be allowed to circulate, like a danger signal. Insistence on respect for ecological values, no less than disclosure of waste and abuse, should be welcomed as a commitment to make government more responsive, more worthy of trust.

2. Take the message from the setting to the people where they live. Russell Dickenson, while he was director, warned, "If we fail to make Americans aware of problems facing the national parks, and to involve them in choosing the right solutions to these problems, then we are failing in our responsibility as stewards of these public resources."[2] But the public has largely been ignored, and well-meant criticism has been stifled rather than heeded, contributing to the agency's difficulties. Make "shared visions, shared responsibilities" the goal and process in public involvement.

3. Set standards for entry into the big parks and standards for minimum length of stay. Visiting a national park has been assumed

as a right, but a sense of privilege and purpose must go with it. Americans should expect to leave the baggage of urban living at home and arrive with a recognition of park values and their responsibility to protect them.

4. Reduce automobile access in some places and eliminate it altogether in others. Downgrade park highways to simpler, slower roads. Substitute shuttle buses where feasible. Encourage restoration and resumption of train travel to the parks.

5. Determine the human carrying capacity of each park, then limit numbers of visitors to provide optimum enjoyment rather than maximum use. Get over the idea that national parks are outdoor amusement centers meant for tourism. Business may benefit, but protection of park values must come first. History demonstrates that whenever a park is treated like a commodity rather than a sanctuary, degradation of the park always follows.

6. Utilize each national park as an outdoor museum of natural history, a field classroom of human history, a laboratory of science, a source of art, literature, and spiritual inspiration. Pay particular attention to school classes and to the underprivileged, based on the premise that Conservation is a point of view involved with freedom and human dignity.

7. Establish vast quiet zones, free of automobiles, snowmobiles, dune buggies, motor-powered boats, and low-flying airplanes and helicopters, in order to ensure preservation of a peaceful environment. Apply this rule to low-level military training flights on the principle that true national defense embraces defense of the natural heritage.

8. Reevaluate the place of each concessionaire. Deemphasize resort hotels and motels in favor of simple low-cost hostels. If the service can be provided just as easily in a nearby community, close the concession. Clean out the souvenir shops.

9. Protect the integrity of national park water, air, and scenic and cultural resources and expand protection for lands surrounding parks through more effective coordination with bordering national forests and communities. Restrain the Forest Service from its damaging commodity-first programs of logging, grazing, and oil and gas exploration.

10. Reconstitute the National Park Service as an independent bureau, distinctly separate from the Department of the Interior and free

of that department's chronic propensity for partisan politics and re-source exploitation. Give it authority to challenge other federal agencies, like the Bureau of Reclamation and Federal Highway Authority, when their activities affect the parks.

Regreening the parks is more than institutional; it is personal and individual. It begins with thee and me. In 1985 I climbed Mauna Loa, the world's largest volcano, a formidable challenge. I ascended to more than thirteen thousand feet. At times I thought I would never make it, but I kept putting one foot in front of another. I felt empowered, realizing anew that the greatest reward comes from doing something on one's own that demands an expenditure of personal energy, that yields the feeling of self-sufficiency away from a supercivilized world. I reflected on the early Hawaiians making their way to the top without benefit of shoes, backpacks, or freeze-dried food, living close to nature as God made them.

Native Hawaiians speak of 'Aina, the traditional love of land, or reverence for life. Their poetic oli, or chants, and the hula recount stories and traditions of humankind woven in the natural universe. Indigenous peoples the world over express their kinship with stars, sun, moon, forests, water, and wildlife through similar rituals. The Navajo and Hopi in the Southwest have their sacred mountains, to which they turn for naturalness, healing, growth, and self-realization.

Each person needs his or her own sacred mountain. I visualize a national park as my sacred mountain even when, as in the Everglades, there is no mountain at all. It speaks to me as a place of spirit. It tells me that transforming society begins with the person. Stealth bombers and nuclear weapons will never force nations to join in recognizing the limitations of a fragile earth, but if I pledge allegiance to a green and peaceful planet, and if others do likewise and we believe strongly, we will make it happen.

Notes

Introduction

1. William C. Everhart, *The National Park Service* (Boulder: Westview Press, 1983), p. 73.
2. For Theodore Roosevelt's interest in conservation see James R. Trefethen, *Crusade for Wildlife* (Harrisburg: Telegraph Press, 1961). "An omnivorous reader with a strong interest in natural history, he had devoured everything that had been printed on hunting and on the wildlife and natural resources of America. His personal observations, on hunting trips to Maine, to the Adirondacks, and finally to the West, confirmed his recognition of the need for leadership in the field of conservation, although the word had not yet been coined, and for vigorous action if any portion of the wild America he loved were to be preserved" (p. 13). See *The Works of Theodore Roosevelt*, 24 vols., Memorial Edition (New York: C. Scribner's Sons, 1923–1926).

I   Women Should Not Go Hiking Alone

1. Thomas Merton, *Raids on the Unspeakable* (New York: New Directions Publishing, 1966), p. 70.
2. Message from President Taft to Congress, February 2, 1912; cited

in Robert Shankland, *Steve Mather of the National Parks* (New York: Alfred A. Knopf, 1954), pp. 52–53.

3. *National Parks Portfolio* (New York: Charles Scribner's Sons, 1916), p. 1. John Ise describes Mather's administration of the fledgling National Park Service, from 1917 to 1928, in *Our National Park Policy: A Critical History* (Baltimore: Johns Hopkins University Press, 1967).

4. Robert Marshall Papers, Bancroft Library, University of California, Berkeley, California; cited in James M. Glover, *A Wilderness Original: The Life of Bob Marshall* (Seattle: The Mountaineers, 1986), p. 175.

5. Irving Clark Papers, University of Washington, Seattle; cited in Glover, *A Wilderness Original*, pp. 180–81.

6. U.S. Department of the Interior, National Park Service Office of Science and Technology, "State of the Parks 1980: A Report to the Congress," May 1980, p. ix. "In many cases this degradation or loss of resources is irreversible," the report continues. "It represents a sacrifice by a public that, for the most part, is unaware that such a price is being paid."

7. *Fresno Bee*, August 22, 1988, reporting on Mott's weekend tour of Sequoia National Park: "In covering a broad range of park issues, the 78-year-old director said the park system is larger and in better condition than it was when he took over nearly four years ago." Mott did warn that developments along park boundaries and the introduction of nonnative species threaten many parks, according to the *Bee*.

8. Associated Press report, June 5, 1988, *Bellingham* (Wash.) *Herald*.

9. In "Patrolling the Park Beat" (*National Parks* [November–December 1987]: 25–29), Lucinda Peach reported on crime in Yosemite National Park: "Between 800 and 900 arrests have been made annually in recent years, and most of those arrested have spent some time in the Yosemite jail." Along with the full-time jailhouse, Peach listed a law enforcement office, a court with authority to dispose of most misdemeanor crimes, and a federal prosecutor, all within Yosemite's boundaries. The park had uniformed patrol rangers, carting visible sidearms, and undercover plainclothes night-patrol rangers; the latter made as many as fifty arrests in one night.

10. See Bernard Shanks, "Guns in the Parks," *The Progressive* (August 1976): 21–23.

11. Letter from Marian Albright Schenck to the author, June 1, 1989: "It's too bad a real leader from their own [National Park Service] ranks couldn't have been appointed as director in 1989. I realize the limitations and pressures from above are formidable, but a Service-oriented director

who could speak out with good ideas (and ideals) along with concrete proposals might make some difference as to how wilderness is to be protected and expanded, how areas around park lands could be saved from developers, etc. I'm not blaming anyone in the Park Service for not doing this, for we all know what would probably happen to an outspoken individualist. In my dad's day, they used to say, 'Well, that poor fool will end up in Platt [National Park, Oklahoma, now Chickasaw National Recreation Area]!' He anticipated this situation back in the 1940s when Shankland was writing *Steve Mather of the National Parks*. He dropped a note to Bob saying, 'As bureaus grow older and men, too, advance in age and as the bureau inevitably takes on new activities and new responsibilities, it tends to become more and more bureaucratic, has more red tape and more rules and regulations, and, in time, gets farther away from the people and ultimately will become just another bureau.'"

12. Secretary Udall supported the Bureau of Reclamation and its director, Floyd Dominy, principally in the Central Arizona Project, a large part of the Colorado River Basin development. The bureau's construction of dams was closely linked to power generation, and to the planning consortium of twenty-three privately owned and public utilities in seven states, called the Western Energy and Supply Transmission Associates, or WEST, formed in 1964. The origins of the initial Four Corners plant went back to the 1950s, leading to leasing of Navajo land and coal rights. The plant started up in 1963 using strip-mined coal; Secretary Udall approved arrangements for additional coal and water to support expansion. See news release, Office of the Secretary, April 12, 1966, "Agreement Reached on Developing Vast Coal-Fired 'WEST' Electric Complex." From the news release: "Regarding the air and water pollution control measures, Secretary Udall said, 'The inclusion of these protective conservation stipulations marks a major step forward in assuring that the development of one natural resource will not lead to the despoilment of other resources. . . . Secretary Udall also indicated that the Department's Bureau of Mines, at the request of the Bureau of Reclamation, studied the possibility of air pollution problems from the Mohave Plant at the Katherine Wash area behind Davis Dam, now under recreational development by the National Park Service. The Bureau reported that it could see no reason why the proposed plant cannot be operated without injury to the recreational area based on a 97 percent dust collection efficiency."

The second plant of the Four Corners complex, the Mohave in southern Nevada, derived coal from Black Mesa. Though many Indians considered Black Mesa sacred, Navajo and Hopi coal was strip-mined and pulverized and sent to the plant in the longest slurry pipeline constructed up to that time. "There could be no doubt at all, of course, that the Interior Department had invited private industry to the Four Corners feast" (William K. Wyant, *Westward in Eden* [Berkeley and Los Angeles: University of California Press, 1982], p. 350). The Bureau of Reclamation was a direct participant in the Navajo plant, which the government helped build in connection with the Central Arizona Project. Another plant was projected for the Kaiparowits Plateau, to which Secretary Udall pledged fealty during 1968 House Interior Committee hearings on the Central Arizona Project. Udall explained that the WEST group felt the Navajo plant should be built first, but the WEST planners were "very enthusiastic" about Utah deep-coal. Udall talked about the "first Kaiparowits plant," indicating there would be more than one. See Wyant, pp. 333–54.

On October 20, 1969, Acting Regional Director James M. Eden, of the Southwest Region, National Park Service, directed a Blue Envelope (urgent, confidential) memorandum to Director George B. Hartzog, Jr., in Washington. Subject: Navajo thermal-electric power plant, Glen Canyon. The memorandum expressed concern about potential air and water pollution from the proposed plant. Eden referred to an earlier memorandum (April 18, 1969) urging intervention for the imposition of strict pollution control measures, to which there was no reply. From the regional director's memorandum: "All preliminary planning and contract negotiations for the Navajo Plant have obviously been conducted with the greatest possible secrecy. Other interested agencies were not invited to participate until we literally forced our way in. . . . We are not technically qualified to debate the requirement for 97% particulate matter removal from the stack emissions as provided in the Interior and Navajo Indian contracts with the Salt River Project. However, we are apprehensive that sufficient air pollutants will still remain in stack emissions to adversely affect aesthetic values of the surrounding area. . . . There is evidence that the 'Four Corners' (Fruitland) coal-fired electric generating plant of the Arizona Public Service Company has contributed to air pollution over an estimated area of 100,000 square miles in the southwestern states of New Mexico, Arizona, Colorado and Utah. . . . what will happen when construction adds almost 11,000 megawatts of additional generating capacity? The broad picture air contamination from coal-fired generating plants in the Southwest is much greater than just the Navajo (Glen Canyon) plant and should be considered in that light. We feel sure the Secretary's Environmental Planning Staff will be interested in what is happening and what the future may hold. We believe consideration should be given to having a thorough analysis of the situation made by a task force of disinterested scientists from outside government circles. It seems regrettable that projects of this nature involving the potential for massive environmental changes are being considered without the input of at least all interested agencies of the Department. Certainly, assimilation of all viewpoints by the Environmental Planning Staff would assist the Secretary to make decisions that reflect the full range of environmental, political, economic and social consequences."

13. Robert Ashton, Jr., Richard Endress, Diane Traylor, and Bruce Panowski (Interpretive Ranger Division, Mesa Verde National Park), press release, September 23, 1970, Boulder, Colorado.

2   Heavy Clouds of Sleaze

1. Comptroller General of the United States, "Effectiveness of the Financial Disclosure System for Employees of the U.S. Geological Survey," March 3, 1975.

2. Stanley Hathaway was a former governor of Wyoming, an archetypical Western conservative, and an opponent of federal public lands, whose interests he could not be expected to uphold as secretary of the interior. The Senate in June 1975 confirmed Hathaway's appointment, though conservation organizations testified against him. He resigned in July after what physicians called "depression brought about by physical exhaustion."

3. See William K. Wyant, *Westward in Eden: The Public Lands and the Conservation Movement* (Berkeley and Los Angeles: University of California Press, 1982).

4. Carl Schurz, "The Need of a Rational Forest Policy," Secretary of Interior Annual Report Public Lands, 46th Congress, 2d session, 1879, Ex Doc 1-5, Serial Set 1910, pp. 26–29. Schurz ten years later was still trying. In an address before the Pennsylvania and American forestry associations he called for a reversal of public opinion "looking with indifference on this wanton, barbarous, disgraceful vandalism; a spendthrift people recklessly wasting its heritage; a Government careless of its future."

5. See Susan R. Schrepfer, *The Fight to Save the Redwoods: A History of Environmental Reform, 1917–1978* (Madison: University of Wisconsin Press, 1983); John B. Dewitt, *California Redwood Parks and Preserves: A Guide to the Redwood Parks and a Brief History of the Efforts*

to Save the Redwoods (San Francisco: Save-the-Redwoods League, 1982); François Leydet, *The Last Redwoods and the Parkland of Redwood Creek* (San Francisco: Sierra Club, 1969).

6. John Ise, *Our National Park Policy: A Critical History* (Baltimore: Johns Hopkins University Press, 1967), p. 90.

7. Wyant discusses the Teapot Dome scandal in chapter 4 of *Westward in Eden*, "The Fall of Albert B. Fall."

8. See Barry Mackintosh, "Harold L. Ickes and the National Park Service," *Journal of Forest History* (April 1985): 78–84; Donald C. Swain, *Wilderness Defender: Horace M. Albright and Conservation* (Chicago: University of Chicago Press, 1970); Harold L. Ickes, *The Autobiography of a Curmudgeon* (New York: Reynal and Hitchcock, 1943).

9. Address of Harold L. Ickes, Superintendents' Conference, Washington, D.C., February 1936. Copy provided by Louise Murie from the files of Adolph Murie.

3   Who Owns Interior?

1. See chapter 1, note 12.

2. Walter J. Hickel, *Who Owns America?* (Englewood Cliffs, N.J.: Prentice-Hall, 1971), p. 294.

3. Edward A. O'Neill, *Rape of the American Virgins* (New York and Washington: Praeger Publishers, 1972), p. 65.

4. Ibid., pp. 65–67.

5. Ibid.; see chapter 4, "The Development Decades."

6. Ibid., p. 92.

7. Ibid., p. 105.

8. Robert H. Boyle, *The Hudson River: A Natural and Unnatural History* (New York: W. W. Norton and Company, 1969), chapter 8, "Power, Power Everywhere."

9. Peter Collier and David Horowitz, *The Rockefellers: An American Dynasty* (New York: Signet, New American Library, 1977), p. 390. The authors add: "But as the infighting intensified, the Rockefellers began to exert leverage on the Secretary. It would have taken a stronger man to withstand their pressure."

10. The Park Service released its report, "The Redwoods: A National Opportunity for Conservation and Alternatives for Action," in September 1964. "The proposal suggested three different plans for a park on Redwood Creek varying in size from 30,000 to 50,000 acres" (Susan R.

Schrepfer, *The Fight to Save the Redwoods: A History of Environmental Reform, 1917–1978* [Madison: University of Wisconsin Press, 1983], p. 121).

11. See Schrepfer, ibid., chapter 8, "The Redwood National Park: 1965–1968."

12. U.S. Department of the Interior, press release, "Excerpts of Remarks by Secretary of the Interior Stewart L. Udall at Glen Canyon Visitor Center Dedication, September 26, 1968."

13. Joseph L. Sax, *Defending the Environment: A Strategy for Citizen Action* (New York: Alfred A. Knopf, 1971), p. 12.

14. U.S. Department of the Interior, press release, March 31, 1967, remarks of Dr. Stanley A. Cain at the New York Botanical Garden members meeting, Hotel Biltmore, New York, March 30, 1967. In a speech titled "New Mechanisms for Conservation" Cain said: "Ingenuity and practicality are being demonstrated by the federal government in developing compromise and cooperative proposals that allow accomplishments that would otherwise risk failure. The art of the possible is being employed instead of the shibboleths of the impossible. Half a loaf is still better than none."

15. Sax, *Defending the Environment*, pp. 33–34.

16. Ibid., pp. 48, 51. Sax cites the "Debacle" report as House Report No. 91-113, Committee on Government Operations, House of Representatives, 91st Congress, 1st session, 1969.

17. Hickel's letter appears on pp. 49–50 of Sax's *Defending the Environment*.

18. Letter to the author, January 1970.

19. See Hickel, *Who Owns America?*, p. 280.

20. See William K. Wyant, *Westward in Eden: The Public Lands and the Conservation Movement* (Berkeley and Los Angeles: University of California Press, 1982) pp. 110–13. Wyant writes: "Morton knew the great world of politics and had the merits and defects of a team player. It was said he had trouble making a decision. He liked to agree with people. When he was chivied on Capitol Hill about things that needed to be done, he had a habit of responding with the disarming assertion, 'I couldn't agree with you more'" (pp. 110–11).

21. Ibid., p. 113.

22. See "The Carter Administration: A Friend or Foe of Wilderness?" *Wild America* (Fall 1980): 3–7, a printed debate between M. Rupert Cutler, president of Defenders of Wildlife, who paints the Carter administration as "as strong an advocate for protection of [our] national heritage

as any in the history of our country," and the author, who criticizes Carter's energy goals and other policies.

23. Conservationists believed the Department of the Interior should have filed suit to force the Virginia Department of Highways and Transportation to consider an alternative route for I-66. Anthony Wayne Smith, president and general counsel of the National Parks and Conservation Association, expressed great concern in a letter to Secretary Andrus, dated April 20, 1979: "No speculation or projected studies are necessary to indicate a 4(f) determination [consideration of feasible and prudent alternatives] is required; the evidence is there. If negotiations between the National Park Service and VDHT do not include a halt in construction until a 4(f) determination is made, a serious and dangerous precedent will be set."

24. Michael Brown, *Laying Waste: The Poisoning of America by Toxic Chemicals* (New York: Pantheon Books, 1980), p. 328.

25. See William Bruce Wheeler and Michael J. McDonald, *TVA and the Tellico Dam, 1936–1979: A Bureaucratic Crisis in Post-Industrial America* (Knoxville: University of Tennessee Press, 1986), pp. 212–13.

26. I examine Andrus's record in Frome, "Andrus Gets Low Marks," *Defenders of Wildlife* (December 1979): 386–88; and "Carter and Friends: Tarnished Halos," *Defenders of Wildlife* (June 1979): 166–68. See also Michael Frome, "Will the Real Cecil Andrus Please Stand Up?" and Bill Loftus, "A Precarious Balance: Andrus, McClure and the Idaho Forest Management Act," *Palouse Journal* (Idaho) (Summer 1988): 14–18.

27. See Bureau of Land Management news release, August 6, 1979, "Interior Secretary Approves Star-Lake Bisti Railroad Proposal," to transport coal from federal, Indian, and private leases in the San Juan Basin to the main line of the Santa Fe Railroad. The secretary is quoted: "The coal which will be transported over this railroad will meet the kind of energy needs which the President is concerned about, and in a way which is extraordinarily useful." See also news release of December 19, 1979, regarding the Intermountain Power Project: "Construction of the largest coal-burning power project in the United States was given the go-ahead by Secretary of the Interior Cecil D. Andrus."

28. In responding to *Washington Post* editorial criticism of an oil lease sale in Georges Bank, a unique Atlantic fishery, Andrus wrote: "The ability of the oil and gas industry and the fishing industry not only to coexist, but also to thrive, is evident in the Gulf of Mexico and the North Sea. With the special protective measures in place for the upcoming sale,

there is no reason these two vital industries cannot do the same in the Georges Bank" (*Washington Post*, October 9, 1979).

29. "In May, Secretary Andrus announced he would not try to stop construction of a nuclear power plant adjacent to Indiana Dunes National Lakeshore, on the southeast shore of Lake Michigan. It was a shocking move; national conservation organizations had rallied to the defense of Indiana Dunes and expected more from him. Yet the Secretary said the utility company involved had already spent too much money to be required to go elsewhere—as though the public investment in the park should count less. It was a curious move. The Interior Department presumably is pressing these days to bring urban parks to the people; there's hardly an area anywhere in urbanized America, however, with higher scenic and natural values than the Dunes at the edge of metropolitan Chicago" (from Michael Frome, "The Yes-But Reformers," *Defenders of Wildlife* [October 1977]: 327).

30. "There is little doubt among most authorities that the 200-plus [uranium] mines studding the hill area [around Cove, Arizona] are largely responsible for much of the lung cancer that has struck ex-miners in Cove and other Navajo communities. Surveys by local social service leaders have found that 40 percent of Cove's families have had at least one member suffer a uranium mining–related disease" (Tony Davis, "Uranium Has Decimated Navajo Miners," *High Country News* [Colo.], June 18, 1990).

31. See Margot Hornblower, "Interior Nominee Is Questioned on Campaign Debts," *Washington Post*, May 21, 1977; Warren Brown, "Controversial Appointee Gets Interior Dept. Post," *Washington Post*, June 6, 1978; Jerry Knight, "Mega-luxury Rises on Banks of Georgetown," *Washington Post*, November 28, 1983; Michael Frome, "How Green Is Their Potomac," *Los Angeles Times*, July 6, 1980.

In the last named, Senator Mark Hatfield of Oregon is quoted as follows: "Even a small area of development on this ribbon of land along the river cannot be justified. It is the most beautiful spot of Potomac River frontage in the capital. The Potomac bends at this point and the views upriver and downriver are unmatched. There is absolutely no reason for destroying this area forever by piling upon it structures of concrete and glass. A people's park on this land would provide the type of waterfront development that is so important for the integrity of Washington as a city of beauty. . . . Through complicated and questionable land exchanges among the National Park Service, Washington city government and developers, Secretary of the Interior Cecil D. Andrus proclaimed accord for construction of a high-rise commercial and condominium complex and designation of a 160-foot-wide strip along the river to be called a public park. 'The plan reasonably meets our objectives,' according to Manus J. Fish, regional director of the National Park Service, 'with a major addition of parkland at no cost.'"

Others disagreed. Lawrence N. Stevens, a former Interior Department official associated with the National Committee for Urban Recreation, declared on behalf of a coalition of twenty-five organizations: "The agreement places the department in the stance of advocating a major commercial-residential structure on a floodplain and of sacrificing an opportunity to provide urgently needed urban recreation in a choice waterfront location."

32. See Roderick Nash, *Wilderness and the American Mind*, 3d ed. (New Haven: Yale University Press, 1982), chapter 14, "Alaska."

33. See Schrepfer, *The Fight to Save the Redwoods*, p. 146.

34. James G. Watt, response to a question about environmentalists in an interview; reported in *Forest Industries* 109, no. 4 (1982): 21–23.

35. *San Diego Tribune*, October 2, 1985.

36. See Jeff Radford, *The People's Victory over James Watt* (Corrales, N.M.: Rhombus Publishing Company). In reviewing Radford's book for the *Amicus Journal* (Spring 1988): 48–49, Charles H. Callison wrote: "Jeff Radford has written a timely reminder in this election year that the Reagan administration's ideological campaign to pass public resources into private hands did not cease when Watt resigned." Callison used Radford's book as a basis for discussing the Powder River and Chaco Canyon coal-leasing scandals.

37. See Ronald A. Taylor, "Interior's James Watt: Hero or Villain?" *U.S. News and World Report*, June 6, 1983; Deanne Kloepfer, Ronald J. Tipton, and Peter M. Emerson, *The Watt Record: James Watt and the National Park System* (Washington, D.C.: The Wilderness Society, 1983).

38. James G. Watt, address to the Conference of National Park Concessioners, International Hotel, Washington, D.C., March 9, 1981, p. 18.

39. Nathaniel P. Reed, from a speech to the annual meeting of the Sierra Club, San Francisco, May 2, 1981.

40. Frederic Golden, "A Sharpshooter at Interior," *Time*, April 16, 1984.

41. See the *Washington Post*, May 20, 1986.

42. *Washington Post*, February 11, 1985.

43. *Christian Science Monitor*, August 1, 1985; Rochelle I. Stanfield, "Tilting on Development," *National Journal*, February 7, 1987; *The Oregonian*, February 6, 1989.

44. *Washington Post*, May 29, 1987.

45. See Michael S. Lasky, "Can He Restore Our National Parks? Director William Penn Mott Is 76, but He's Going Like 60," *Parade Magazine*, November 24, 1985.

46. According to the *Los Angeles Times* of February 5, 1987, National Park Service Director William Penn Mott gave Western Regional Director Howard Chapman an efficiency rating of "level 2" in fall of 1986. On a scale of 1 to 5 (1 being best), Mott's evaluation indicated that Chapman had "exceeded performance standards." Horn wanted to change Chapman's rating to an "unsatisfactory" level 4, and recommended Chapman be immediately reassigned. On resistance from Mott, Horn compromised on a level 3, or "average," rating. Chapman resigned May 2, 1987. See also *High Country News*, June 22, 1987.

47. *Anchorage Daily News*, June 16, 1988.

48. *Washington Post*, May 15, 1989.

49. *Los Angeles Times*, April 30, 1989.

4   Why Directors Get Fired

1. Robert Shankland, *Steve Mather of the National Parks* (New York: Alfred A. Knopf, 1954), pp. 215–16.

2. Kent was a member of the Cosmos Club from 1911 until his death in 1928. In the club bulletin of April 1985, William F. Whitmore decribed William Kent as a commanding personality and expert outdoorsman. "In business deals, his word was his bond. He spoke his mind vigorously but without malice." Whitmore's vignette was based largely on Kent's biography, published privately by his wife, Elizabeth Thacher Kent, a crusader for woman suffrage.

3. See John B. Dewitt, *California Redwood Parks and Preserves: A Guide to the Redwood Parks and a Brief History of the Efforts to Save the Redwoods* (San Francisco: Save-the-Redwoods League, 1982).

4. For discussion of the proposed Grand Canyon cableway, see Shankland, *Steve Mather of the National Parks*, pp. 207–8.

5. Ibid., p. 287.

6. Horace M. Albright and Robert Cahn, *The Birth of the National Park Service: The Founding Years, 1913–33* (Salt Lake City and Chicago: Howe Brothers, 1985), p. 225. See also Donald C. Swain, *Wilderness Defender: Horace M. Albright and Conservation* (Chicago: University of Chicago Press, 1970).

7. "Keep it Youthful, Vigorous, Clean, and Strong," Horace Albright's "unpublished farewell" of 1933, in the 1985 Annual Report, Eastern National Parks and Monuments Association, unpaged.

8. Swain, *Wilderness Defender*, pp. 310–16.

9. Horace M. Albright, "The Paradox in Resource Conservation," statement for the Eleventh Cosmos Club Award, April 15, 1974 (Washington, D.C.: Cosmos Club, 1974), pp. 6, 13.

10. See Barry Mackintosh, "Harold L. Ickes and the National Park Service," *Journal of Forest History* (April 1985): 78–84.

11. Horace M. Albright, interview with the author, Los Angeles, 1984.

12. Donald C. Swain, "The National Park Service and the New Deal, 1933–1940," *Pacific Historical Review* 41 (August 1972): 312–32; *The Secret Diary of Harold L. Ickes*, 3 vols. (New York: Simon and Schuster, 1954); Ickes's typescript diary is at the Library of Congress, Manuscript Division. Cited in Mackintosh, "Harold L. Ickes and the National Park Service," pp. 79–80.

13. "Mr. Cammerer, when Assistant Director, was the Interior Department's representative in inspecting the lands and determining the boundaries for the Park, and perhaps is better acquainted with the scenic qualities of the Great Smokies than any other Government official" (Laura Thornborough, *The Great Smoky Mountains* [New York: Thomas Y. Crowell, 1937], p. 11).

14. "In elaborate ceremonies on the roof of the Interior Department Building in Washington on February 20, 1930, the first deeds were presented to the government before a large delegation, which included the governors of Tennessee and North Carolina, the chairmen and other members of both Park Commissions, and National Park Service officials. Governor Henry Horton, of Tennessee, presented three separate deeds— one for each of the three Tennessee park counties—for a total of 100,176.63 acres. Governor O. Max Gardner, of North Carolina, presented two deeds for a total of 52,000 acres in that state" (Carlos C. Campbell, *Birth of a National Park* [Knoxville: University of Tennessee Press, 1960], p. 96).

15. Lucy Morgan and LeGette Blythe, *Gift from the Hills: Miss Lucy Morgan's Story of her Unique Penland School* (Indianapolis and New York: Bobbs-Merrill Company, 1958), p. 83.

16. See Susan R. Schrepfer, *The Fight to Save the Redwoods: A History of Environmental Reform, 1917–1978* (Madison: University of Wisconsin Press, 1983).

17. John Ise, *Our National Park Policy: A Critical History* (Baltimore: Johns Hopkins University Press, 1967), p. 475.

18. Conrad L. Wirth, *Parks, Politics, and the People* (Norman: University of Oklahoma Press, 1980), p. 349.

19. "Just prior to his resignation, Park Service Director Drury authored his agency's official reaction to the CRSP (Colorado River Storage Project), declaring that the proposed dam in Dinosaur National Monument, in particular, 'would result in nationally significant scenic, scientific and other recreational values being irreparably damaged or lost all together'" (Russell Martin, *A Story That Stands Like a Dam: Glen Canyon and the Struggle for the Soul of the West* [New York: Henry Holt, 1989], p. 55).

20. *National Parks Magazine* 97 (April–June 1949): 28. Cited in Ise, *Our National Park Policy*, p. 7.

21. Transcript of Albright's remarks at commemorative dinner for Save-the-Redwoods League's fiftieth anniversary, Eureka, California, June 16, 1968, p. 7.

22. Transcript of Wauer's remarks to the Tenth Annual Southwest Studies Summer Institute: National Parks and Wilderness on the Colorado Plateau, Colorado Springs, Colorado, July 20, 1981, p. 13.

23. Interview with the author, "A Kind of Special Breed," *American Forests* (January 1964): 4–5, 36–37.

24. Wirth, *Parks, Politics, and the People*, p. 304.

25. U.S. Department of the Interior, Office of the Secretary, "Remarks by Assistant Secretary of the Interior John A. Carver Jr. at the National Park Service Conference of Challenges, Yosemite National Park, October 14, 1963," p. 4. In *Parks, Politics, and the People*, Wirth comments (p. 311): "The auditorium was full of very angry people after Carver's speech. He left immediately."

26. U.S. Department of the Interior, Office of the Secretary, press release, "National Academy of Sciences Recommends Positive Research Program for National Park Areas; Secretary Udall Orders Corrective Steps," October 18, 1963.

5   Directors of the New Age—Innocence Lost

1. Biographical data: George B. Hartzog, Jr., July 1971. Sent to the author by U.S. Department of the Interior, Office of Information, on March 23, 1972. See McPhee, cited in text.

2. *New York Times*, June 14, 1966.

3. George B. Hartzog, Jr., "The Wilderness Act and the National Parks and Monuments," in *Wilderness and the Quality of Life*, Proceedings of the Sierra Club Biennial Wilderness Conference, San Francisco, April 7–9, 1967, ed. Maxine E. McCloskey and James P. Gilligan (San Francisco: Sierra Club, 1969), p. 17.

4. "In developing recreation opportunities in the area, management might well borrow from the imaginative mass transit approach of European recreation managers who have utilized—perhaps for different economic reasons but with very successful results—the funicular, the monorail, the tramway and other dramatic but relatively inconspicuous means of access up into the mountains" (from "National Park Service Management Proposals for the North Cascade Mountains Study Area," *The North Cascades Study Report* [Washington, D.C.: U.S. Department of the Interior and U.S. Department of Agriculture, 1965], p. 179).

5. George B. Hartzog, Jr., *Battling for the National Parks* (Mt. Kisco, N.Y.: Moyer Bell Limited, 1988), p. 106.

6. Robert Ashton, Jr., Richard Endress, Diane Traylor, and Bruce Panowski (Interpretive Ranger Division, Mesa Verde National Park), press release, September 23, 1970, Boulder, Colorado. See chapter 1 in this volume.

7. The protest letter from the "Glacier 14" was published in the *Hungry Horse News*, September 24, 1971. See chapter 8 in this volume.

8. Reported from notes by Riley McClelland; provided to the author in correspondence.

9. See chapter 8 in this volume. In a letter to the *Hungry Horse News* (April 28, 1972) McClelland wrote: "The central issue in need of attention is one of principle, not of specific details of a particular employee's rights . . . I have said that substantial opposition to environmental and other management practices elicits a reaction of harassment, reassignment or transfer. Failure to transfer apparently results in being fired. The threat of transfer or being fired is obviously a potent form of intimidation."

10. Bernard Shanks, interview with the author, Phoenix, December 2, 1984. See chapter 7 in this volume.

11. *San Francisco Examiner*, October 10 and 11, 1971.

12. Hartzog, *Battling for the National Parks*, pp. 228–29.

13. Interview with Roger Allin, Whidbey Island, Washington, 1985.

14. Biographical information on National Park Service directorate, sent to the author from the U.S. Department of the Interior, Office of Information, March 23, 1972.

15. See Hartzog, *Battling for the National Parks*, chapters 18 and 19.

16. U.S. Department of the Interior, National Park Service, press release, July 11, 1971; *Los Angeles Times*, April 4, 1971; *New York Times*, May 16, 1971; Commonwealth of Pennsylvania, Office of the Governor, Harrisburg, press release, July 20, 1971; *Harrisburg Patriot*, July 26, 1971.

17. A National Park Service news release dated July 11, 1971, quoted Hartzog in the first paragraph as announcing the agreement, then in the second paragraph referred to Interior Department Special Assistant J. C. Herbert Bryant, Jr., a political appointee, as the negotiator with Ottenstein, the promoter of the tower. See Bill Richards, "Tower Power," *Washington Post*, October 28, 1973. Hartzog is quoted as follows: "I O.K.d the agreement by phone from the Grand Canyon. When I got home and saw that access I tried to cancel it but it was too late."

18. *Alaska Conservation Review* (April 1972): 11.

19. Ron Walker related the story of his appointment in an interview with the author in Washington, D.C., 1985.

20. See Frank C. Craighead Jr., *Track of the Grizzly* , 1st softcover ed. (San Francisco: Sierra Club Books, 1982); see also chapter 9 in this volume.

21. "Walker Emphasizes Preservation Role," *National Park Service Newsletter*, February 18, 1974.

22. For discussion of MCA's desire for an aerial tramway and other developments in Yosemite, see Alfred Runte, *Yosemite: The Embattled Wilderness* (Lincoln: University of Nebraska Press, 1990), pp. 203–5; see also chapter 10 in this volume.

23. Dickenson, interview with the author, Seattle, Washington, 1987.

24. "Secretary Morton told Walker that under his leadership 'significant strides have been made in protecting the natural environment and in providing for the enjoyment and education of people in areas under your jurisdiction'" (U.S. Department of the Interior, Office of the Secretary, press release, September 11, 1974).

25. Walker, interview with the author, Washington, D.C., 1985.

26. See the *Washington Times*, September 13, 1985.

27. Gary Everhardt, interview with the author, Waynesboro, Virginia, 1985.

28. Chapman, interview with author, Washington, D.C., 1980.

29. See chapter 1, note 6.

30. Morris Udall's letter is printed in full in Don Hummel's book, *Stealing the National Parks: The Destruction of Concessions and Public Access* (Bellevue, Wash.: Free Enterprise Press, 1987), p. 361.

31. Andrus, interview with author, Boise, Idaho, 1985.

32. Dickenson, interview with the author, Seattle, Washington, 1985.

33. Ibid.

34. Jack Hughes, interview with the author, Olympic National Park, 1985.

35. See *National Parks in Crisis* (Washington, D.C.: National Parks and Conservation Association, 1982), published following the conference at Jackson. It includes three parts: discussion papers serving as background information, addresses to the conference, and recommendations reached at the conclusion.

36. Memorandum from Deputy Director Grier to the National Park Service Directorate and WASO Division Chiefs, March 25, 1982. Grier replaced Ira Hutchison as deputy director after he left the Park Service for another position in the Interior Department. She was without experience in national parks and clearly the appointee of Secretary Watt, for whom she had worked in the Bureau of Outdoor Recreation during the Nixon administration. Subsequently, and before joining the Park Service, she worked in the district office of a Texas congressman and as a business entrepreneur (service stations and construction). William Penn Mott replaced her as deputy director with Denis P. Galvin in October 1985.

37. Dickenson, interview with the author, Seattle, Washington, 1985.

38. Columnist Tom Diaz interviewed Donald E. Sowle, an OMB administrator, about the A-76 program for the *Washington Times*, August 13, 1984.

39. The *Tribune* (Oakland), March 11, 1985; *San Francisco Chronicle*, February 9, 1985.

40. Mott, interview with the author, Washington, D.C., 1986.

41. According to an Associated Press account, Mott also denied any administration interference (*Bellingham Herald*, June 5, 1988).

42. *Sacramento Bee*, December 9, 1986; *Federal Times* (Washington,

D.C.), January 12, 1987; *High Country News*, June 22, 1987. See chapter 3, note 46.

43. *Los Angeles Times*, April 30, 1989.

44. See John Kenney, "Interior Sub Rosa: Political Appointees Use the Parks as Pawns," *National Parks Magazine* (September–October 1989): "Though Galvin had done an outstanding job as deputy director, he was unceremoniously removed from his position in April. [Assistant Secretary Becky Norton] Dunlop engineered his ouster" (p. 13).

6   Perplexity of a Park Superintendent

1. For discussion of the Cataloochee Road issue see the *Knoxville Journal*, August 8, 1974; the *Mountaineer* (Waynesville, N.C.), August 9, 1974; *Asheville Citizen*, June 8, 1974; *Asheville Times*, July 12, 1974.

2. The cabin in question is located bordering Hazel Creek, across Fontana Lake from the Fontana Village resort; it provides access to choice mountain fishing. The National Park Service maintains a small chain of guest facilities, or "VIP houses," including Brinkerhoff House, Grand Teton National Park; Camp Hoover, Shenandoah National Park; Little Cinnamon Bay, Virgin Islands; Pink House, Virgin Islands; an apartment at Fort Jefferson National Monument; and Good Luck Lodge, Catoctin Mountain Park, Maryland. These are made available to public officials and special contacts.

3. U.S. Department of the Interior, Office of the Assistant Secretary for Fish, Wildlife, and Parks, "The European Wild Boar Issue, Great Smoky Mountains National Park," February 15, 1978.

4. Don Gillespie, interview with the author, Salt Lake City, 1987. See Jim Woolf, "Lobbyist Says Garn Aide Threatened Him," *Salt Lake Tribune*, October 12, 1988.

5. National Park Service, *Glacier Bay General Management Plan*, September 1984; Gary W. Vequist, "Whales Are Visitors, Too," *Courier* (February 1987): 12–13.

6. Tollefson, interview with the author, Glacier Bay, Alaska, 1985.

7. See Robert Shankland, *Steve Mather of the National Parks* (New York: Alfred A. Knopf, 1954), pp. 248–49.

8. John R. White, "Atmosphere in the National Parks," address to Special Superintendents' Meeting, Washington, D.C., February 10, 1936; from files of National Park Service, furnished by Boyd Evison.

9. Boyd Evison, interviews with the author, Bellingham, Washington, 1988, 1989.

10. George B. Hartzog, Jr., minutes of October 19, 1983, meeting between Park Service and GSI on Sequoia–Kings Canyon National Park; response letter from Russ Dickenson to GSI president S. J. DiMeglio, November 22, 1983.

11. Beck told the *Missoulian* (April 23, 1972): "Each one of us who has left Glacier has been threatened in a verbal manner. It's never in writing." Beck also charged that civil service personnel regulations were not enforced: "There's no real examination of what's going on. It's all on a cursory or approval level. The civil service agency isn't doing the job it was set up for."

12. In *The Monkey Wrench Gang* (Philadelphia: Lippincott, 1975) and other works.

13. Dickenson, interview with the author, Seattle, Washington, 1989.

14. Parry, interview with the author, Moab, Utah, 1986.

15. Statement of Mary Lou Grier before the Subcommittee on Energy and the Environment of the Committee on Interior and Insular Affairs, "Concerning the Department of Energy's High-Level Radioactive Waste Repository Siting Program in Utah," October 12, 1984.

16. *High Country News*, October 29, 1984.

17. See Jim Woolf, "Artifacts Looters Systematically Rape Indian Ruins in Southeastern Utah," *Salt Lake Tribune*, October 28, 1984. See also Scott S. Warren, "Crackdown on Shard Thieves," *National Parks Magazine* (September–October 1984): 12–16. Warren writes that while antigovernment sentiment may spur acts of wanton vandalism to archaeological sites, profit drives theft of artifacts: "Decorated Anasazi pots and other relics command high prices from collectors. Pothunters, or 'moki poachers' as these folks are referred to in parts of southern Utah, usually resort to actual digging in ruins, sometimes with backhoes and other heavy equipment."

18. See chapter 5 in this volume.

7   When Ranger Rick Becomes a Renegade

1. The National Park Service in the early 1930s reconsidered its policy on predators, particularly with publication of *Fauna of the National Parks of the United States: A Preliminary Survey of Faunal Relations in*

the National Parks, by George M. Wright, Joseph S. Dixon, and Ben H. Thompson (Washington, D.C.: Government Printing Office, 1933); and *Fauna of the National Parks of the United States: Wildlife Management in the National Parks*, by Wright and Thompson (Washington, D.C.: Government Printing Office, 1935). Nevertheless, in the latter book the authors noted: "There is sometimes a tendency in men in the field to hold any predator in the same disreputable position as any human criminal" (p. 48).

2. Gifford Pinchot, *Breaking New Ground* (New York: Harcourt, Brace, 1947), p. 321.

3. See Irving Brant, *Adventures in Conservation with Franklin D. Roosevelt* (Flagstaff: Northland, 1988); and Ben W. Twight, *Organizational Values and Political Power: The Forest Service versus the Olympic National Park* (University Park: Pennsylvania State University Press, 1983).

4. *Daily News Record* (Harrisonburg, Va.), December 6, 1977.

5. See George Freeman Pollock, *Skyland: The Heart of the Shenandoah National Park* (Berryville, Va.: Virginia Book Company, 1960).

6. The congressman's letter was printed in the *Madison County Eagle* of December 8, 1977. The response letter from Superintendent Jacobsen, printed in the same issue, stated: "Though Federal Regulations authorize the destruction of animals observed by authorized persons in the act of killing, injuring or molesting wildlife . . . it is not the policy in this Park to do so except under extreme circumstances and when other feasible efforts to intervene have failed."

7. *Richmond Times-Dispatch*, December 8, 1977.

8. For Jackson Hole, see John Ise, *Our National Park Policy: A Critical History* (Baltimore: Johns Hopkins University Press, 1967).

9. "When I lived and worked in the park as a ranger, the contrast of the hunt with the park was more than dramatic; it was painful" (Bernard Shanks, *This Land Is Your Land: The Struggle to Save America's Public Lands* [San Francisco: Sierra Club, 1984], pp. 217–18).

10. Ibid., p. 212; Shanks, interview with the author, Phoenix, Arizona, December, 1984.

11. Shanks, *This Land Is Your Land*, p. 212, and interview with the author, Phoenix, 1984.

12. Shanks, interview with the author, Phoenix, 1984.

13. Alfred Runte, interviews with the author, Seattle, Washington, Bellingham, Washington, and Moscow, Idaho, 1984, 1985, 1988, 1989.

8   Showdown at Logan Pass

1. Riley McClelland, letter to the author, July 31, 1973. Much of the material concerning Riley McClelland that was used in this chapter, including clippings, correspondence, and reports, was provided in bound notebooks by Dr. James R. Habeck, Department of Botany, University of Montana, Missoula.

2. *B. Riley McClelland* v. *Cecil D. Andrus, Secretary of the Interior, et al.* Appeal from the U.S. District Court for the District of Columbia, U.S. Court of Appeals, D.C. Civil Action no. 75-1969, printed, unbound decision, August 17, 1979, p. 4.

3. National Park Service, Settlement Agreement with Riley McClelland, August 7, 1980. Signed by McClelland and Nancy Garrett, associate director, administration, National Park Service.

4. See "Snowmobile 'Died' 10 Years Ago in Park," *Hungry Horse News*, January 10, 1985.

5. For the history of Glacier National Park's establishment, see John Ise, *Our National Park Policy: A Critical History* (Baltimore: Johns Hopkins University Press, 1967), chapter 9.

6. Riley McClelland, interview with the author, Missoula, Montana, 1984.

7. "What we hope to achieve is a professional approach to the management of resources for their perpetuation as elements of the total environment" (memorandum from Lyle H. McDowell, Chief, Branch of Resources Management, to Riley B. McClelland, Park Naturalist, June 20, 1967).

8. Riley B. McClelland, "The Ecosystem—A Unifying Concept for the Management of Natural Areas in the National Park System" (Master's thesis, Colorado State University, June 1968), pp. 38–41, 90. (The thesis was also published in the *Rocky Mountain–High Plains Parks and Recreation Journal* [Colorado State University] 3, no. 2 [1968].)

9. Beatrice E. Willard, "Effects of Visitors on Natural Ecosystems in Rocky Mountain National Park," Report 5, final report on the 1962–1963 contract between the park and the University of Colorado, 1963.

10. McClelland, "The Ecosystem," p. 92.

11. See "Conservationists Join in Seeking Glacier Park Probe," *Seattle Times*, April 30, 1972; Dale A. Burk, "Union Throws Support behind McClelland," *Missoulian* (Missoula, Mt.), August 3, 1972.

12. Memorandum from Chief of Park Maintenance to Glacier Superintendent, August 12, 1971.

13. The protest letter from the "Glacier 14" appeared in the *Hungry Horse News*, September 24, 1971.

14. Best's letter to the editor, *Hungry Horse News*, October 1, 1971.

15. The *Missoulian*: undated news clip of firing of boardwalk protesters; October 5, 1971, report of rescindment of firing; May 21, 1972, report of complaints of demotion.

16. Habeck quote from unpublished manuscript for *National Parks* magazine.

17. After examining the Logan Pass boardwalk and surroundings in early August, Habeck reported in a letter to Briggle, dated August 4, 1972: "The chemical or chemicals used to treat the wood in the boardwalk construction show a high degree of mobility. . . . Direct plant mortality was observed to be taking place in several instances. Plants located beneath the decked materials are the recipients of concentrated doses of the treatment chemical."

18. In a letter to the Montana congressional delegation (April 10, 1972), Habeck wrote: "The sewage disposal problems in Glacier Park are not yet solved. . . . A secondary treatment plan being seriously considered will involve spraying nutrient-rich liquid waste-water over a 27-acre native grassland meadow near St. Mary Lake. This system is given 'support' because similar systems are used elsewhere in conjunction with golf courses. The nutrients will alter the native grasslands seriously. On golf courses, the grass is clipped and harvested; this isn't intended on the Glacier prairie spray field. Air-borne virus and bacteria spores may also endanger nearby campers. Additional nutrients may end up in St. Mary Lake."

Notable headlines that appeared over some of the many letters James Habeck wrote for the "Local Comment" section of the *Missoulian*: "Briggle's Strange Tale" (November 19, 1971); "Parks Need a Change at the Top" (March 13, 1972); "Logan Pass Boardwalk Halted" (April 4, 1972); "Glacier Park Needs Probing" (April 25, 1972); "Park Officials Ignorant of Law" (June 14, 1972).

19. Briggle responded to Habeck's criticism in a letter to Senator Lee Metcalf, published in the *Missoulian* (November 15, 1971). Concerning the Logan Pass sewage system: "Mr. Habeck claims that sewage from the pass was dumped into an unsealed pit near McDonald Creek and for the most part drains into the stream. The disposal pond is unlined and was

left so on the best advice of Public Health Service officials and the Environmental Protection Agency who inspected it. The effluent did not
drain into the stream, and I invite Mr. Habeck to prove differently. This
stream was monitored at regular intervals and we found no evidence of
seepage."

Habeck later stated: "Mr. Briggle claimed he had approval from the
U.S. Public Health Office and the Environmental Protection Agency to
dump the sewage in this unsealed pit. It wasn't until after the dumping
had started that an effort was made, using color dyes, to see where the
sewage might be going. I do not know the results of this testing, but it
has been announced through Mr. Briggle's office that the sewage this
summer (1972) was to be hauled to a treatment plant at Hungry Horse,
Montana. I have learned that Riley McClelland had advised Mr. Briggle
that the pit should be sealed, but he ignored this advice. Now we discover
that the unsealed pit is not being used during 1972, even though it had
full 'approval'" (notarized letter from Habeck to Robert Nogler, national
representative for the eleventh district of the American Federation of
Government Employees, August 4, 1972).

20. Letter to the author, June 7, 1972.

21. Riley McClelland, memorandum to National Park Service director (summary of formal grievance), April 25, 1972.

22. On January 17, 1972, Taylor addressed a memorandum to Arthur
L. Sullivan, superintendent, Bighorn Canyon National Recreation Area,
on the subject "Inventory of historic and archaeological properties in National Park Service areas," in which he proposed listing on the National
Register of Historic Places recently discovered historic and prehistoric
sites, in addition to nineteen already nominated, thus assuring their protection within historic districts of the national recreation area. Superintendent Sullivan in a memo of response dated January 20, 1972, rejected the proposal with very specific reasons. Establishing historic
districts would: preclude construction of the transpark road; eliminate
grazing and other agricultural uses, causing economic loss to Indians and
non-Indians; cause removal of facilities—including high-power transmission and telephone lines—not associated with archaeological values;
preclude tourist developments and thus establishment of Crow-operated
concessions. The big issue was the road: "Without the transpark road,
visitation would remain stagnant and the proposed Pretty Eagle recreational complex would not be economically viable. Again a loss of jobs
and revenue." The superintendent concluded: "Historic districts are pri-

marily applied to a grouping of historic structures within an urban area, such as was established at Boston, Charleston, New Orleans, etc. The approach taken by Historian Edwin C. Bearss [later chief historian of the National Park Service], that is of nominating individual sites, is, I believe, the correct approach to take in this matter."

23. Riley McClelland, memorandum to National Park Service director (summary of formal grievance), April 25, 1972.

24. George B. Hartzog, Jr., letter to Richard Boyer, April 26, 1972.

25. Notes on conferences with National Park Service officials provided by Riley McClelland.

26. Elbert F. Floyd, chief appeals officer, U.S. Civil Service Commission Denver Field Office, transmittal of findings and recommendation in McClelland appeal, to Richard Robbins, Office of the Solicitor, U.S. Department of the Interior, July 29, 1974.

27. U.S. Civil Service Commission Appeals Review Board, decision in the matter of B. Riley McClelland, November 25, 1974.

28. U.S. Court of Appeals, unbound decision, p. 26.

29. McClelland, interviews with the author.

30. See B. Riley McClelland et al., "Habitat Management for Hole-Nesting Birds in Forests of Western Larch and Douglas fir," *Journal of Forestry* 77, no. 8 (August 1979): 480–83.

31. National Park Service, Denver Service Center, Midwest/Rocky Mountain Team, "Environmental Assessment for Reconstruction of Comfort Station and Accessible Ramp at Logan Pass: Package No. 243," February 1985.

32. National Park Service, "Finding of No Significant Environmental Impact for the Proposed Comfort Station Reconstruction and Accessible Ramp at Logan Pass," approved by the acting Rocky Mountain regional director April 4, 1985; sent to the public April 24, 1985.

33. Robert T. Pantzer, letter to William Briggle, October 3, 1972.

9   The Nature of Naturalness

1. "The poison used is called by the Park Service 'an approved non-persistent pesticide,' otherwise known as Sevin-4, a product of the Union Carbide Company. It is patently non-selective and kills virtually all insects, threatening to eliminate or contaminate fledgling birds' food supply during the nesting season, with long lived adverse effects upon the

food chain. According to Woodrow A. Miller, president of the Miller Honey Company of Colton, California, discussing an incident in his region, 'It stays lethal for seven days and seven nights when it was used on cotton crops. Bees and butterflies were completely wiped out.' David Graves, of the Cucamonga Honey Company, adds, 'It's the worst I've seen for bees. It doesn't just kill the bees in the field like DDT does, but kills them in the hives.' He said 350 of his colonies were killed from a Sevin spray, with bees in hives 2½ miles from the spray area wiped out" (from Michael Frome, *American Forests Magazine* [August 1970]: 44–45). See also Ted Williams, "Ardis and the Gypsies," *Horticulture* (September 1979): 19–26.

2. National Park Service, "Draft Management Plan for Blacktailed Prairie Dog, Badlands National Park," May 1979.

3. Among public comments the Park Service received on its draft prairie dog management plan for Badlands National Park in 1979 were the following: "The Pennington County Commissioners are pleased to learn that you are proposing to control prairie dogs. It is our opinion that prairie dogs are nothing more than a rodent (prairie rat might be a more appropriate name) and to continue to allow them to infest good grazing land and to re-infest private land is beyond our comprehension."

"I am a producing farmer and rancher in the adjoining neighborhood and this is affecting my livelihood. The Park Service is causing my operation undue loss because they are not concerned for my future or the future of the consuming public for whom I produce food. . . . We have faced the influx for five years with an unending and unsuccessful fight to control the dirty dogs. We are losing the war. We cannot continue to spend thousands of dollars out of our own pockets for a problem that started with the Park Service."

On the other side: "Whenever poison is suggested as a means to control animal populations, we wonder if such a method might be an efficient manner of curbing the prolific nature of mankind. How much of this earth's resources is man entitled to devastate? Why do people insist on the destruction of other living creatures to assume the appearance of power and superiority? . . . the introduction of more natural predators would be far more efficient, much safer, and less costly than the suggested program."

4. "Virtually every piece of up-to-date literature stresses this [zinc phosphide] to be an intense, extremely dangerous and long-lasting poison. Warnings such as the following are plain and plentiful: 'Zinc phos-

phide must be used with care, as it is toxic to all forms of animal life. It has poisoned humans, as well as domestic and wild animals.' 'Secondary hazards do exist. Dogs, cats, or other animals can die from eating zinc-phosphide-poisoned rodents'" (from Michael Frome, *Conscience of a Conservationist* [Knoxville: University of Tennessee Press, 1989], pp. 66–67).

5. Adolph Murie, "Pesticide Program in Grand Teton National Park," *National Parks Magazine* (June 1966): 17–19: "All this wildness has beauty and harmony for those who have a feeling for wildness. We have set aside national parks to protect this natural ecology with all its variety and change. National parks should not be tamed, subdued, and managed into units as prosaic as tree plantations."

6. Letter from Mount McKinley Superintendent Duane Jacobs to Adolph Murie, November 15, 1956.

7. Brothers Frank and John Craighead studied Yellowstone's grizzlies for more than a decade, tagging and tracking them with radio transmitters, attempting to quantify the age and sex ratios of the grizzly population and compiling data on social organization, feeding habits, and other aspects of grizzly life history. From 1959 to 1967 the Craigheads collaborated with the Park Service on a friendly basis, enjoying valuable information from park personnel while helping the park manage troublesome bears. The relationship changed, however, in 1968, when a new Yellowstone Park administration instituted changes in grizzly bear management policy that were "in response to external pressures and in complete disregard of scientific information we had made available," according to Frank Craighead, writing in *Track of the Grizzly*, 1st softcover ed. (San Francisco: Sierra Club Books, 1982), p. 11.

Thus the research team was in the position of "opposing the official line on management"; over the next few years "the climate for independent scientific research in Yellowstone steadily worsened, and our work was in various ways impeded, misrepresented, and publicly disparaged by park officials because its results did not conform to the changed position of management," Frank Craighead continues. "More important, the new policies were very nearly disastrous to the grizzly community." These events and the ensuing controversy "resulted in the untimely termination of our field work in Yellowstone in 1971."

8. See Glen F. Cole, "Preservation and Management of Grizzly Bears in Yellowstone National Park," *BioScience* (August 15, 1971): 858–64. Cole cites an increase in annual visitor numbers from about 1000 to

260,000 between Yellowstone's establishment in 1872 and 1929. Average annual numbers were about 0.3 million during the 1930s, 0.5 million during the 1940s, and almost 2 million during the 1960s.

9. See Adolph Murie, *The Wolves of Mount McKinley* (Washington, D.C.: U.S. Government Printing Office, 1971; reprint of National Parks of the United States Fauna Series, no. 5, 1944).

10. Preface to Adolph Murie, *The Grizzlies of Mount McKinley* (Seattle: University of Washington Press; originally published as National Park Service Scientific Monograph Series, no. 14, 1981), pp. xi–xii.

11. Adolph Murie, *Mammals of Mount McKinley National Park, Alaska* (Mount McKinley Natural History Association, 1962), p. 1.

12. Theodore Roosevelt, *A Book-Lover's Holidays in the Open* (New York: Charles Scribner's Sons, 1916), p. 22. See Richard A. Bartlett, *Yellowstone: A Wilderness Besieged* (Tucson: University of Arizona Press, 1985), chapter 12, "Beginnings of Wildlife Policy."

13. Describing findings of his extensive studies of wolf–Dall sheep relationships, Adolph Murie cited studies of sheep skulls. Among four age groups (lamb, yearling, "prime," or two- to eight-year-olds, and nine years and older), Murie found that few sheep died while in the prime of life— and most of these were severely diseased. "The largest number of skulls belonged to the old-age group. There was a heavy mortality among young sheep in their first winter. Because so few sheep died in their prime, it is obvious that any wolf predation affects mainly the weaker animals. . . . Wolf predation probably has a salutary effect on the sheep as a species" (*The Wolves of Mount McKinley*, p. xvii).

14. The Leopold Committee, officially the Advisory Board on Wildlife Management (A. Starker Leopold [chairman], Stanley A. Cain, Clarence M. Cottam, Ira N. Gabrielson, and Thomas L. Kimball) delivered its report, "Predator and Rodent Control in the United States," to Interior Secretary Stewart L. Udall on March 9, 1964. It followed the earlier Leopold Committee report on managing wildlife in national parks. The full text of its report is found in *Predator Control and Related Problems*, Senate Hearings before the Committee on Appropriations, December 14–17, 1971 (Washington, D.C.: Government Printing Office, 1972).

15. "I was disappointed in the failure of the Department, under former Secretary Udall to stop the slaughter of predators. After publication of my article on 'Predators, Prejudice and Politics,' in *Field & Stream* of December 1967, I wrote Secretary Udall, for whom I normally have high regard and esteem, pleading that he stop the use of 1080. On February 17,

1968, he responded: 'Mike, 1080 is not being misused or used indiscriminately. I have made personal inquiry on several occasions and it was considered by my Advisory Committee. They concluded that "When properly applied, according to regulations, 1080 stations . . . do an effective and humane job of controlling coyotes and have very little damaging effect on other wildlife.'" This conclusion is not ecologically valid or defensible. Compound 1080 is not humane. It is a nonspecific poison; therefore, proper application is impossible. It has a widespread damaging effect on other forms of life, both directly and indirectly. I quote the following: 'It has been found to be highly toxic to most forms of life on which it has been tested, including dogs, cats, rabbits, mice, field rodents, chickens, ducks, pigeons, goats, horses and monkeys—This rather general toxicity requires that this poison be used with the utmost caution even by persons accustomed to handling toxic materials. It should never be entrusted to inexperienced people, the danger of accidental poisoning is too great.' I am quoting from Wildlife Leaflet 287 titled 'Facts About 1080,' prepared in the Division of Wildlife Research, of the Interior Department" (testimony of the author, ibid., pp. 302–3).

16. George M. Wright, Ben H. Thompson, and Joseph S. Dixon [U.S. Department of the Interior, National Park Service], *Fauna of the National Parks of the United States: A Preliminary Survey of Faunal Relations in National Parks*, by (Washington, D.C.: Government Printing Office, 1933). See Alfred Runte, *National Parks: The American Experience* (Lincoln: University of Nebraska Press, 1987), pp. 139–40.

17. Murie, *The Grizzlies of Mount McKinley*, p. 239.

18. Advisory Board on Wildlife Management (appointed by Secretary Udall), "Wildlife Management in the National Parks," March 4, 1963, pp. 4–5.

19. Edward E. C. Clebsch, "Concerning the Values to Science of Wilderness in the Great Smoky Mountains National Park, North Carolina-Tennessee," June 23, 1969.

20. See chapter 5 for reference to the transmountain road, strongly advocated by George B. Hartzog, Jr., director of the National Park Service.

21. Adolph Murie's problems with superiors derived in large measure from publishing independent and critical views in scientific and popular periodicals. *National Parks Magazine* featured his articles deploring expansion of the road in Denali (then Mount McKinley) and pesticide spraying in Grand Teton. His classic, *A Naturalist in Alaska*, was reissued by the University of Arizona Press in 1989.

22. See "The Yellowstone Fires: A Primer on the 1988 Fire Season," National Park Service, Yellowstone National Park, October 1, 1988.

"One area fire commander in Yellowstone dryly commented to a reporter, 'We just spent a million dollars to save a $100,000 rubber tomahawk shop,' and Dr. Tom Power, Chairman of the Economics Department at the University of Montana, questions other aspects of the economic rationality of our present fire policies. 'We dump money on fires that are about to go out anyway and chase after fires we cannot stop, throwing money on them too. We spend hundreds of millions of dollars, but fires sweep across the mountains regardless—giving rise to demands that we spend even greater sums of money. In the end we accomplish little except providing summer work for our young and unemployed" (from George Wuerthner, "The Flames of '88," *Wilderness Magazine* (Summer 1989): 41–54.

10   Concessionaire Profits and Public Access

1. See transcript of Russell Dickenson's address to the Conference of National Park Concessioners, International Hotel, Washington, D.C., March 9, 1981, p. 15.

2. Don Hummel, *Stealing the National Parks* (Bellevue, Wash.: Free Enterprise Press, 1987), p. 12.

3. Ibid., pp. 16–17.

4. Buddy Surles, interview with the author, Estes Park, Colorado, December, 1985.

5. Transcript of address by James Watt to the Conference of National Park Concessioners, International Hotel, Washington, D.C., March 9, 1981, p. 9.

6. Hummel, *Stealing the National Parks*, pp. 25–26.

7. See Morris Udall's letter to Secretary Cecil Andrus, printed in Hummel, ibid., p. 361. "In some quarters of the bureaucracy, I got the credit for Whalen's release," Hummel wrote (p. 363).

8. See Alfred Runte, *Yosemite: The Embattled Wilderness* (Lincoln: University of Nebraska Press, 1990).

9. See Richard A. Bartlett, *Yellowstone: A Wilderness Besieged* (Tucson: University of Arizona Press, 1985).

10. Ibid., p. 19.

11. See "The Concessionaires & Their Personnel," chapters 4–6 in ibid.

12. George Freeman Pollock, *Skyland: The Heart of the Shenandoah National Park* (Berryville, Va.: Virginia Book Company, 1960), pp. 266–67.

13. Bartlett, *Yellowstone*, p. 178.

14. See Dyan Zaslowsky, "'Black Cavalry of Commerce': Hotels, Hot Dogs, and the Concessioner Syndrome," *Wilderness* (Spring 1983): 25–32.

15. Robert Herbst, letter to the author, March 8, 1978.

16. Bartlett, *Yellowstone*, p. 202.

17. Ibid., p. 169.

18. George B. Hartzog, memorandum to Stewart Udall, March 30, 1966, in National Park Service, Yellowstone Concessions Study Team, "Yellowstone National Park Concessions Management Review of the Yellowstone Park Company," October 1976, appendix B.

19. Ibid., p. 11.

20. Hardy, interview with the author, Yosemite, 1985.

21. *Hamilton Stores, Inc.* v. *Donald Hodel, Secretary, Department of the Interior, et al.* Brief in Support of Plaintiff's Motion for Preliminary Injunction, September 5, 1985, p. 7.

22. Hamilton Stores, Inc., claim signed by HSI president Trevor H. S. Povah May 28, 1985, p. 2.

23. Yellowstone Concessions Study Team, 1976 report, pp. 7–8.

24. In an affidavit dated September 12, 1985, HSI president Povah said HSI met with the Park Service in Denver in 1979 "in an attempt to define, what is a souvenir?" Povah stated that the result was the wording given in the text.

25. "The National Park Service and the U.S. Fish and Wildlife Service have currently backed off on plans to close facilities at Fishing Bridge, after Wyoming's congressional delegation objected" (*Cody* [Wyo.] *Enterprise*, June 4, 1984).

"The Park Service has recommended removing the campground, picnic area, recreational vehicle park and store from the Fishing Bridge area, saying it was prime grizzly bear habitat. . . . But representatives of the Cody Chamber of Commerce complained, saying it would hurt their business as a gateway community" (*Billings Gazette*, October 27, 1986).

26. In their booklet *Life in the Geyser Basins* (Yellowstone Library and

Museum Association, 1971), scientists Thomas and Louise Brock describe diverse life forms that use hot springs and their overflow channels for habitat or feeding grounds: algae, bacteria, flies, mites, dragonflies, spiders, beetles, wasps, and even a shorebird, the killdeer.

27. Joint House study described in Zaslowsky, "'Black Cavalry of Commerce,'" p. 26.

28. Edward L. Curran, "Inspection and Evaluation at Main Hotel Buildings in Glacier National Park, December 9–14, 1979"; William A. Penttila, investigator and fire safety consultant, "Inspection and Evaluation Report Concerning Concession Facilities at Many Glacier, Lake McDonald and Apgar in Glacier National Park"; W. J. Callabresi, United States Fidelity and Guaranty Company, "Accident and Loss Control Recommendations," January 2, 1980; "Life-Safety—Glacier National Park," statement of objectives of work to be completed prior to opening for public occupancy in June 1980, signed March 14 and March 20, 1980.

29. U.S. General Accounting Office, draft report, "Facilities in Many National Parks and Forests Do Not Meet Health and Safety Standards," July 1980.

30. Ibid., pp. 13–17.

31. Prepared statement to a conference of concessionaires and conservationists at Yosemite, March 29–31, 1987. The meeting was convened by the Sigurd Olson Environmental Institute, of Ashland, Wisconsin, where the author was then located, and supported by the Yosemite Park and Curry Company and the National Parks and Conservation Association.

32. For discussion of MCA's desire for an aerial tramway and other developments in Yosemite, see Runte, *Yosemite*, pp. 203–5.

33. Hardy, interview with the author, Yosemite, 1985.

34. See Gene Rose, "GAO Examines Probe of Drugs," *Fresno Bee*, November 1, 1985; and Jack Fischer, "Beleaguered on Several Fronts, a Park Faces Another Test of Endurance," Knight-Ridder News Service, *Philadelphia Inquirer*, June 1, 1986.

35. See Gene Rose, "Binnewies Admits Ordering Recording," *Fresno Bee*, May 9, 1986. According to the account, Binnewies asserted he did nothing illegal: "This action on my part was a lapse in judgment, but my intentions have always been to further the interests of the NPS."

36. In response to a letter from the author (May 1, 1986), Morehead telephoned on May 15: "I decided it would be better to call and answer

your questions than to write. I admit reflecting [Director] Walker's views about the TV program. I expected it would show a ranger from park to park, his duties and involvement in public health, safety, rescue, snowplowing, and make the public aware of the ranger and the National Park Service, and the pressures of the public. . . . I made dozens of trips to Los Angeles. As technical adviser, I was constantly telling directors and writers they couldn't plan to shoot in certain settings. I was constantly restraining their actions. I learned to be very cautious. . . . Those in the field who hear the director wants something want to help. Today I would tell the director not to do it. It failed miserably and gave us a black eye with the public."

37. Hardy, interview with the author, Yosemite, 1985.

38. Alfred Runte, interview with the author, Seattle, 1988.

39. *Los Angeles Times*, January 20, 1990. The enterprising journalist was Kevin Roderick, writing under the headline "Big Yosemite Concession Take Bared."

40. *San Francisco Examiner*, January 21, 1990.

11   Crashing through the Snow

1. National Park Service, Yellowstone National Park, press release, May 20, 1973.

2. International Snowmobile Industry Association, *Snowmobiling and Our Environment—Facts and Fancies* (October 1976), p. 10.

3. "Voyageurs National Park," Hearings before the Subcommittee on National Parks and Recreation of the Committee on Interior and Insular Affairs, House of Representatives, 91st Congress, 2d session, 1970. Quoted in "Legislative History of Voyageurs National Park with Regard to Proposed Kabetogama Peninsula Snowmobile Trail," memorandum from Voyageurs Region National Park Association to William Penn Mott, Jr., National Park Service director, September 9, 1988, p. 6.

4. Letter from William Penn Mott, Jr., to A. David Kelly, chairman of Voyageurs Region National Park Association, November 15, 1988.

5. See the *Jackson Hole Guide*, October 18, 1979. On October 17 the *Jackson Hole News* ran an advertisement from the Jackson Hole Snow Devils, which invited supporters to a victory party to celebrate "saving" the Potholes for snowmobiling.

12   The Silly Souvenirs They Sell

1. Lloyd H. New, letter to Stewart Udall, December 2, 1968.
2. Charles Eames, letter to George Hartzog, Jr., August 13, 1968.
3. Letter from the author to Hilmer Oehlmann, October 11, 1968.

13   Conservationists and Compromise

1. Nancy Newhall, *A Contribution to the Heritage of Every American: The Conservation Activities of John D. Rockefeller, Jr.* (New York: Alfred A. Knopf, 1957), p. 175.
2. Conrad L. Wirth, *Parks, Politics, and the People* (Norman: University of Oklahoma Press, 1980), pp. 356–57.
3. U.S. Bureau of the Census, *Statistical Abstract of the United States: 1974,* 95th ed. (Washington, D.C.: Government Printing Office, 1974), p. 204; cited in Alfred Runte, *National Parks: The American Experience,* 2d ed., rev. (Lincoln: University of Nebraska Press, 1987), p. 173.
4. Devereux Butcher, *Exploring Our National Parks and Monuments,* 8th ed. (Cambridge, Mass., and Boston: Harvard Common Press, 1985).
5. Brock Evans, interview with the author, Bellingham, Washington, 1989.
6. Interviews with Litton 1980–81, by Ann Lage. From *Martin Litton: Sierra Club Director and Uncompromising Preservationist, 1950s–1970s,* Sierra Club History Series (Berkeley: University of California, Bancroft Library, and the Sierra Club, 1982), p. 73.
7. Morris K. Udall, *Too Funny to Be President* (New York: Henry Holt and Company, 1988), pp. 59–60.
8. Quoted by the author in "Carter & Friends: Tarnished Halos," *Defenders of Wildlife* (June 1979): 166.
9. Ibid.
10. Ibid.
11. "The Environmental Decade (Action Proposals for the 1970s)," Hearings before a subcommittee of the Committee on Government Operations, House of Representatives, 91st Congress, 2d session (Washington, D.C.: Government Printing Office, 1970), p. 225.

12. Stephen Fox, "We Want No Straddlers," *Wilderness* (Winter 1984): 4–19.

13. Sources for Wilderness Society field representatives backpack in Sierra Nevada: interviews with Dick Carter, Salt Lake City, 1986, 1987; interview with Jim Eaton, Visalia, 1989; interview with Dave Foreman, 1986.

14. Dave Foreman, interview with the author, 1986, Tucson, Arizona.

15. Newhall, *Contribution to the Heritage*, p. 177.

14   Regreening the National Parks

1. Judy quoted this letter from Mark H. Brown, *The Flight of the Nez Percé* (New York: Capricorn Books, 1971), p. 41.

2. Russell Dickenson, interview with the author, Washington, D.C., 1983.

Sources

The following is a list of the principal books I have found useful in my research and recommend for study connected with history, policy, and future prospects of the national parks.

Albright, Horace M., and Robert Cahn. *The Birth of the National Park Service: The Founding Years, 1913–33*. Salt Lake City and Chicago: Howe Brothers, 1985.

Bartlett, Richard A. *Yellowstone: A Wilderness Besieged*. Tucson: University of Arizona Press, 1985.

Butcher, Devereux. *Exploring Our National Parks and Monuments*. 8th ed. Cambridge, Mass., and Boston: Harvard Common Press, 1985.

Collier, Peter, and David Horowitz. *The Rockefellers: An American Dynasty*. New York: Holt, Rinehart, and Winston, 1976.

Connally, Eugenia H., ed. *National Parks in Crisis*. Results of a Conference held in Jackson Hole, Wyoming, in September 1981. Washington, D.C.: National Parks and Conservation Association, 1982.

Conservation Foundation. *National Parks for a New Generation: Visions, Realities, Prospects*. Washington, D.C.: Conservation Foundation, 1985.

——. *National Parks for the Future*. Washington, D.C.: Conservation Foundation, 1972.

Craighead, Frank C., Jr. *Track of the Grizzly*. 1st softcover ed. San Francisco: Sierra Club Books, 1982.

Darling, F. Fraser, and Noel D. Eichhorn. *Man and Nature in the National Parks: Reflections on Policy*. Washington, D.C.: Conservation Foundation, 1969.

Frome, Michael. *Strangers in High Places: The Story of the Great Smoky Mountains*. Knoxville: University of Tennessee Press, 1980.

Hartzog, George B., Jr. *Battling for the National Parks*. Mt. Kisco, N.Y.: Moyer Bell, 1988.

Hickel, Walter J. *Who Owns America?* Englewood Cliffs, N.J.: Prentice-Hall, 1971.

Hummel, Don. *Stealing the National Parks*. Bellevue, Wash.: Free Enterprise Press, 1987.

Ise, John. *Our National Park Policy: A Critical History*. Baltimore: Johns Hopkins University Press, 1967.

Leydet, François. *The Last Redwoods and the Parkland of Redwood Creek*. Introduction by Edgar and Peggy Wayburn. San Francisco: Sierra Club, 1969.

Martin, Russell. *A Story That Stands Like a Dam: Glen Canyon and the Struggle for the Soul of the West*. New York: Henry Holt and Company, 1989.

Muir, John. *Our National Parks*. Foreword by Richard F. Fleck. 1901. Reprint. Madison: The University of Wisconsin Press, 1981.

Murie, Adolph. *The Grizzlies of Mount McKinley*. Seattle: University of Washington Press. Originally published by the National Park Service in 1981 as Scientific Monograph Series, no. 14.

———. *The Wolves of Mount McKinley*. Washington, D.C.: U.S. Government Printing Office, 1944, 1971.

Newhall, Nancy. *A Contribution to the Heritage of Every American: The Conservation Activities of John D. Rockefeller, Jr.* Prologue by Fairfield Osborn. Epilogue by Horace Marden Albright. New York: Alfred A. Knopf, 1957.

O'Neill, Edward A. *Rape of the American Virgins*. New York: Praeger Publishers, 1972.

Runte, Alfred. *National Parks: The American Experience*. 2d ed., rev. Lincoln: University of Nebraska Press, 1987.

——. *Yosemite: The Embattled Wilderness*. Lincoln: University of Nebraska Press, 1990.

Sax, Joseph L. *Defending the Environment: A Strategy for Citizen Action*. New York: Alfred A. Knopf, 1970.

——. *Mountains without Handrails: Reflections on the National Parks*. Ann Arbor: University of Michigan Press, 1980.

Schrepfer, Susan R. *The Fight to Save the Redwoods: A History of Environmental Reform, 1917–1978*. Madison: University of Wisconsin Press, 1983.

Shankland, Robert. *Steve Mather of the National Parks*. 2d ed., rev. and enl. New York: Alfred A. Knopf, 1954.

Shanks, Bernard. *This Land Is Your Land: The Struggle to Save America's Public Lands*. San Francisco: Sierra Club Books, 1984.

Swain, Donald C. *Wilderness Defender: Horace M. Albright and Conservation*. Chicago: University of Chicago Press, 1970.

Whitaker, John C. *Striking a Balance: Environment and Natural Resources Policy in the Nixon-Ford Years*. Washington, D.C.: American Enterprise Institute, 1976.

Wirth, Conrad L. *Parks, Politics, and the People*. Norman: University of Oklahoma Press, 1980.

Wyant, William K. *Westward in Eden: The Public Lands and the Conservation Movement*. Berkeley and Los Angeles: University of California Press, 1982.

Interviews on tape were conducted with the following: Horace M. Albright and Marion Albright Schenck, at Los Angeles; Roger Allin, Whidbey Island, Washington; Cecil Andrus, Boise, Idaho; Bruce Babbitt, Phoenix; Anthony Bevinetto, Falls Church, Virginia; Robert Binneweis and Edward C. Hardy, Yosemite National Park; Dick Carter, Salt Lake City; Walter (Scotty) Chapman, Gardiner, Montana; David Condon, Vernal, Utah; Robert Cunningham and Charlie Ott, Denali National Park; Lee Davis, Roderick Hutchinson, and Terry Povah, Yellowstone National Park; Russell E. Dickenson, Bellevue, Washington; Peter Donau, Robert Howe, and Michael Tollefson, Glacier Bay National Park; Gary Everhardt, Waynesboro, Virginia; Dave Foreman, Tucson, Arizona; James R. Habeck, Missoula; Walter J. Hickel, Anchorage; Jack Hughes, Olympic National Park; Marvin Jensen, Sequoia–Kings Canyon National Park;

Riley McClelland, Glacier National Park; William Penn Mott, Jr., Washington, D.C.; Louise Murie, Margaret Murie, and John Turner, Jackson, Wyoming; Alfred Runte, Seattle; Noble Samuel, Virgin Islands National Park; Bernard Shanks, Phoenix; Gilbert F. Stucker, Mount Vernon, New York; L. E. (Buddy) Surles, Estes Park, Colorado; Stewart L. Udall, Phoenix; Ron Walker, Washington, D.C.; William J. Whalen, San Francisco; and Tobe Wilkins, Dinosaur National Monument.

These tapes are available in the Special Collections section of the library of the University of Idaho, at Moscow, Idaho, together with correspondence and other source materials. Students of national park history and policy may wish to examine the letters in the Frome File from many of the individuals cited in this book.

About the Author

MICHAEL FROME has been a newspaper reporter and columnist, a successful travel writer, an outdoorsman, and an eloquent conservationist. Since 1987 he has been a member of the faculty of Huxley College of Environmental Studies, a division of Western Washington University at Bellingham, Washington. His books include *Strangers in High Places*, the classic work on the Great Smoky Mountains; *Conscience of a Conservationist*; *Promised Land—Adventures and Encounters in Wild America*; *Battle for the Wilderness*; and the *National Park Guide*, which has sold more than half a million copies in twenty-five annual editions. In 1986 he received the Marjory Stoneman Douglas Award from the National Parks and Conservation Association for his many years of work on behalf of the national parks.